Sustainable Pathways

Sustainable Pathways: The Role of Indigenous Tribes and Native Practices in India's Economic Model

BY

NISHI MALHOTRA
Indian Institute of Management, India

United Kingdom – North America – Japan – India – Malaysia – China

Emerald Publishing Limited
Emerald Publishing, Floor 5, Northspring, 21-23 Wellington Street, Leeds LS1 4DL

First edition 2024

Reprints and permissions service
Contact: www.copyright.com

British Library Cataloguing in Publication Data
A catalogue record for this book is available from the British Library

ISBN: 978-1-83549-491-2 (Print)
ISBN: 978-1-83549-490-5 (Online)
ISBN: 978-1-83549-492-9 (Epub)

Printed and bound by CPI Group (UK) Ltd, Croydon, CR0 4YY

INVESTOR IN PEOPLE

This book is dedicated to the rural India and the courageous rural women who have time and again showed us the way to empowerment and sustainable growth. This book is dedicated to the artisans, handicraft makers and the tribes of India for their contribution to the heritage and our culture. Above all, I dedicate this book to my parents.

Contents

List of Abbreviations

AYUSH	Ayurveda, Yoga, Naturopathy, Unani, Siddha and Homoeopathy
BARC	Bhabha Atomic Research Centre
CAQDAS	Computer-Assisted Qualitative Data Analysis Software
CIF	Community Investment Fund
CLF	Cluster Level Federation
CMIE	Centre for Monitoring Indian Economy
COVID 19	COronaVIrus Disease of 2019
DAY NRLM	Deen Dayal Antodaya Yojan National Rural Livelihood Mission
DMMU	District Mission Management Units
DRDA	District Rural Development Agency
HDI	Human Development Index
IIT	Indian Institute of Technology
IRB	Institutional Research Board
LOHAS	Lifestyle of Health and Sustainability
MAC	Mutually Aided Cooperatives
MCP	Minimum Credit Plan
MFI	Microfinance Institution
MIS	Management Information System
MYRADA	Mysore Resettlement and Development Agency
NABARD	National Bank of Agriculture and Rural Development
NABARD	National Bank for Agriculture and Rural Development
NARI	Nimbkar Agricultural Research Institute
NGO	Non-Government Organization
NPA	Non-Performing Loans
NRHM	National Rural Livelihood Mission
PLR	Prime Lending Rate
PMAAGY	Pradhan Mantri Adi Adarsh Gram Yojana

PMJANMAN	Pradhan Mantri Janjati Adivasi Nyaya Maha Abhiyan
PRADAN	Professional Assistance for Development Action
RBV	Resource Based View
ROSCA	Rotating Savings and Credit Association
RPL	Recognition for Learner
SBLP	Self-Help Group Bank Linkage
SC/ST	Scheduled Caste/Scheduled Tribe
SDGs	Sustainable Development Goals
SEWA	Self-Employed Women Association
SHG	Self-Help Group
SHPI	Self-Help Promoting Institution
SRYEA	Society for Rural & Youth Educational Advancement
SWP	Solar Water Purifiers
UN SDGs	United Nation Sustainable Development Goals
UV	Ultraviolet
VKY	Van Bandhan Kalyan Yojana
WHO	World Health Organization

About the Author

Dr Nishi Malhotra is an Assistant Professor, Finance Accounting and Control at Indian Institute of Management (IIM), Sambalpur, India. She has completed her PhD in Finance, Accounting and Control from IIM Kozhikode, India and MBA from MDI Gurgaon. She also holds an MCom degree from IGNOU, India and has done her BCom Hons from Shri Ram College of Commerce, Delhi University, India. She has approximately 4 years' experience in teaching and 11 years in industry.

Preface

The United Nations has adopted the Sustainable Development Goals to build equitable societies and achieve equity for all. Reducing inequalities and building sustainable communities is one of the major objectives of the Sustainable Development Goals. The Indian Government has transitioned the sustainable development goals into agenda for action. India is home to around 705 ethnic communities, and each has its own rich heritage and culture. Hon'ble Prime Minister Shree Narendra Modiji has started various schemes and initiatives for the inclusion and development of the indigenous communities and tribes. With increasing environmental challenges and dynamic environment myriad with climatic changes, ecological imbalances inclusion of the tribes and leveraging their indigenous knowledge for the preservation of the nature and ecosystem becomes extremely important. Despite the rich culture and knowledge, the tribal people do not have access to resources and are not included in the mainstream to be part of the economic growth and development. Many of the tribes are nomadic and migrate frequently making social and financial inclusion a distant dream. Since 2014, many developmental initiatives have been started by the government to facilitate the progressive development of the tribes and the indigenous people. Exclusion mainly pertains to keeping a particular community away from the resource sharing and positions of authority and roles of leadership. However, the Indian Government has carved out the special niches and roles for the communities in the development of the nation through initiatives such as the self-help group linkage programme. To give a boost to the unique skill of hand and the art possessed by these communities, the Government of India has started various schemes such as MUDRA financing and Sabka Sath Sabka Vikas and many more mission initiatives under the aegis of Ministry of Handicraft and Ministry of Textiles. To provide the livelihood to millions of artisans and craftsmen, the government has started the DAY NRLM (Deen Dayal Upadhyay National Rural Livelihood Mission) to provide employment to the marginalised craftsmen. The Hon'ble Prime Minister Shri Narendra Modiji has declared this period as Amrit Kaal of the Indian economic growth story and has identified four Amrit Stambh namely the *nari shakti, farmers, cattle rearing and fishermen and youth* and *the middle class* and *poor marginalised* sections of India. 15th November, Bhagwan Birsa Munda birth anniversary has been declared as the Jaan Jati Gaurav Diwas. During this Amrit Kaal, the Government of India aims to include all the marginalised sections of society in the development of the nation through sustainable initiatives. The preservation of the heritage indigenous art and culture provides us a unique opportunity to enrich our civilisation and pass on the knowledge to the future generations through artistic expression, literature, culture, traditions and practices. This book is aimed at highlighting the various sustainable practices and traditions of the tribes in our country and celebrating the spirit of naturalism. The tribes are indeed the pride and add colours to mosaic of rich Indian culture and traditions. Financial inclusion is the key to the economic upliftment of the marginalised, but in deficit of the skills and craftsmanship, this objective of financial inclusion seems like a distant dream. But the tribes in our nation are in possession of most valuable skill, the craftsmanship that is passed on to them from generations to generations. This book aims to celebrate the social capital, the rich cultural identity, the craftsmanship of the tribes, without which the history of evolution of mankind and its progress is incomplete. I take this opportunity to present this book for the academicians and researchers who are keen to research the financial inclusion of the tribes and the native people in India.

Acknowledgement

This book is dedicated to my parents, teachers, sister, Delhi University, MDI Gurgaon, IIM Kozhikode, and all my professors and teachers without whom I would not have been able to accomplish this dream. Above all, I would like to thank the Government of India and our military armed forces for their relentless, selfless service to the nation, and a special thanks to the State Government of Kerala and the people of the state. I wish to thank Emerald Publishing, especially Daniel Ridge and his team for their relentless motivation and support.

And above all, I would like to thank the tribes and indigenous people of India. I would like to thank Sh Rati Kanta Nayak, Director, Jana Jagran Kendra, Sh Narayan Das, Orissa, Rural and Urban and Producers Association, Sh Krishna Moorthy, Rural Education and Action for Change, Dr Sudha Malaiya – Multiple Crafts, Ojaswini Samdarshi, Sh. Dhananjay Bhatt, Uttarakhand SLBC Member, and all other people who helped me in completing this prestigious assignment. I extend my heartfelt gratitude to the Principles for Responsible Management Education (PRME) chapter for their guidance and for giving a sense of direction to the cause of responsible growth. And I thank DAY NRLM (Deen Dayal Antodaya Yojana, National Rural Livelihood Mission) chapter run by the Government of India and Hon'ble PM Shri Narendra Modiji for this great initiative that is a beacon of hope and livelihood for many people below the poverty line.

Chapter 1

Introduction to Indigenous Tribes

Abstract

The indigenous and sustainable knowledge possessed by the tribal people and communities plays an extremely important role in the conservation of the climate. As per the United Nations Sustainable Development Goals (UN SDGs), tribal communities play an important role in preserving traditional knowledge, culture, food practices and textiles. The remains of the Indus Valley civilisation highlight the importance of the culture and religion. Animism and the worship of nature to achieve success in routines and tasks have been practised by these tribes for centuries. India is a mosaic of more than 705 different colourful tribes, and each of these tribes has their own identity that differentiates it from the other tribes. With increasing ecological complexities, the knowledge owned by the tribes is extremely useful in the preservation of the climate. This chapter seeks to explore the various hues and colours that constitute the mosaic of Indian tribal culture.

Keywords: Sustainable culture; indigenous knowledge; tribal community; local climate preservation; tribal culture

India is a confluence of many cultures, it assimilates in itself different tribes, sects and foreign influences. Tribes and indigenous people form an extremely important part of Indian culture, and their customs, traditions and rituals have become part of the treasured heritage of the country. Over and above the class stratification based on birth, the Indian culture assimilates anyone who wants to be part of it irrespective of caste, creed and colour sect. What is the indigenous culture of India, and how is it celebrated today? This is the main theme of this chapter. India has a rich heritage of cultures and traditions which have become part of popular culture and give it a unique identity.

Sustainable Pathways, 1–39
Copyright © 2024 Nishi Malhotra
Published under exclusive licence by Emerald Publishing Limited
doi:10.1108/978-1-83549-490-520241003

Introduction

The word tribe is derived from the Latin word "tribus". In traditional societies, a tribe is a social division comprised of families united by blood, economic, social or religious connections, and sharing a common language and dialect. Tribal communities in India are officially recognised under Schedule 5 of the Constitution of India. Thus, the communities that the Constitution designates as "Scheduled Tribes" are so named. There are 705 tribes in India. These people are also known as Adivasis. However, the modern literature refers to them as Vanyajati, Vanvasi, Pahari, Adimjati, Adivasi, Anusuchit jati. Tribal culture, festivals and traditions in India are well known all over the world. These have changed over the years to reflect the people's beliefs and practices. The variety of ethnic groups, cultural practices and modes of life in India is unparalleled. Indian clans are characterised by unique social, cultural and political attributes. A considerable number of subcontinental Indian communities did not adhere to the social customs and rituals of the Brahmanas, nor were they stratified into a variety of unequal classes. The tribal population is dispersed in numerous regions across the Indian mainland, encompassing nearly all states and union territories. They predominantly inhabited secluded areas, including deserts, forests and hills. Strangely, the native tribes have not only blended in with the rest of the people, but they have also married into the priest clans and created many of the traditions and customs. From an idealist point of view, Sri Aurobindo's article "Jagannath Rath Yatra" (The Chariot of Jagannath) is a great way to describe how the different ethnic groups and the main population come together. There's no doubt that an educated society is like Lord Jaganath's chariot – a vehicle of the holy. The chariot shows up as the Global spirit. The four wheels of this heavenly chariot are thought to represent power, freedom, unity and knowledge. Researchers who study the future think that in an idealist society, the age of truth and morals will come when work, emotion and knowledge will all come together smoothly. An excellent example of this coming together is the state of Odisha. Many of Odisha's native cultures and practices can be seen in the form of *Bratkatha*, which are the stories of brata, or *Osha*, which are the famous fasting rituals. Indigenous cultures' ways of life and accepted norms are shown through their traditions, stories and festivals, like the Raja Doli Gita (Raja Swing Songs). They show how readily these rules are accepted, and how important they are in shaping the social environment and fabric of the mainstream. Numerous changes and additions to current cults and religious practices are proof of this practice. Three new religions, Mahima Dharma, Khumbipatia Dharma and Alekh Dharma, came into being in Odisha in the 1800s. Pre-independence, there was more discrimination based on caste, the East India Company started revenue settlements and certain practices in temples made it easy for new groups to grow. Therefore, indigenous tribes are very important for both keeping heritage and creating new cultures. Of course, Lord Jagannath in Odisha has a strong tribal identity, and many stories about him as a god mention the presence of native tribes in his royal arsenals. The word 'Scheduled Tribes' first appeared in the Indian Constitution. The provisions of Article 366 (25) defined Scheduled Tribes as "such tribes or tribal communities or parts of or groups within such tribes or tribal communities as are deemed under Article 342 to be Scheduled Tribes for this constitution". The President may, concerning any state or union territory, and where it is a state, specify the tribes or tribal communities or parts of or groups within tribes or tribal communities that shall, for this constitution, be deemed to be scheduled tribes about that state or union territory, as the case may be. Parliament may by law include or exclude any tribe or tribal community, or part of or group within any tribe or tribal community, from the list of Scheduled Tribes specified in a notification issued under clause (1), but, except as aforesaid, a notification issued under the said clause shall not be varied by any subsequent notification.

Philosophy of the Indigenous and Native Tribes

The indigenous peoples' culture, beliefs, attitudes and values are influenced by their experiences in the natural environment, according to the texts. Participation in the natural environment and landscape results in a wide range of experiences. Human evolution is shaped by the time when humans first learn about and interact with nature. The approach of Claude Levi-Strauss is examined via the theoretical prism of structuralism. This method refers to the bricolage technique, which is used to adapt and adopt existing traditions. Philosophers once believed that the Earth housed the ultimate spirit of the cosmos and cosmology and that humans interact with and express themselves through nature. People, nature and natural objects such as trees and animals are all interconnected and reliant on one another. In addition, indigenous people have a strong connection to the environment and locality, which is reflected in their language. They have a strong connection to nature, which they express via their culture, beliefs and values. This bond is passed down from generation to generation. Because they are physically tied to the earth and all the aspects of nature and the world in which they dwell, these native groups view themselves as the forefathers of all humans. Nature and people have interacted over time, resulting in religious practices, folktales, myths and concepts that are passed down from generation to generation. Indigenous people studies and research are techniques to discover the truth about where people came from. Native Americans and indigenous tribes are founded on animism and the ability to interact with and comprehend the natural world. Natural impulses or a mind that can shift into different forms are what have propelled the human species forward through language, spoken words and symbols. Native traditions assist people in connecting with cosmology and the universe. As a result, it is critical to preserve their history and culture and to bring that history and culture into mainstream society. Through bricolage and modifications, these indigenous people are adapting to their changing surroundings. This chapter discusses how distinct indigenous communities live in different regions and have different traditions. Few other works emphasise the relevance of acculturation as the convergence of cultures from many geographies leads to the basic development of culture and traditions. Historians previously hypothesised that the Aryan conquerors who entered the Indian subcontinent were the originators of Hinduism. Later discoveries modified the theory that Hinduism arose after the arrival of the Dravidians. Until recently, the origins of tribes were assumed to be due to cultural differences, language disparities and religion. Later, studies on race and genetic inheritance became the driving force for the development of tribes. T. Kivisild et al. (2003) have studied the genetic distinctions between the Chencu and Koyas tribes in this regard. The literature emphasises the great genetic unity of Indian tribes and their ancestry with some Eurasian and European tribes. Thus, there are two schools of thought in India about the origins of caste and tribe. One school of thought links caste and tribes to primordial Brahmanical beliefs and another links caste to beliefs derived from texts such as the Vedas and Puranas based on occupation. The modern world considers their concept of caste and tribe origins as very artificial and the product of Brahmanical clan activities. The Vedic song discusses the origin of castes and clans from Adipurush's human form. According to the Vedas, Brahman arose from the mouth, Rajanya from his arms, Vaishyas from his thighs and Sudra from his feet. Similarly, early literature emphasises the disparities between races based on occupation, and the literature emphasises the presence of clans of smiths, artisans, and weavers. The presence of Aryans and Dasyus is also discussed in the Vedas. The Aryans are thought to be the extraordinarily fair-skinned group who gave birth to handicrafts. The Dasyus are jungle inhabitants who were eventually assimilated into the Aryan bloodline. The tolerant acculturation of the clans and tribes resulted in the growth of society and the invention of the moral code. Some historians praise the fourth-century enlightenment and reformation brought about by the advent of Buddhism and Jainism, led by Lord Buddha, the nobility and Lord Mahavira. To rid popular culture of biases and discrimination, the Hindu religion undertook extensive reformation. Though the Puranic texts depict castes in various ways, new literature with a higher moral code of equality emerged in the form of Jatakas. The Jatakas discuss caste mixing through marriages and alliances, with Buddha marrying a low cultivator's daughter as an example. The varnas as a birthright are abolished in the Jatakas, as anybody can become a Brahmin through penance. It evolves into an occupational idea in which trades and occupations like barbers, weavers and potters are mentioned. This period, which overlaps with the Bhakti movement in Hinduism, saw the rise of powerful occupational guilds and corporations in the fourth and sixth centuries. The Indus Valley culture, which lived 2,500 years ago, had a similar distinction based on profession. These guilds are referred to as Sresthi, and a subsequent section of the text discusses the Sresthi. The key example of this blurring of caste and varna borders is seen in the fourth-century literature called Mrchchhakatika (Toy Cart), which recounts the merger of a Brahmin clan with the lower varna, which leads to upheavals in society and law and order. This was the age of social emancipation when many reformers left up nobility and took employment as Jogi's, sanyasi and garland makers to transform society and attain the aim of inclusivity. Thus, the period from the fourth to sixth centuries is significant in terms of the creation of thought surrounding the paradigm of inclusivity and reformation in the Indian subcontinent. During this time, Megasthenes or Seleucus visited India and spoke with and offered a description of Indian society to the Greek civilisation and philosophical community, which included prominent philosophers such as Pliny, Strabo and Arian. Hiuen Sang visited India around this time and confirmed the presence of caste in primitive Indian society, where Chandalas reside apart from the community, and their entrance into the village is marked by the banging of a piece of wood. This time was followed by enormous invasions, which gave rise to another hypothesis of caste formation as the mingling of alien races with Indian tribes and castes. Thus, in addition to the distinctions of Brahmins, Kshatriyas and varnas, the concept of varnasanskaras, or mixed race, arose. However, there is disagreement among experts over the origins of classes and clans. A new class of people emerged as a result of the blending of Indian roots and their foreign invaders such as Sakas and Hun. The invasion of the White Huns from Central Asia's steppes in 465 AD which led to an intermixing that had a huge impact on the mosaic of Hindu society. The Gujar tribe of North India, situated in Jammu and Kashmir, Rajasthan and Haryana, is thought to be descended from Huns. These Gujar tribes are prominent in Hun and Indian subcontinent archaic writings; they are thought to be descendants of the Pratihara and Rajputana clans. Thus, many influences were assimilated into the Indian mosaic of Hinduism, and this culture was accepted and expanded to the diversities of various cultures, which became an insignia of the castes and clans known today as tribes. With the birth of the Prophet Mohammed in the seventh century, Islam gave further impetus to the elimination of the caste system and clans in the subcontinent, and gradually, the thin lines of birth as the reason for class and clans blurred, leaving only the belief in occupation as the insignia of caste and clan. The ownership of family skills, pursued since time immemorial, became the basis of classification; but, with mass foreign incursions, when the peasant clan began experiencing mass atrocities, the ruling military classes and nobles gained importance (Sir Edward Blunt, 2010). Then some anthropologists thought of physical characteristics and aspects such as facial features, colour and hair as differentiating elements. However, renowned anthropologist William Flower claims that physical characteristics are not used to identify people based on race (Fuller, 2022). Indeed, tribes created their rituals, language and traditions, but the occupation and possession of a distinct heritage, became the distinguishing element for tribal classification. Foreign invasions and mixing resulted in the formation of new customs, as seen in the Bengali speaking Kochh people. Because of the Mughal conquest, the Kamrup kingdom, to which they belonged, was split, resulting in racial mixing and the development of a new language. This resulted in the creation of the Rajbanshi language. As a result of so many invasions and conquests, it is considered that the Asian subcontinent has seen a great deal of race mixing. The Himalayas act as a shield, thwarting the dry cold winds that would otherwise sweep across the Indian subcontinent, causing potential natural disasters. Historically, the formidable Himalayan range has acted as a natural fortress, creating a formidable barrier to invading forces from the north. Its rugged terrain and harsh climate have made it a challenging barrier for infiltration, contributing to the defense of the Indian subcontinent. While the Himalayas present a formidable barrier, the narrow passageways between the mountains have facilitated cultural confluence and exchange in the northern region. Similarly, in the East, the impact of the Burmese and Chinese on the people living on the periphery has given rise to numerous tribes and tribal communities. Many foreign conquerors, merchants and traders have made incursions into the Indian subcontinent in southern India, near the Indian Ocean and the Arabian Sea.

Constitution of India and Tribes

Lokur Committee (1965) has given the characteristics of the tribal community as distinctive culture, distinctive primitive traits, geographical isolation, shyness and, as described at the time, backwardness. The constitution of India provides for political safeguards, such as in Articles 330, 332 and 243 provide for the reservation of the seats in Lok Sabha, legislative assembly and panchayat, respectively. India has undertaken various initiatives such as TRIFED, digital transformation of schools, development of particularly vulnerable tribes, Pradhan Mantri Jan Dhan Yojanas and Eklavya Model Residential School for the welfare of tribes. Tribal peoples various problems and challenges in India, such as loss of control over the natural resources, lack of education, displacement and rehabilitation of tribes, problems of health and nutrition, gender issues and loss of identity. The 15th November of every year has been declared as the Janjatiya Gaurav Diwas by India.

Origins of Tribal Population

In the pre-independence era, the British considered implementing a regulation in 1833 to safeguard the indigenous populations for a variety of reasons. In 1874, the British Government passed the Scheduled Area Regulation Act. Meanwhile, the notion of a tribe emerged as a social category that was intended to differentiate them from the Hindu, Muslim and other organised religious groups employ an overly simplistic approach. In the aftermath of independence, the protection and development of the tribe-identified population became a constitutional mandate. In pursuit of this objective, a roster of tribes was ratified. This list, which comprised 212 names in 1950, was revised by subsequent presidential decrees. The provisions of Article 366 (25) defined Scheduled Tribes as "such tribes or tribal communities or parts of or groups within such tribes or tribal communities as are deemed under Article 342 to be Scheduled Tribes for this constitution". The President may, concerning any state or union territory, and where it is a state, specify the tribes or tribal communities or parts of or groups within tribes or tribal communities that shall, for this constitution, be deemed to be Scheduled Tribes about that state or union territory, as the case may be. Parliament may by law include or exclude any tribe or tribal community, or part of or group within any tribe or tribal community, from the list of Scheduled Tribes specified in a notification issued under clause(1), but, except as aforesaid, a notification issued under the said clause shall not be varied by any subsequent notification.

Importance of Tribal Communities in India

India boasts an unprecedented diversity of ethnic groups, cultural practices and ways of life. Indian lineages are distinguished by distinct cultural, political and social characteristics. A significant proportion of subcontinental Indian communities were not stratified into an assortment of unequal classes, nor did they observe the social rituals and practices of the Brahmanas. The tribal populace is geographically scattered throughout various regions of the Indian subcontinent, including the majority of states and union territories. They inhabited sequestered regions predominately, such as deserts, forests and hills. The perceived advantages of the tribal communities are as follows:

Preserving Biodiversity: The ethnic communities of India have been instrumental in conserving the fauna and flora of sacred groves of tribals and in preserving the biodiversity of numerous primeval forests. They possess invaluable ancestral knowledge and expertise regarding the adaptation, mitigation and reduction of climate and disaster risks.

Sustainable subsistence practices: The indigenous population cultivates crops that exhibit remarkable adaptability. They are resilient to altitude, drought, inundation and all temperature extremes. These crops contribute to the development of resilient agriculture. Regarding social harmony and gender equality, tribal communities are among the most progressive. The status of women is significantly elevated due to their substantial contributions to activities of basic subsistence.

The tribes in India are facing various challenges such as cultural extinction, and impinged rights to natural resources such as land and water. The numbers of many tribal groups are dwindling fast.

Case Study of Toda Tribe of Nilgiris

Approximately 3,500 years ago, arid regions with limited summer monsoon activity were more susceptible to wildfires. A mere 1,500 Todas individuals practiced controlled burning in high-altitude meadows. The findings contribute valuable insights into the paleoecology, archaeology and human ecology of the highland Nilgiris and peninsular India during that period. A study found that climate change in peninsular India may have forced a pastoralist community, possibly the Todas and their buffalo herds, to the highest Nilgiris in the Western Ghats at least 1,500 years before historical reports suggest. Todas are one of six indigenous tribes of the Western Ghats' Nilgiris highlands. The 1,500-member Todas are a Vulnerable Tribal Group. Based on the Toda language's linguistic connections with southern Indian Dravidian languages, the Nilgiris' Toda origin is believed to be less than 2,000 years old (Mongabay, 2020). However, scientists at the Indian Institute of Science, Bengaluru, and Inter-University Accelerator Centre, New Delhi, hypothesise that the discovery of "intense fire activity" and signs of humans, herbivores, and grasslands in the Sandynallah basin in the upper Nilgiris in the Western Ghats 3,500 years ago indicates the movement of a pastoralist community and their herds from lower to cooler higher realms to manage better (Ghosh, 2020). Six ancient indigenous tribes live in the Nilgiris: Badagas (traditionally settled agriculturists and the largest numerically), Todas (pastoralists on the upper plateau), Kotas (artisans) and Irulas, Kurumbas and Paniyars. They live in thatched huts with half-barrel roofs, built on wooden frameworks by the Toda in groups of three to seven on the grazing slopes. The villages of Toda people are known as munds, and it consists of several thatched huts with barrel roofs. Toda people are known for their beautiful embroidery work known as puthkuli, which comprises of red and black thread work on white fabrics. Toda women do embroidery in home, and they join the self-help groups and cooperatives to market their craft work. In their wedding ritual, the Toda people gift bow and arrow to each other. Toda people are facing the challenges in terms of ecological balance, and there is need for sensitivity to preserve their culture. The Toda trade dairy, cane and bamboo with other Nilgiri peoples, exchanging Badaga grain, cloth and Kota tools and pottery. Kurumba bush people supply forest items and play music for Toda funerals (Britannica, T. Editors of Encyclopaedia, 2014). Besides this, the tribes are also known for their royal lineage and affiliations.

Jenu Kuruba Tribe of Karnataka

Jenukuruba tribal people live in the forest corridor between Karnataka, Tamil Nadu and Kerala (Devadasan, 2016). This tribe lives mainly in Mysore and Coorg, Karnataka encompassing about 3,000 km. Over 40,000 people live there. This tribe's culture is unique. The major profession was food gathering in the forests and collecting minor forest products like honey. They are skilled elephant tamers. They worked in logging and firefighting. They reside in Hadi villages and settlements. Their nomadic lifestyle stems from food gathering and shifting crops. Recently, they've moved to larger hamlets with government help. Agriculture is their side business. They use a bamboo spear to scratch the field instead of ploughing.

Classification of Indian Ethnic Communities or Tribes

In contemporary research and academia, there is a significant emphasis on ethnicity as the foundation of classification for human populations. This focus on ethnicity reflects a recognition of the cultural, social and historical dimensions of human diversity. From the acculturative perspective, with several incursions and invasions, the interracial mixing of tribes has led to the emergence of the shared cultural meanings, beliefs and value systems that have become the basis of classification. India is the world's seventh largest country, with a total land area of 3,287,263 square kilometres. The country's coastline is 7,517 kilometres long, and the longest river is the Holy Ganga or Ganges, which is 2,510 kilometres long. The country is divided into four distinct regions: the plains, the mountains, the southern peninsula and the desert. The productive Indo-Gangetic plains cover the eastern and central parts of India. Rajasthan's Thar Desert is located to the northwest. The Deccan plateau constitutes virtually the entire terra farma in southern India. The Western Ghats and Eastern Ghats mountain ranges are two prominent mountain ranges in South India that are near banjara seashores. The two well-known mountain ranges in India are the Himalayas, upper, middle and lower Himalayas, and Shivalik's. The Indian subcontinent is open to the confluence of many foreign cultures and influences, and the classification of ethnicities is possible only through homogeneity in terms of culture, language, beliefs and attitudes. Different researchers have given different classifications of the races and ethnicities, and the most popular ones have been (1) Sir Herbert Hope Risley and (2) B.S. Guha.

Classification by Sir Herbert Hope Risley (1915)

Sir Herbert Hope Risley attempted to categorise the Indian population using anthropometric measures. When he managed the conduct of the Census for India in 1901, he established a strong concept about the ethnic elements of India. Later, he used anthropometry to justify these assumptions and published the results under the title 'The People of India' in 1915. He opined three major racial types in India: Dravidian, Indo-Aryan and Mongoloid.

The Dravidian Clan

Risley considered these people to be the original inhabitants of India, who had been altered by the infiltration of foreign invaders.

The Indo-Aryans

This group is most similar to the traditional Aryans that invaded India and are found in Punjab, Rajasthan and Kashmir, where members are known as Kashmiri Brahmins, Rajputs, Jats and Khattris.

The Mongoloids

This group can be found throughout the Himalayan region, particularly in the North East Frontier, Nepal and Burma. The Kanets of the Lahul and Kulu Valleys, the Lepchas of Darjeeling and Sikkim, the Limbus, Murmis and Gurungs of Nepal and the Bodo of Assam are the some examples.

B.S. Guha Classification

Dr B. S. Guha's racial classification is based on anthropometric measurements obtained during his research from 1930 to 1933. Guha identified six primary racial strains and nine sub-types among modern Indians.

Geographical Distribution of Tribes in India

Bakarwal, Gujjar, Tharu, Busha, Shouka, Bhoutia, Gaddi, Kinnauri, Garo, Khasi, Jaintia, Bru, Naga, Mog, Bodo, Konyak, Apatini, Chakma and Chakpa are the major tribes found in India's north and north-eastern region, which includes Jammu and Kashmir, Himachal Pradesh, Uttarakhand, Uttar Pradesh, Bihar and Northeast, etc. Madhya Pradesh, South Rajasthan, Gujarat, South Uttar Pradesh, Bihar, Jharkhand, Chhattisgarh, Odisha and Andhra Pradesh are home to the major tribes of Bhil, Gond, Reddy, Santhal, Ho, Dongria, Kondh, Munda, Korwa, Oraon, Kol, Banjara, Meena and Koli. Irula, Korma, Gond and Kadar tribes are found in the southern states of Kerala, Karnataka and Tamil Nadu. The Sentinelese, Jarawa, Shompen, Tebow and Org tribes are found in the Andaman and Nicobar Islands.

Peninsular India includes the Deccan plateau and the Chota Nagpur plateau, which covers the plains of Bombay, Madhya Pradesh, Orissa, Southern Bihar, and West Bengal. The Principal tribes of this peninsular India are Gond, Santhal, Birhor, Bhil, Paharia, Oraon, Kondh, Munda, Bhuiya, Ho, Savara Kol, Korka and Baiga. They mainly practise hunting, agriculture and shifting cultivation. While Birhor live on hunting and Baiga live on shifting cultivation, Munda, Santhal and Bhumij live on settled cultivation. Baiga are a subtribe of Gond and semi-nomadic. The largest number of Baiga is found in Southern district of Mandla and Balaghat districts of Madhya Pradesh. The ancestors of Baiga spoke the Austroasiatic language and they are now speaking Baigani through a variety of Chhattisgarhi influenced by Gondi and Western Hindi used by Baigas. The Panchas of Baiga Panchayat are Mukdam, Deewan, Samrath, Kotawar and Dawari. The Baigas eat coarse grain Kodo and Kutki and drink pej. Bhil from Central and Northern India speak Indo-Aryan language with modifications, while the Gond and Kadar speak the Dravidian language that originated in the Deccan peninsula. Guha, a renowned anthropologist, describes them as Proto Australoid (Guha, 2018).

The Hindu Mythology and Tribal Heritage

The Indian epics and holy texts such as Ramayana and Mahabharata make mention of the tribal culture and deity. In the holy scripture Ramayana, Shri Valmiki make mention of two tribal characters, Sabri and Guhan. The tribals from Bhil, Gond and Kol tribes find mention in Ramayana in Ayodhyakanda, Aranyakanda and Kishkindhakand. The brief description of narratives pertaining to existence of the tribal characters in the holy books is given below.

Kevat Guha

Nishada monarch Guhan (Guha) organised boats and boatmen to ferry Ram, Lakshman and Sita over the Ganga. Guha, the Nishadraj, led Ganges-side tribes. He was powerful and the first to welcome Ram. Guha served high-quality cooked rice and other sweets after his warm welcome. Ram quickly lifted and hugged Guha after he prostrated.

Sabri

Sabari, sage Matanga's attendant, is another Ramayana legend. She appears in Valmiki's epic's third book, *Aranya Kanda* (the woodland incident). Kambar's *Ramavataram* mentions Sabari's hospitality for Ram and Lakshman. As per many studies, the Kol tribe is considered to be the descendent of Shabri (Times of India, 2020). Rather, the studies propagate that more than 80% of the existing descendants in Western India and Haryana have their DNA and genetic sequencing matching with three tribes Kol, Bhils and Gonds or with people from the Indus Valley civilisation that existed 2,500 years ago (Chaubey et al., 2015). Though, the Ramayana is supposed to be some 7,000 years old.

Lord Hanuman is a tribal deity and finds a link with the practice of animism and worshipping the animals and has mention in epics and scriptures of Indus Valley and Greek civilisation of few. Similarly, the lions and other animals are worshipped as the vehicles and carriers of the deity and lords. Thus, tribal practices and rituals find lot of relevance in the Hindu mythology. The epic of Mahabharata also makes mention of a tribal character Eklavya. A monument of Dron Acharya, a Kauravas and Pandavas teacher, inspired the Nishada prince, a self-taught archer. Ekalavya always respected Dron Acharya, even if he wanted his right thumb for guru Dakshina.

Major Tribal Communities in India

There are more than 705 tribes in India Eighteen of the 50 states and one union territory in the country are home to particularly vulnerable people. There are 95 notified tribes in the nation, and a stable and declining population is the criterion for identifying the most vulnerable group. The different government programmes are causing the tribal communities to experience extensive development and welfare (India.gov.in national portal in India, 2024). Some groups avoid contact with the outside world because they are wary of outsiders and antagonistic to the populace. Seventy-five tribes out of the total 705 have been identified as being highly vulnerable. According to the Fifth Schedule of the Indian Constitution, private mining and exploration corporations cannot be permitted access to indigenous people's territory. The Fifth Schedule contains information on the Scheduled Tribes, their places of residence and the Scheduled Areas. Ladakh and the union territory of Jammu & Kashmir are the primary locations of this group. They move from one location to another as a semi-nomadic community. The Bhil or Mina tribe is the most populous in India, and it is followed by the Chenchu, Khasi, Santhal, Dhodia, Gaddi and Chakma tribes. According to the census, there are 104 million tribal peoples in India, making up about 8.6% of the country's total population. Lakshadweep has the highest percentage of tribal people in the nation (94.8%), whereas Madhya Pradesh has the largest population (around 15.3 million or about 21%). With over 46 lakh individuals, the Bhils are the largest tribe, while the Andamanese are the smallest tribe with only 19 members.

Juangs are Odisha Indian tribes that specialise in animal dances. The animal dances are mainly done by girls dressed in glass and brass jewelry and a garment made entirely of leaves. During the torchlight night, the women execute various dances in the background. The males sing while the women dance in a circle, executing various dances. In other dancing genres, they march in circles while keeping their hands on the shoulders of the girls ahead of them. They sing numerous bird melodies, such as the pigeon dance, quail dance, pig and tortoise dance and vulture dance. In the in-pigeon dance, the dancing girls imitate the act of a hungry vulture pouncing upon its prey, the carcasses of a dead man. The Baigas and Gonds, who perform the parrot dance, also do the Juangs, the animal dances. Turtle dance is particularly popular among the indigenous tribes of Andamans, and the Gond custom is said to be founded in peacock dance, in which the Gond men began to imitate and dance with the peacock after observing the peacock dancing on the sacred hill. Similarly, the Baiga tribe is said to have learned to dance after seeing tigers, peacocks and panthers on moonlit nights. Men on tambourines frequently accompany the dancing girls. The hills dances feature a strong storyline as well as rites and rituals. The rites performed by the tribals of Orissa's Ganjam and Koraput hills are noteworthy. Odisha has a Hill Savara theory that is completely committed to the discovery of the art of dance. Savara dances are performed for a variety of rituals, including weddings, harvest festivals, animal sacrifices and ceremonies. This art form is performed in rectangles and does not have a tune or rhythm. The tribal individuals performing the Savara dance follow no rules; they simply swirl their bodies, pacing up and down, while carrying a prop such as an umbrella, peacock feathers, a sword or a stick. The Savara dance is also known as the Shaman dance, in which the shaman is possessed by an ancestor's ghost and subjected to torment. As a result, there are dances for every occasion. The person dances with the deceased's ornaments and belongings or property on his head as part of the Guar ceremonial on his death. The shaman shoots the arrow at the time of the goat sacrifice. Dances are also classified as those that are in harmony with the body and those that are convulsive to the body and cause the person to lose control. The residences of these indigenous tribes are decorated with animal sculptures and artifacts such as bison horns, python skin and peacock feathers, and the head of the household wears a turban while wearing numerous musical instruments. Hulki, the expedition dance, the Mandri dance, the Muria dance, and the religious dances of the Hill Maria of Abhujmahar mountain Karsana are dances that imitate animals.

The Tewa Lalung tribe observes the Wanchuwa ceremony, during which tribal members pray for a successful harvest and pest-free crops. They predominantly grow Jhum and live in Assam and Meghalaya. Meghalaya and Arunachal Pradesh also have them. Members of the organisation identify as Tiwa, which means "people who were lifted from below." They are divided into two subgroups: Hill Tiwas and Plain Tiwas. Hill Tiwa lives in the Westernmost section of the Ancient Lalung, once known as the Tiwa Hills and today known as Umswai Valley. Tiwa is a subset of the Tibeto Burman language spoken by the Bodo-Garo. They are divided into various clans, which are distinguished by the distinctive names they use as patronymics. The term "ambilineal" alludes to their lineage. The husband continues to live in the area with the wife's family, and the children are part of the mother's family. In 30% of marriages, the woman moves in with her husband, and the children take on the mother's clan name. The Irula tribe is mostly found in Tamil Nadu and is well known for their snake charmer performances. The Abujh tribes are noted for their vulnerability and live in the Abiymad district of Chhattisgarh's Bastar region. Big cat conservation is also substantially supported by the donations of Indian tribes. They are mostly found in Telangana and Andhra Pradesh. They are listed as a particularly fragile tribe. The Bru are a north-eastern ethnic group who live in Tripura, Assam and Mizoram. During the ethnic violence with Mizo tribes in Mizoram in 1997, several members of the Bru tribe fled to camps in Tripura. The Zomi tribe is found in Nagaland, Mizoram, Assam and Manipur. The Zomi tribe includes the Gonte, Kom, Pete, Mate, Simte, Tedim, Chin, Jou and Weifei tribes. The Konyak Naga tribe is found in Nagaland's Mon district. Konyak dancing is recognised in the *Guinness book of World Records*. The Chakpa community in Manipur is the country's first carbon-positive community. The title was bestowed upon the Fayeng tribe, which is governed by the Chakpa. The Chippa are a well-known community in Rajasthan, producing hand-block prints. The Chippa community is also featured at the Titanwala Museum in Bagru, Rajasthan. The Negrito tribe's most aggressive members are the Sentinelese of the Andaman and Nicobar Islands. They take hostile action against the outside world. The Yanadi tribe of Andhra Pradesh cast their first vote in the 2019 Lok Sabha election. The Apatini tribe of Arunachal Pradesh is well known for living in harmony with the environment. The Tharu tribe lives in the Terai lowlands, in the lower Himalayan or Shivalik range. They currently live in Nepal and India. The government of Uttar Pradesh has devised a strategy to acquaint the world with the peculiar Tharu ethnic culture. They mostly inhabit the Indian Terai in Uttarakhand, Uttar Pradesh and Bihar. The bulk of them live in forests, although some are farmers as well. The name "Tharu," which means "Buddhist follower," is said to be derived from the word "Sthavir." The Bonda are an ethnic group who live in isolated portions of the Malkangiri district in south-western Odisha, Chhattisgarh and Andhra Pradesh. The Bondo tribe is said to have been the first to depart Africa some 60,000 years ago. Bonda is referred to as Remo.

Madhya Pradesh is well known for its art and culture and is regarded as the nexus of numerous art forms. The art form is transmitted from one generation to the next. The Gondwana region, which encompasses Balaghat, Chhindwara, Seoni and Shahdol, is regarded as Madhya Pradesh's cultural centre and is famed for producing the renowned art known as Gond art. The term Kond, which signifies mountains in Dravidian, is the ancestor of the word Gond. Mountains, rivers and animals are the inspirations behind this expression. Using these components, Gond artists tell a variety of stories. The artist uses a variety of organic pigments, such as plant, charcoal and cow dung. According to the Gond culture, maintaining a positive reputation brings luck. This idea has allowed Gonds to utilise animals, mountains, rivers and other motifs and tattoos to decorate their homes and floors. Another well-known art type that can be discovered as cave drawings is Pithora. This style of art is accompanied by song and dancing and has significant religious importance. This genre of art honours several eras of rural living. The indigenous people utilise paints to decorate their homes with a variety of murals. The first step is called Lipai. Setting the house in cow dung is a part of it. The painting of saplings on the walls is done next, then paintings of hunting, dancing and singing scenes. These activities aid in fostering societal harmony and cohesiveness. The importance of worshipping the gods is paramount in tribal culture. Paintings by Chitravan, Mandana and Panna are well known in Madhya Pradesh. This state is home to some of the world's most gifted craftspeople. Bamboo art is produced by the Baiga, Gond and Korku tribes. The kids sing well-known religious tunes like Relo songs. The well-known dance styles are Saila, Sua, Karma, Pandvani and Panthi. Raut Nacha is the famous dance form in Madhya Pradesh practised by Yadavas. This dance is dedicated to Lord Krishna and is performed on Ekadashi, 11 days after the occasion of Diwali. Fag, Karma, Cher Chera, Chau Mau, Sawnahi, Bhojali, Fugdi, Leha, Dhankul and Chait Paran are the famous song styles. The state observes several festivals that either signal the beginning of the seasons or include the worship of regional deities.

Jarawa tribe comprises 400 members of the nomadic tribe of Jarawa that live in groups of 40–50 members in Chaddah which they call homes. They survive by hunting for seafood such as the toothed pony fish, turtles, pigs and coral-fringed reefs for crabs and fishes. They gather fruits, tubers and honey. They collect the wood from the Baratang island to make their bow and arrow from the Choi woods. Jarawa women collect honey bees, and they sing songs of happiness while collecting the honey. Jarawa men always bathe after collecting honey. Jarawa tribes are less in number, and there is immense pressure to include these tribes into the mainstream.

The Sentinelese are indigenous people who live on North Sentinel Island in the Bay of Bengal in the northern Indian Ocean. They are also known as the Sentinel and the North Sentinel Islanders. They are a Scheduled Tribe and a particularly vulnerable tribal group within the larger class of Andamanese peoples. The Sentinelese, along with the Great Andamanese, Jarawas, Onge, Shompen and Nicobarese, are one of the six native and often secretive peoples of the Andaman and Nicobar Islands. The Sentinelese, unlike the others, appear to have steadfastly refused any contact with the outside world. They are hostile to visitors and have slain any who have attempted or landed on the island. The Indian government proclaimed North Sentinel Island a tribal reserve in 1956, prohibiting navigation within 3 nautical miles (5.6 kilometres). It also maintains a continual armed patrol in the nearby waterways to deter strangers. Photography is not permitted. There is considerable uncertainty about the group's size, with estimates ranging from 40 to 400 people.

Artisan Communities in India

The Scheduled Tribes as per the latest census form approximately 7% of the total population. The tribal people form the majority of the population in the north-eastern states and union territories of India, out of which 80% are in Nagaland and 70% in Arunachal Pradesh. More than half of the tribal population resides in Madhya Pradesh, Bihar and Orissa. The majority of these tribes are found in Central India, Western India and Eastern India. Approximately four million Gond people reside in Central India, particularly in the states of Madhya Pradesh, Maharashtra, and Andhra Pradesh. The Gond community is renowned for its rich cultural heritage and traditions. Western India is home to around four million members of the Bhil tribe. This indigenous community is prevalent in the region and contributes significantly to the cultural diversity of India. Aboriginals are considered tribal communities, and the social system has time and again highlighted the importance of respecting the culture and treating them with affection. The literature highlights the importance of preserving the tribal language and culture, to protect the economic rights of people and integrate them with the rest of India. The artisan community in India is known for the skill of their hand, and they play an extremely important role in preserving the heritage of India. The most prominent among these art forms are bamboo work, metal casting, fisheries and fish farming. This section presents the excerpts from the interviews of some of the members of the artisan communities.

Tribes of Kerala

The Kadar community lives at the periphery of the states of Kerala and Tamil Nadu. There are various narratives attached to the origin of the Kadar tribe. They live on the fringes of the forests in Kerala and Tamil Nadu and near the highways. The Kadar men move with the women, and once they have expanded the family, they leave the establishment and the caravan. Once the spring has spread its mantle over the Earth, they once again migrate to the forest. They are nomads who move from village to village in search of food and livelihood. The major vocation of the Kadar clan is the maintenance of the coffee estate and tea plantations. Their life is based on hunting and gathering, and they specialise in making honey wax, argot, sago, cardamom and ginger. They are often also called the people of the Pariyar community who live and take care of the forest. Kadar community mainly depends on hunting and farming for earning their livelihood. Due to deforestation, the Kadar community is losing its home in the forests, and due to the frequent hunting, the animals are also becoming extinct. The Government has undertaken various initiatives for the upliftment of tribal people and communities, providing them with housing settlements and livelihood training (Davey, 2016). The Government has established the Kuriarkutty colony in the jungle, with roads well-built to provide the access to village. Besides, the Government is also fighting for the electorate of the tribal people. Kadar has the tradition of passing on their ways of living by the way of oral folklore and storytelling, which include the folklores of the spirits of the ancestors and the tribal members having an innate sense of the direction in the forest. These tribal people are known for their intricate relationship with nature, and they have a keen sense for the plants and the smells in nature. Yet another tribe inhabiting the forests of

Kerala are Mailvan, and they live near Kannur and Kasargod. They perform the Mangalam Kali dance, and they affiliate with the Dravidian culture. They dance to the beats of the percussion instrument called Thudi. Just as other tribes, the tribal people have migrated from the forests to the plains, and their life is impacted by the regulation of the forests. There is yet another tribe known as the Adiya tribe that pursues the Gadhika art, to cure disease and miseries. This art form has two major variations known as Nattu Gadhika and Pooja Gadhika. Changpa community lives mainly in the state of Uttarakhand, and they rear the Pashmina goats that yield fine wool.

Tribes of Rajasthan

The tribes in Rajasthan constitute more than 10% of the total population. After Madhya Pradesh, Rajasthan is the 6th largest state with a tribal population. The state of Rajasthan comprises various tribes including Minas and Bhils, and these tribes can be classified according to their culture, customs, trades, fairs and festivals. Bhils are the largest tribe in the state of Rajasthan and are spread from Banswara to Jaisalmer. Bhils are found in large numbers in the district of Banswara, and they mainly pursue the art form of archery and shooting. They are experts in hunting using the bow and arrow. The Bhils have found a mention in various holy epics including the Holy Ramayana. These tribals were originally food gatherers, but with time, they have taken up the vocation of agriculture. Tribals celebrate various festivals including the Baneshwar fair and Holi. Ghoomar is one of the major art forms that is celebrated with fervour in the state of Rajasthan. People from far and distant parts of India come to witness this art form. In the background of the dunes in Jaisalmer, the Bhils perform this art form to the delight of the visitors and tourists. Mina is another clan that is found in Rajasthan, and it seems to have originated from the Matsya Puran. These minas are spread across the state of Rajasthan. In the Dungarpur, Udaipur region of Rajasthan, the Damor clan is found. This clan mainly speaks the Vagri Indo-Aryan language. This clan is claimed to have originated from the Rajputs. They pursue polygamy, and they also accept the money from the bride's family, which is known as Dapa. They also celebrate the Chela Bawaji festival with much pomp and show. Near the Sirohi district of Rajasthan, the famous Garasias tribe inhabits near the Abu Road. The Rajasthan desert, known as the Thar Desert, is known for the Khejdi tree. The Kathodi tribe is known for making the Katha from the Kher tree. The women from the tribe make tattoos on their bodies, and they worship the Gods known as the Dungar dev, Bagh dev, Bhari Mata and Kansari Mata. The Sahariya tribe from Rajasthan is an indigenous tribe from Kishanganj. Kishanganj is known for its beautiful paintings and pursues the occupation of cultivation, hunting and gathering. Kanjar is another tribe that is found in the Hadauti area of Kota, Bundi, Baran, Jhalwar and Sawai Madhopur, Alwar, Bhilwara and Ajmer. The family deity of this tribe is Chauth Mata, and these females are known for singing and dancing. Bhils has the largest population in India.

Kumbhar Community

Kumbhar community is an indigenous community that pursues the art form of making earthen wares and utensils with terracotta. This community is often known by the name Prajapati. As part of the research, one of the potters was interviewed, and he has been pursuing this art form since time immemorial. Terracotta art form is a heritage art form, and the artisans have been pursuing this art form for more than 70 years now. This art form has been passed on from generation to generation. The group pursues terracotta art forms to make utensils, sculptures and decorative art forms. This art form plays an extremely important role in enhancing the lifestyle of people. The artisans face various challenges, which include getting the clay and mud for making earthen wares and pots. The master artists also saw the challenge of getting fuels for making earthen wares and utensils from mud and terracotta. The artist has the distinction of getting a National award for Matti kala during the handicraft carnival. The Barasingha sculpture made by the artist was appreciated by the public at large and received state recognition. The group is trained by the master artisan to make intricate designs and carvings without the use of dyes with hand only. The artisans have recently completed making sculptures on designs like Khajuraho. The veteran artist plays an extremely important role in protecting the Kumbhar community. There is yet another community of potters in Dharavi, that is working to promote pottery making and protect this heritage art form. The village of the potters is normally called Kumbha wadi, and they make earthen wares with black and red earth mud. During the festivities, they make the earthen diyas and decorative items for the house. Their products are in large demand in national and international locations and markets. This foundation provides support to the artisans and handicraft makers through training and marketing. This community has a great role to play in the preservation of the environment and protection of the age-old art form that is widely recognised as the heritage of India. Besides, there are many nomadic tribes in Rajasthan which include Baldias, Gadias Lohars, Jogi Kalbela, Jogi Kanphata, Khurpalts and Ghisadis. Other semi-nomadic tribes include the Sarangiwala Bhopas, Raths, Bhayas, Kannis, Janglus, Jhangs, Sindlus, Jogis, Ramaswamis and Bharati Jadhavs.

Tribal Art and Culture

Paintings

Madhubani art, which originated in the Mithila region of Bihar, is one of the most well-known styles of Indian paintings. This painting was created using natural colours and a variety of materials such as fingers, twigs, brushes, nib pens and matchsticks. Madhubani paintings are distinguished by their goal to establish a balance between the brilliance of colours and the simplicity of their designs. *Bharni, Katchni, Tantrik, Godna and Kohbar* are the five distinct styles of Madhubani painting. Madhubani paintings can be easily identified because of the use of tribal patterns and vibrant earthly hues. Warli paintings are a more than 2,500-

year-old Thane and Nasik tradition that is intricately interwoven with nature and social rituals. Their paintings depict everyday activities of that community's residents such as hunting, farming and playing. To commemorate harvest or weddings, women traditionally use twigs to sketch with rice paste on the mud walls of tribal huts. To reflect everyday life, simple geometric designs are white on a red or yellow background. The style of Kalighat paintings started at Calcutta's Kali temple and was drawn on paper by a group of patuas. They show ordinary life in indigo, ochre, Indian red, grey, blue and white. Phad paintings are Rajasthani devotional scroll paintings. These paintings on canvas are known as Phad. The women of the Meena community pursue different kinds of paintings and arts. Mandana Art is the oldest form of art in India and is created using mud. This art form is predominant in Jaipur, Swai Madhopur, Alwar, Hadoti, Tonk, Bharatpur and Bundi, and the paintings are referred to as Meena paintings. Kolam art in South India and Aripana in Madhya Pradesh refer to another form of popular art forms pursued by the tribes in India.

Rajasthan is known for its beautiful Banithani paintings and Kishangarh paintings, which are based on narratives of Radha and Krishna. Kajali paintings and Hadoti paintings feature gold panel work.

Colours form an important part of art and culture in India, particularly in Rajasthan. Various schools of art developed in Rajasthan namely Mewar School of Painting, Bundi School of Painting, Kota School of Painting, Jodhpur School of Painting and Amber School of Painting. The earliest paintings are small narratives on palm leaves in the form of Jain Tirthankaras and episodes from Kulpasutras. From the 15th to 16th century, palm leaf was replaced by paper. Gold was extensively used in the Hadoti paintings.

In India there are various schools of arts and paintings, and most prominent among them are found in Rajasthan. The school of paintings comprises Mewar School, Marwar School, Hadauti School, and Dhundha School to name a few. Mewar School comprises Nathdwara, Devghar, Udaipur, Bagur, Saavr and Kelowna. The Marwar School comprises Bikaner, Jodhpur, Ajmer, Kishangarh, Nagur, Sirohi, Jaisalmer and Jooniya and the Hadauti School comprises Bundi, Kota and Shalwar. The Dhudha School contains Ajmer, Shekhawati, Jaipur and Alwar to name a few. Before the advent of the Mughal empire, the paintings were made on thin sheets of paper called waslis, and they were painted in pigments rich in colour. A brush made from camel and squirrel hair was used for making the paintings. In the 16th century during the Mughal rule, Vaishnavism emerged as a trend, and the scenes from the Bhakti movement were depicted in the paintings of Mewar School major cult in the paintings. This included the scenes from The Holy Ramayana and poetic narratives of love songs of Radha Krishna in the form of the famous Rasa Manjari by Bhanu Datta a Maithili Brahmin, Gita Govind. Along with the depiction of narratives of affection of Lord Krishna and Radha, shringar ras emerged as another prominent theme in the paintings of this era. Raskipriya is the poetic interpretation of love lores and songs of different emotions and emotive states. The psyche and emotional interpretations reached an altogether different stature with the emergence of Ragamala paintings Dhola-Maru, Sohni-Mahiwal, Mrigavat, Chaurpanchashika and Laurchanda. Many more paintings emerged on the theme of the court scenes and accoutres. Mewar paintings are considered to be the centre of the confluence of the Mughal style and Rajasthani style of paintings. The Ragmal paintings, Raskipriya, Bahgvat Purana and Yudha Kanda were the popular themes of paintings till the end of the 18th century.

At the end of the 18th century, the textual representations were replaced by the depiction of the courtly activities and past times of the Royales which included the Vaishnava paintings of Nathdwara including the famous Pichwai paintings. Inclusiveness and gender parity became the common theme of the paintings at Mewar School in the 18th century with the emergence of the women courtiers and zenana activities in the painting styles. Bundi style of painting is known for its depiction of the lush green vegetation, wildlife, hunting scenes of the Royales, flora, thick jungles, and particularly elephant was the central theme of all the paintings. The feminine characters in Bundi paintings are depicted as women with petite round faces, receding foreheads, sharp noses, full cheeks, sharply pencilled eyebrows and pinched waists. The important themes of Bundi paintings are Baramasa and Dipak Raga, and the palaces have domes that are flat inspired by the Mughal form of art. Silver and gold are used extensively in the Hadoti paintings.

The Kota School of Paintings very similar to the Bundi School of Painting emerged as the epitome of calligraphy, which depicted the scenes of chase and hunting. The hue is often vibrant. Female characters in Bundi paintings are tall with a thin waist, wearing a short choli, colourful ghagra and translucent odhni that partially covers the head; facial traits include a sharp nose, receding chin, almond-shaped eyes and a reddish brown skin colouring. The landscape background (Bundi – Kotah Region is noted for its attractive terrain) with hills, flowing rivers, lush foliage and brilliant flowers is the most prominent element of Bundi paintings. However, the terrain depicted in Kota paintings is very naturalistic, with the monarch and his followers dispersed among bare rocks, stylised trees and animals, as seen in the hunting scenes. The elephants are portrayed with amazing realism and awareness of their dignified behaviour, whether they are battling another elephant or hunting a rhino or wild buffalo. The landscape in contemporary Bundi paintings serves as a flat, decoratively designed backdrop and is not an important feature of the picture. Amber School established a vast studio with over 50 painters who produced excellent miniatures in several manuscripts of Durga-Path, Ramayana, Bhagvata Purana and Krishna Lila, among others. During his reign, painters like Gopal, Udai, Hukma, Jiwan, Saligram, Ramasevak, Lakshman and others produced many miniatures depicting Ragamala, court scenes, festive scenes and so on. In the 13th century, the Rathors established their empire with its capital at Mandor, which was later relocated to Jodhpur in 1459. Though samples of wall paintings have been discovered at a Jain Temple at Nadol and contact with the Mughals was established during Udai Singh's reign in 1581, dated examples of Jodhpur school from the 16th century have been discovered. Among the earliest examples of miniature paintings found in the Marwar region are a profusely illustrated Bhagavata Purana dated 1611 previously in the Jodhpur Pothi Khana and a set of Ragamala miniatures painted in 1632 by an artist named Virji at Pali and now in the collection of Kumar Sangram Singh of Nawalgarh. Another very famous work is the narrative of the folklore of Dhola Maru. On horizontal cloth in red, yellow and orange, stories of local deities and heroes are painted. Several stories are told in these paintings. Kalamkari is a type of hand painting or block-printed cotton textile created in Andhra Pradesh and Telangana, and it is done in 23 complicated processes using natural dyes and colours. Srikalahasti and Machilipatnam are two painting styles that use free-hand painting. Kalamkari pens are used for free-hand sketching as well as colour filing. Indigo, crimson, black, green and mustard are among the earthy colours employed. The well-known artist is Revered Kamladevi Chattopadhyay.

Miniature painting arrived in India with the Mughals, who influenced it with Islamic, Persian and Indian elements. They are fashioned from materials such as palm leaves, paper wood, ivory, marble and fabric to tell stories. Stone, dust, actual gold and silver dust are examples of natural minerals employed. These paintings are created on a special paper known as Wasli. Gond paintings include elaborate designs made up of dots and dashes. They tell legendary stories and describe different stages of life. Plant saplings, charcoal, soil, cow dung, flowers and leaves are used to create the colours for the paintings. Watercolour is also used by Gond painters. Kerala mural paintings are one of the most popular kinds of frescoes, depicting Hindu mythology epics through Krishna folktales. This art form dates from the seventh to eighth centuries and is distinguished by vibrant images, strokes and colours. They are available in ochre, yellow, blue, green and white. Patachitra is a type of scroll painting based on religious themes and mythology. This style of painting is distinguished by bold outlines, brilliant colours such as white, red, yellow and black and decorative borders.

Pichwai painting, also known as the Nathdwara painting, is a hanging artwork devoted to Lord Krishna. Tanjore painting is a famous south painting from Thanjavur done with gold foils. These are panel paintings honouring gods and goddesses. Nakashi Art refers to Cheriyal paintings and scroll paintings. It is well known as a Telengana indigenous theme. These scrolls are illustrated in narrative styles. Pithora painting on walls is done by the Rathwa and Bhilala tribes of Gujarat and MP. They are carried out within inner walls.

Tribal Communities and Textiles in India

Indian tribes are renowned for their inventive art and dexterity. Bharat is renowned for its exquisite patterns and motifs found in its textiles. Kashmiri pashmina shawls are among the most sought after. This is the craft of creating opulent clothing accessories by hand. The goat lives in the Indian Ladakh region of Changthang. The Changthang goats have dense coats, and their cashmere wool, which is just 12–16 microns thick and incredibly warm, prevents animals from dying from the cold. The wool is hand treated and spun on a wooden spinning wheel as soon as it is obtained. This stage is essential since cashmere wool is sensitive. In Varanasi, Uttar Pradesh, Banaras sarees are manufactured. Because of the intricate stitching, these are among the best traditional sarees in

India and are rather heavy. The Mughal dynasty introduced banarasi silk, which is known for its exquisite weaving and design craftsmanship. Banarasi silk comes in a wide range of designs, such as organza, satin borders, jangle, cutwork, anchor and Reshambutti. Intriguing geometric patterns and animal, avian, floral and fruit designs can be found there. Indian designers often incorporate Persian themes to produce unique floral patterns. The name Kullu shawls comes from the Kullu valley in Himachal Pradesh. Among the best woollens are the women of Kullu. They are renowned for their reversible weaving technique, which features the same colours and patterns on both sides. Shawls made of Kullu are worn by both genders. The terms Loi and Pattu refer to the men's shawls. Every design uses eight classic, vivid colours. The fibre Pashmina angora is used to make merino wool. Pashmina angora is woven with yak hair. The ladies of Uttarakhand who live close to the Indo-Tibetan border in the foothills weave these textiles. Women from Panchachuli weave merino wool and wool from sheep. Every fabric, including blankets for home décor, wool, scarves and shawls, is knitted and weaved by hand. Only natural colours are utilised as dyes for these textiles. Another well-known fabric with elaborate patterns and decorations is chikankari. Chikankari, which implies making delicate patterns, comes from the root words chakin and chakeen. This type of stitching is extremely delicate and shadow-like. Originally, it was done on colourless muslins called tanzeb using white yarns. These days, textiles such as cotton, georgette and chiffon are utilised to create chikankari fabrics. Additionally, table linens, pillows and cushion covers are used. The Sanskrit term bandhani, which means to tie and die, is the source of the phrase bandhani weaving. The fabric is coloured with colours and designed patterns using impermeable thread. It is let to dry in the open after drying. Suitmaking is a common application for bandhani fabric. Boonds are tiny dots that have darker centres. The Indian silk city of Bhagalpur, Bihar, is the inspiration behind the name Bhagalpuri silk.

Bhagalpuri silk is made from the cocoons of Antheraea Pahia silkworms. Another type of silk that doesn't include chemicals is kuchai silk, which is made from cocoon cultivated in Arjun, Sal silks. The Lepcha handloom is woven by the women of the Lepcha community and is used in the rear straps of loin looms. This fabric, which is composed of yarn made of wool and silk, is distinguished by its elaborate designs. The Assamese tribal people weave muga silk, which is renowned for its sturdiness. It was created by the Garo community and is golden-yellow. The Apatani tribe of Arunachal Pradesh, who reside in Ziro in the lower Subansiri, is the maker of the Apatani fabric. It is well known for having zigzag patterns and geometric elements. The inhabitants of Maharashtra, India's Paithan region, make the Paithani saree. The Paithan sarees are woven using the labour-intensive tapestry technique with gold and silver threads. This saree is very bulky and has elaborate borders and decorations. The history of Chanderi fabric dates back to the hand-woven turbans worn by the Maratha rulers in 7 BC, and it originates from Chanderi, Madhya Pradesh. Chanderi is renowned for its nobility and was once a symbol of it. Figurines of animals, such as peacocks, flowers, money and celestial bodies, are among the motifs employed. Ikat, or Sambhalpuri, sarees are created by tribal people in Sambhalpur and are renowned for their graphic motifs. Like Sankha, Chakra and Phula, the fabric used to make this saree has its roots in Bandhkala. The communities that manufacture Kancheevaram sarees claim ancestry from Sage Markanda. Kanchipuram is a small town known for its mulberry weaving. After dipping the silk thread in rice water, it is sun-dried. Another popular fabric is Mysore silk, which was initially produced in a factory in Mysore by the Maharaja of Mysore in 1912. The cocoon is the source of the raw material used to make sarees. Its inherent lustre is derived from the use of genuine zari and silk. Cocoons cultivated on Arjun, Sal and Saja are used to make silk. It is constructed from organic hues like fire flowers. A jamdani saree, which is handmade by the communities, is an essential piece of clothing for Bengalis. Another name for it is Dhakai. It is constructed of cotton and is incredibly lightweight, and the motif is inlaid with denser threads. Gujarati artists need about five to six months to create the exquisite patan patola saree. Double Ikat is used to make it.

Bamboo Art Form

The artisans in the Dawod region of Gujarat pursue Bamboo beads production and marketing. This art form is almost 40–45 years old, and this community plays an extremely important role in the preservation of the tribals and the indigenous people. The community dwellers pursue this art form to make baskets and wares and utensils. Many of the tribal people face the challenge of earning a livelihood, and through marketing support and exhibitions, the artisan people can earn a respectable livelihood. Indeed, bamboo is the identity of the Indian people and tribes in India. I had the opportunity to speak to the master craftsmen and he provided the following information:

The group is involved in the training of the SC/ST and tribal groups. The master artist trains the artisans and teaches them the art of making handicrafts using bamboo leaves and bamboo products. These communities play an important role in the preservation of dying art forms such as terracotta pottery making. The society has given grants to the museum for the preservation of different art forms. The society also arranges the handicraft carnival for 5–7 days, during which the cultural troupes from different parts of the world come together to celebrate the various art forms such as terracotta, ceramics, wood carving, bhittichitra and other forms of kalamkari and ancestral art forms. Yet another community group comprised of 12 artisans from below the poverty line is formed by the people from the community pursuing handicrafts and different art forms. These artisans make various handicrafts which are sold through the conventions and the exhibitions. The artisans are mainly from the Kumbhar community, and they make various terracotta figurines from clay and mud. The artisans mainly make sculptures of various animal forms such as bulls, horses, elephants, etc. Handicraft makers face various challenges such as lack of marketing support and demand for the products. Indigenous communities follow various practices that help in the conservation of the ecology and the protection of the environment. The indigenous people are helping the existing institutions and organisations to improve land practices by bringing about reduced rates of greenhouse emissions. Due to the ecological differences, the land cultivation practices are not uniform across the ecologies. Thus, there is a need for the assimilation of the ecological practices and natural conservation practices pursued by the indigenous people and to take steps to reduce the deterioration of the climate. Various initiatives can be taken to resolve the conflicts between the indigenous and non-indigenous stakeholders.

There is an increasing conflict between the indigenous groups and the state over the use of the resources. The fire is frequently used for clearing the forests, and it is often used for signalling to the other tribes the presence of a particular tribe. And fire is also used to remove the reptiles, snakes and scorpions, and fire is an extremely powerful tool for protecting the fallow lands and improving the productivity of soil. Fire knowledge is transmitted to the members of the indigenous groups through observation. Burning of the fields is fairly common for cultivation, hunting, harvesting, protection of lands, livestock grazing, eliminating pests and putting off the outsider fires. To harvest the forests, fire is used for honey extraction and for keeping the aesthetic clean. The fires are also used for promoting the grass regrowth, eliminating pests, putting off the fires, harvesting natural fires, hunting and promoting good cultivation. Indigenous people use the fire and the moon for sowing and harvesting; this lunar cycle becomes an important indicator for agricultural practices. Fire is increasingly being used for the conservation and enrichment of biodiversity. Gradually, the burning regimes are becoming extremely important for protecting the ecology.

Metal Casting

The self-help promotion institution (SHPI) highlights the importance of joint liability groups to promote the empowerment of women by providing them their own livelihoods (Interview taken with the SHPI). In the rural sector, the artisans get an opportunity to undergo training under the Pradhan Mantri Kaushal Yojana and Recognition for Learner (RPL) that aims to certify the works of artisans. The artisan is given the certificate after the training in the handicraft. Fish farming and fishery is one of the most important vocations, and the National Bank of Agriculture and Rural Development (NABARD) plays an important role in promoting this vocation. Another such vocation is goat rearing, where poor people earn their livelihood through joint liability group lending. These self-help groups play an important role in promoting the livelihood among the people and empowerment of women.

Another such vocation is the oil spillways and oil extraction through the farming of the oilseeds. Hastshilp is another such vocation in which artisans pursuing stone carving and making of marble wares earn their livelihood through the sale of stone-made artifacts. These artisans suffer from various challenges such as the diversion of the savings and earnings of the small artisans by the other members of the group. To help the artisans, the banks have introduced various schemes such as providing machinery tools and equipment directly to the artisan himself (Interview taken with the SHPI). Other artisan communities are involved in the making of the leather products and weaving work on traditional artifacts. They also highlight the importance of the training and support from various Government schemes in promoting the artists and the craftsmen. The artisans highlight the various art forms pursued by the craftsmen are ancestral, and the artisans have been pursuing this art form from generation to generation. Similarly, there are the artisans who are pursuing the art of incense making, while promoting the disabled and blind people.

The indigenous tribes and the artisans are playing an extremely important role in promoting the heritage art form. Elsewhere, the artisans pursue embroidery and crouchea artwork that has great demand in the markets, both domestic and international. This is a dying art form, and there is a need to promote this art by providing financial support and providing training in the use of medical equipment. These all remain attached to the Ajeevika programme. These groups are from the different regions but the same village. Our team helps the artisans to improve their business, and it is not that we leave these villages, our different teams work in a different area. There is a regular meeting of groups, and one person also remains present in their meetings. There is need for intense motivation of these groups. For around 3–6 months, we have to remain attached with them, and only then they come on line. When we make SHG, it is not that if there are 10 or 14 candidates, then all are illiterate or literate. We put at least one or more member in the group who can read and write. Today, no body is illiterate; everybody let's say in a group of 15 members, at least 12 can do something.

Foods of Tribes in India

Indian tribes are known for their cuisines and food dishes. The tribal foods are made from the most natural and nutritious sources. Tribal foods do not use much of spices, and use of the traditional methods of cooking is the main hallmark of all the tribal dishes. These dishes include Dhuska (deep-fried snack made of powdered rice), Thapdi Roti, Khapra Roti with Mutton, wild fruits, etc. The tribal foods are a delight for any gourmet or connoisseur of good food. Dhuska is the tribal food that is popular in Jharkhand, and it is made from urad dal and chana dal and sometimes potatoes. Thapdi Roti is extremely popular in Chhattisgarh and Jharkhand, and it is made from nachni or ragi flour. Another very popular dish from Gujarat is Muthia, which is made from batter of gram flour and methi leaves. Maahni is a food of Himachal Pradesh. It is a curry and is generally eaten with steamed rice and rajma. This dish is made from the stew or maand of the starch flour rice. In West Bengal, an extremely popular tribal food is teliya maach, and it is made from fish, onion, tomato, mustard, oil, spring, onions and melange of whole powdered spices. Yet another mouth-watering dish is Dubki Tiyan, that is made from urad dal batter, and it is steam cooked and is enjoyed with pork curry. The Bafuri dish is made from garlic chana dal paste, garlic, coriander and green chilies. This food is extremely popular in Madhya Pradesh. In the state of Meghalaya, an exotic dish made from red rice and pork is cooked with spices. This dish is an absolute treat for any gourmet. Jharkhand has another recipe that is extremely popular among the connoisseurs of good food, Marh Jhor. It is a soup made from herbs and green leafy vegetables. Most of the leaves used to make this dish are sun dried, powdered and stored for the entire period. Black rice kheer made from black rice and sugar is extremely popular all across the globe. Another delicacy is made from steamed fish, which is steamed using a bamboo steamer. This dish is known for its rich aroma of bamboo, and it is served with plain steaming rice.

Sustainable Food Habits

Tribal culture is known for its sustainable food habits, which include honey and millet. Paliyars are commonly known for extracting honey from honeybee hives, and they use honey in almost all type of cuisines and foods. Due to the medicinal properties, the honey is used by the tribal people. In many parts of India, tribal people consume millets and use millets in their cuisine. In the interior of Odisha, the Laato Jel and Laad are extremely popular tribal dishes. These dishes are also popular in West Bengal. North-eastern India is known for its some of the best cuisines, including the Eromba, which is stem of mixed vegetables and potatoes, and Mui Borok, the dried fish Barma without the use of oil. Aptani tribe in Andhra Pradesh makes an extremely popular dish known as Pika Pila; Malpua is another famous dish of Jharkhand and is made during Holi. Balu Shahi is another famous sweet from the north that is made from jaggery, sesame seeds, peanuts, and muri (Puffed rice). Jujube is made with fermented rice and is extremely good for health and skin generation.

Millets Indigenous Food for a Healthy Body and Mind

India celebrates August 9, as Indigenous People's Day everywhere. In the year 2023, another milestone under the aegis of the Indian Government was the declaration of this year as the Millet's year. This event aims to create a linkage between traditional food and the sovereignty of the indigenous tribes. It is also emphasised that the local millet value chain is leading to a sustainable and inclusive ecosystem. Millet is eaten and celebrated by many indigenous communities, and in a recent conclave hosted by the World Food Programme, many organisations from the southern part of the world emphasised the importance of saved millet seed in ensuring food security for future generations. Slowly and gradually, the world is realising the importance of connecting with nature and leveraging the knowledge of indigenous communities. Millets play an extremely important role in the conservation of the environment and promoting food security, good health, culture and protecting the economy. In indigenous households, millets are primarily produced by the women in the household. Through the oral traditions in the form of stories and poems, the women pass on the knowledge regarding the benefits of the millets. Millet harvesting also drives the philosophy of the indigenous economy. Various natives and agricultural communities are also developing various smart agricultural practices. The self-help groups run by women are particularly promoting the consumption of millet in the hinterlands of the nation. The millets are leading to a major society transformation. The millets are usually grown in sandy and mountainous zones. The land used for the cultivation of the millets can be later left as fallow to be used for grazing purpose. Since millet is resistant to pest and spoilage, it can be grown without the use of fertilizers. The millets have many medicinal properties and can be used to treat blood clots, uterus ulcers, cysts and ailments of stomach. The straw left from millet cultivation can be used as fodder for the cattle and the ruminants.

Some Unique Economic Systems of Tribes in India

Bhils of Rajasthan are the biggest tribe in India, and they are extremely independent, and they frame their own rules and customs. Bhils are one of the most open tribe in the mosaic of Indian culture today. The Bhil women often have multiple partners. Bhils are extremely fond of music, dance and flute. They are found in parts of Madhya Pradesh, Gujarat, Malwa and Bihar. They believe in the afterlife and the spirits, and they follow exotic rituals to appease the Gods for the muksha. They follow the gathala pratha, the journey of the dead which they celebrate in the form of the folklores, stories and rituals. *The other tribe of Rajasthan is Meenas.* Meenas are the subtribe of Bhils, and they claim a descent from the Matsya Avatar or fish incarnation of Vishnu. These tribes have oral traditions and folklores which have been passed on from generation to generation. Meenas are one of the biggest tribe in Rajasthan, and they are known for their vibrant culture and dresses. They are famous for their ethnic dress, the Mina Lugdi, which is worn by the tribals across the tribal areas of Udaipur, Dungarpur and Banswara. The dress is an exotic wear with a golden kinari and embroidery which makes it attractive. This dress is worn on special cultural occasions, and the dress is marked with the ethnic mirror work and consists of Lugdi and Angrakha, a flowing dress, skirt with embroidery and Odhni.

Damors are the tribals of the Western India, and they mainly sustain themselves on the agricultural practices. They are found in Panchmahal, Dahod and Sabar kantha, and they speak Bhili. There main sub tribes are Parmar, Rathore, Sisodia, Chauhan, Solanki, Saradia and Karadiya. They do not marry outside their clan or with their sisters and are Hindus by belief. They worship God Surya and also serpents. They speak the language Bhili, and unfortunately, they lack the access to the basic facilities like electricity and clean drinking water. They are mostly found in the Dungarpur and Banswara region of Rajasthan. They are also known as Damariya and speak Vagri, the Indo-Aryan language, and they consider their descent from the Rajput. They organise the Chadiya festival during the Phalgun and Holi festival.

Dhanak is another tribe that has derived its name from the Dhanush which means bow and arrow. They are very similar to and share many cultural similarities with other tribes. They are Hindus by faith and practice agriculture and hunting. Garasia tribe is also said to have originated from the Rajputs, and they are found in the Sirohi region of Rajasthan. The word Garasia is derived from the word gras, which means the substance. It is believed that this tribe safeguarded the people who were uprooted from the plunder of 13th century by Aluiadin Khilji. They speak local dialect blend of Bhili, Marwari and Gujarati language, which is known as Nyar ki Boli. They reside in one-room homes made of mud and bamboo. The polygamy and joint family system is still prevalent among the Garasia clan. Kathodi is a tribe of Jhadol region in Rajasthan, and they are known to make Katha from the Kheir tree found in Rajasthan. The women do not wear any sort of jewellery, and they make tattoos on their body. The head of their tribe is known as the Nayak. They worship Dungar Dev, Bagh Dev, Bhari mata and Kansari mata. Sahariyas are identified as the most backward tribe in Rajasthan, and they are identified as the most vulnerable group in Rajasthan. Kanjars are found in Hadauti, (Kota, Bundi, Baran, Jhalawar) and Swai Madhapur, Alwar, Bhilwara and Ajmer. They are fondly known for not speaking the lie after sipping the "Hakim Raja ka Pyala". They are known for singing and dancing, and the head of the tribe is known as Patel.

Uttarakhand has five major tribes that are identified as Tharu, Jaunsari, Buksa, Bhotia and Raji. Tharu are the tribals of the Eastern Uttarakhand, and they are found in the lower Terai region of the state of Uttarakhand. The peculiar feature of the Tharu tribe is that they follow the matriarchal culture. They have the strong panchayat and joint family system, and widow remarriage is also allowed among the Tharu tribals. Jaun sari is one of the rare polyandry societies in India and they worship their local god known as Mahasu devta. They inhabit the regions of Upper Dehradun called Jaunsar Bawar and Rawain or Uttrakashi. The forest plays an important role in the subsistence of these people. They consider themselves to be the descendants of the Pandavas. They are known for their witchcraft and treat diseases with chandeliers. The dress of the Jaunsari tribe is unique. They wear elaborate Ghagras, Jhaga and Dantu, and their females are very fond of the jewellery. They wear silver and gold jewellery which comprises of the Kadahs, bangles, panjebs or anklets and necklace known as the mangla sutras.

Bhoska tribe found in Pauri Garwhal and Terai region of Uttarakhand is another major tribe that has many characteristics similar to the Mongoloids. They believe themselves to be the descendants of the Rajput tribes, and they speak Buxuari dialect. The Bhutia tribe are found in upper Himalayan region of Kumaon and Garhwal regions of Uttarakhand. They speak the language called as Bhoti, and they are Buddhist, and they are known for their yarn and woollen weavings, and the Bhotia women weave the Pattu and dye them in the natural vegetable colours.

Van Raji is another prominent tribe that is found in the upper Himalayas, Pithoragarh, and they are cave dwellers. They are hardly 679 in numbers, and the Rajis are also known as the Ban Rawat, Ban Raji or Ban Manus. Rajis has many sub-castes or sub-clans. Each sub-caste within Raji caste has its own deity. Kanyal among the Rajis worship Dhanelinag, Rakal worship the Ghurmal, Pachaypa worship Malkarjun, Badwal worship Betal, Dayakori worship the Bhagwati and the Galdiyar worship Kedar tree.

In the state of Jammu and Kashmir, the main tribes found are Gujjar, Gaddi, Bakkarwal, Sippi, Purigpa, Mon, Garran, Changpa, Dard, Drokpa, Brokpa, Beda, Bot, Bota, Balti to name a few. Bakkarwal is one of the pastoral communities found in the state of Jammu and Kashmir. They use Arabic script and speak Kashmiri language and known as the sheep herders. Balti are the Muslim tribes that are found in the state of Jammu and Kashmir. They speak Arabic, and they believe in endogamy. Their women go to the interior of the forests to collect the juniper bushes. They are Tibetic ethnic groups.

Another prominent tribe found in the Northern Himalayas is the Gujjars, and they are a pastoral and semi-nomadic community. They are found in Srinagar, Pulwama, Anantnag, Doda and Kishtwar region which is surrounded by the Pir Panjal ranges in Himalayas.

The Gujjars wear salwar kameez, and the women wear a special headgear, and they speak Gujjari. The males dye their beards with mehndi. They eat maize, rice, gram, wheat, pulses and take salty tea with bread. There are two types of Gujjars found in the Jammu and Kashmir known as the Jamindars and Dodhi. They are the ardent followers of the prophet.

Mons is another tribe which is found in Ladakh, and they are assumed to be the original dwellers of the Indian subcontinent. They are also called as the water dwellers and said to have originated from the Tibetian community. They are Austroasiatic in the origin, and they are assumed to have settled in the Indian sub-continent much before the coming of the Aryans and the Dards. The historians believed that prior to the coming of the Aryans, the Bhots and Mons arrived in the fertile meadows of the Indian upper Himalayas. The Mons constructed beautiful castles, and the early chronicles and the literature mention about the songs and the music played by the Mons and the Bedas. The Mons drums are still beaten in the lectures of the Their Holiness Dalai Lama. The Ladakhi Mons are considered to be of the lower tribe, and they are known for supplying the music to the villages in the upper slopes of Himalayas. The Mons are believed to have come from the south, and they play the drums to please the Gods and the dignatries in return for which their land was returned to them. The Ladakhi music played by the Mons is appreciated by even the veteran musicians from the west who appreciate their music for the notes that go up in a stepwise fashion, and in the down notes, they move in an interlocking pattern. Another class similar to the Bheda is Garhwali caste, and the monasteries in Ladakh every year organise the music confluences in which the Mon and Bheda tribe play the music. Bodh tribe in Ladakh is another tribe that has its descent in the Mahayana sect of Buddhism with Gelukpa (Yellow shirts) and Drokpa (Red shirts) and the Lamas as they are popularly called as are proficient in making paintings, art and drawings. Gara are the blacksmith clan in Ladakh. The Garas are known for their typical Ladakh dress, which is gamcha, goncha, perak, firoz and scarf. They mainly consume non-vegetarian food. Gaddis are the shepherds that are found in the state of Jammu and Kashmir. They chew tobacco and play a musical instrument which is known as ponoth, and besides the Hindu religion, they also celebrate another festivals called as Pitrolu and Shari. Orissa is known for its tribes such as Kondh, Bonda, Sauras, Santhals, Gond, Bhumias, Koyas, Parajas and Oraons.

The Gonds are the most artistic tribe that is known for its art. By occupation, they are the warrior tribe that is found in the hills of Koraput, Kalahandi, Sambalpur and Gonda. Gonds is the largest tribe that is found in the world, and their staple food is kodo and kutki, and they believe in the Gods of the Earth, Air and Water. They speak Gondi, and they practice stick dance, and they celebrate the Hindu language. The Gond paintings of Mandla are famous across the world for the colourful depiction of the flora, humans and animals. The paintings have motifs of gopis with pots on their head and portraits of Krishna with cows. Santhals are worshippers of the spirits, and they do not believe in the worship of idols. The tribals speak the language Santhali.

Gadava is the most ancient tribe of Orissa, and they belong to the Munda group in the Lamataput, and they speak Gutab and Desia dialect of Austroasiatic language, and they practice the shifting cultivation. The women from the Gadaba tribe wear the Kereng.

The major popular tribes found in the state of Jharkhand include Banjara, Bhatudi, Chik Baraik and Mahli. Asur tribe is another tribe that is found in Dumla, Palamu and Latehar districts of Jharkhand. They are the Austroasiatic tribe, and they stay in the houses that are made with clay. There houses do not have any windows, and they paint the external walls of the house with paintings. The epic Ramayana has a mention of this tribe Asuras, where it mentions of the righteous king Bali who is sent to the pataloka by Vamana. These people possess various tools and equipment for iron smelting, baskets, dresses, ornaments, and their houses are rectangular in shape. Their houses have a door and a wooden gate, and they believe in animism. They worship the animal gods which include Singbhonga, Dharati mata, and Duari, celebrating many different local festivals. Baiga is another tribe which is known as the medicine men.

Festivals of Indigenous Communities

The indigenous seed festival is celebrated and is termed Burlang Yatra. This festival is celebrated in the Kandhamal district of Odisha. This festival promotes the sociocultural harmony in the indigenous community and also leads to the generation of a culture of sustainable farming. It promotes socio-learning and helps in resolution of the indigenous conflicts and ecological imbalances.

To adapt to the adverse climatic conditions, farmers from all over the world are adopting sustainable eating habits. Farmers are increasingly growing millets, and the cultivation is picking pace mainly in the tribal zones of the state of Orissa. Indigenous seed festivals are celebrated with fervour to cherish the spiritual and religious values in the preservation of the indigenous communities. Due to the importance of seed cultivation for the human race, India has promoted the use of millet through self-help groups. In the Koli hills region in Tamil Nadu, the leaders of the native or tribal communities play an extremely important role in protecting the traditional knowledge and narratives. The convention on biological diversity held in 1992 at the Rio Earth Summit did recognise the importance of traditional knowledge and indigenous communities in promoting sustainable agricultural practices. Malayali people living in the western belt of the Koli Hills region in Tamil Nadu have originated from the proto Australoid group. This practice is mainly undertaken by the local communities, which belong to the same proto Australoid group that has a linkage with the Harappan civilisation. The storage of the millet in clay pots is a practice that has been followed from time imme-morial. The communities are still holding to the practice of storing the millets seed in the clay pots. Out of the many traditions attached with millet cultivation, one of the important traditions is the Kolli Malai songs. From the birth till death, there are various practices for the conservation of millet seeds. Millets are increasingly being used for promoting culinary habits among the tribal people and communities. In a labour-intensive society, millets provide fortitude and strength to the labour class. *Oor Mugatham* is the group leader, and he onsets the farming season. Thus, millet growing is fast emerging as a sustainable farming practice in Tamil Nadu. Millet farming is a practice that is embedded in the social fabric of tribal society in India and Orissa. The major factor behind the sudden popularity of the millets is the cultural practices that are promoted through various songs and rituals, and the musical practices play an extremely important role in the adoption of sustainable practices in India through millet cultivation. In order to enhance household consumption, India has undertaken various initiatives, including organising the millets festival, cooking competitions, awareness cam-paigns and training with competitions to invite various millet recipes. India is providing various incentives to promote the cultivation and production of millets.

Dhinga Gavar festival in Rajasthan is celebrated by the tribal women of Rajasthan. These women adorn themselves with gold, and no unmarried men are to come near to these women, and if they do, they are beaten with the sticks. If the stick touches the men, it is believed he will be married soon. Similarly, Bhagoria festival in Chhattisgarh is dedicated to the lovers, and during this festival, the lovers are given the permission to run away, before they have applied colour to each other and eaten on betel leaf. Kila Raipur rural sports festival is celebrated in Punjab. This festival is celebrated in Qila Raipur (Ludhiana) in Punjab, India, and the competition is held for major Punjabi rural sports, including cart race, athletic events and rope pulling; in the month of February, this festival is India's rural Olympics. This festival is celebrated at Kila Raipur since 1933. Moatsu Mong festival is celebrated in Nagaland, and it is celebrated in the first week of May and is known as the spring festival of Nagaland. Sammakka Sara Lamma is celebrated in Jatara, Telangana, and it is believed to be approximately 1,000 years old and is one of the biggest festivals after the Kumbh mela and gold is offered to the goddess to honour. Vautha fair is held in Gujarat, and this is the largest animal fair in India. The main attractions of the fair are the donkey and camels decorated with colour. Made Made Snana, Karnataka is the festival celebrated to throw some light on the atrocities meted out to the lower caste. This is organised at the Kukke Subramaniam festival, and lower caste people are made to roll over the left-over food of Brahmins. The Gauchar Mela, Uttarakhand, is a popular fair among the Garhwali's; Gauhar mela is the weekly fair held on 14th November. This festival is famous for food stalls, handicrafts, dance and music to enthral the visitors. Rongali Bihu Sentinelese is another festival celebrated thrice a year in January (Bhogali Bihu), April and October (Kongali Bihu). Rongali Bihu also marks the Assamese new year in April. Minjar, Himachal Pradesh, is generally held in the month of July and August. During this festival, the locals are dressed up in colourful silk dresses and offer prayers at Laxmi Narayan temple.

Hornbill festival is celebrated from December 1 to 10 in Northeast, India, and it is called as festival of festivals. The state of Nagaland is home to various tribes which have their own distinct tribes, and this festival is named after the Indian hornbill, the large and colourful forest bird. Madhya Pradesh is home to various tribes and cultures, and Madai festival is celebrated to celebrate ritualistic performances like folk dance, prayers and sacrifices of the goats. These sacrifices are dedicated to goddess Kesharpal Kesharpalin Devi, one of the tribal deities. Bhagoria festival is celebrated among the young boys and girls to elope with the partners of their choice, and during this festival, the Bhilala tribe boys put red powder on the face of the girl whom they want to marry. Mim Kut, the maize festival, is aimed to celebrate the harvest maize, during the August and September. And Sekrenyi festival is celebrated among the Angami Naga tribe and Tsukheyi festival is celebrated by Chakesand Naga tribe. To mark the end of the harvest, the Kut festival is celebrated by Kuki Chin Mizo tribe in Nagaland. In the Imphal valley of Nagaland, a particular festival, Ningol Chak Kouba festival, is celebrated by the Meiti women, when they feast at the paternal home. If the substantial part of the harvest remains unconsumed, then Sikpui Ruoi festival is celebrated by the Kuki Chin Mizo tribes. Chiithuni festival of the Maos Nagas is the new year post-harvest festival that is celebrated in Nagaland. The post-harvest celebration of Gaan Ngai of the Zeliangrong tribe is a seven day post-harvest celebration. Gang Ngai festival is celebrated in Manipur, Nagaland to worship the ancestors with feasts, cultural performances and followed by the dancing of the girls and boys. Sulia festival is celebrated in Orissa by the Kandha tribes to mark the sacrifice of the animals and the birds in Balangir district in Odisha. The forefather of the Balangirs, Sulia Budha, is worshipped by the Balangir. In Arunachal Pradesh, the Apatani tribes celebrate the Myoko festival.

On the 14th November of every year, the Garhwalis celebrate the Gauchar mela. Nilachal mountains close to river Brahmaputra is the seat of Goddess Kamakhya where Ambuabachi festival is celebrated with pomp and splendour. During the Dusshera festival, lathi-wielding devotees from Karnataka and Andhra Pradesh gather at the Devaragattu Temple in Kurnool to hit each other on the heads to commemorate the killing of a demon by Mala-Malleswaram (Shiva). Pnars tribe in Jaintia Hills celebrate the Behdienkhlam festival in Meghalaya to chase away the demon of cholera. Koya tribe in Koraput, Orissa, celebrate the Chaitra Parva which is also known as Bija Pandu festival. A 10-day long Sume Gelirak festival is celebrated in Odisha for 10 days. Kang, the Rath Yatra of Manipur Meiteis, is a 10-day festival that is celebrated in Manipur. This is the festival when the Lord Jaganath leaves his temple in car known as the Kang. The famous Ras Leela dance is performed on this day too. Tangkhul Naga post-harvest is a weeklong festival for merrymaking and social bonding on last three days.

As the spring spreads its mantle over the Earth, the flowers bloom and the mother Earth takes a full turn, and the seasons change. To celebrate the change in seasons, the blooming of the flowers and the returning of the soldiers back home, the tribal people celebrate various festivals. The Rung tribe of Pithoragarh, Uttarakhand, in India celebrate the Kandali festival, and this festival coincides with the blooming of the Kandali flower, which blooms once in 12 years in the Chaundas valley. The three tribes namely Rung, Bangbanis and Joutiya celebrate this festival. General Zorawar Singh Kahluria who was military head of Dogra Rajput, along the river Kali and after returning from the loot, was resisted by the women of the village and the victorious folklore of the Kandali is still famous across the globe. This festival is also known as the Kirji festival.

Sarhul festival is celebrated in April, and this festival marks the beginning of spring and dedicated to the worship of the Earth and nature. This festival is celebrated by the tribes known as Ho, Oraon and the Munda tribe. The Sarhul festival has its origin in the myth of the Mahabharat. It is believed that Munda tribal helped the Kauravas to the fight the Pandavas, and the bodies of the Mundas who died fighting the Kaurvas were covered with the leaves of the sal tree; this kept the bodies safe, and this gave rise to the Sarhul tribes. The other famous folklore is of the Bindi tribe, the only daughter of the mother Earth. One day when Bindi did not return home from bathing in the pond, her mother searched for her daughter. Bindi was with the God of underworld, and they appealed for her return. The God of Death settled for a compromise that Bindi will spend half of her time in the underworld and other half of the time on the Earth. Since that time, this festival is celebrated every winter by the Ho, Oraon and Munda tribe in Jharkhand, India.

Another interesting tribe is the Dimasa tribe of Northeast. The most populous tribal groups in north-eastern India are Dimasa. Assam's North Cachar Hills, Cachar and Karbi Anglong districts are home to these tribes. Bodo-Kachari clan includes Dimasa tribal community. According to history, the Dimasa tribes were the first Brahmaputra Valley residents. The term "Dimasa" refers to the Brahmaputra River and its children. Hilltop dwellings with rivers or streams are common among Dimasa tribes. Most houses are built on earth plinths in two rows with a considerable gap between them. An important village institution is "Hangsao". The village's unmarried youths and girls form it. Religion is important to Dimasa tribes. Festivals, music, religious rituals and customs enrich this tribal culture. The Dimasa believe Banglaraja is the highest deity. Tribal people revere Lord Banglaraja, Sibrai, spirits of good and evil, Sakainjeek, and Madai. Rikaosa, Richa, Paguri Rimchau and Rimchaoramai are traditional men's clothing, while ladies wear Rikhra, Jingsudu, Rijamfini, Rikaucha, Rijamfinaberen, Rigu, and more. Dimasa Daikho reflects their religion. A Daikho has a territorial deity and Khel followers. Dimasa Kacharis worship their ancestral deity annually before sowing paddy. The name is Madai Khelimba. Dimasa indigenous people celebrate Bushu and Hangsao with music and dance. Dimasa daily life revolves around music and dance. This community's men and women dress in traditional attire and perform folk dances during these festivities. They perform Baidima, Jaubani, Jaupinbani, Rennginbani, Baichargi, Kunlubani, Daislelaibani, Kamauthaikim Kaubani, Nanabairibani and others utilising their traditional musical instruments like Muri, Muri-wathisa, Supin Khram, Khramdubung.

The Hornbill festival in Nagaland is the festival celebrated by various ethnic groups in Nagaland, North-eastern India. More than 60% of the population depends on the agriculture, and this festival celebrates agriculture. This festival is celebrated in Kisama Heritage Village, and the objective of this festival is to promote the heritage. During the week-long festival, the people relish the fairs, food, games, rituals, performances and the handicraft and crafts of Nagaland. The ethnic tribes found in North-eastern India are known as Nagas; however, it includes various tribes which include Konyak, Lainong, Makury, Nokko, Para, Somra Tangkhul and Tangshang. The languages spoken by the Naga tribes include the Sal languages. The Nagaland has 16 recognised tribes which include Angami, Ao, Chakhesang, Chang, Khiamniungan, Konyak, Lotha, Phom, Pochury, Rengma, Sangtam, Sumi, Yimchunger, Zeme-Liangmai (Zeliang), Kuki and Kachahri. Naga people, prior to the Sanskritisation and Westernisation through Christianity, mainly believed in animism. The festivals celebrated by the Nagas mainly include forests, the fertility, community bonding, sowing and harvesting and merry-making after harvest. The other festivals celebrated by the Nagas include Thuni festival as a post-harvest festival, Poang Lum as premier festival of the Chang Nagas, Sukrunye festival by Chakhesang, Mimkut festival the post-harvest festival by Kuki tribe, Bishu as post-harvest festival by Kachari tribe, Ngada festival, Ahuna festival, Wangala festival, Chaga festival, Hega festival celebrated mainly by Zeliang tribe to name a few. The state of Jammu and Kashmir celebrates various festivals. The most important festival is the Hemis festival in the Hemis Monastery, and this festival is celebrated every 12 years. This festival is celebrated to celebrate the mental and physical health of the people. Spituk Gustor Zanskar is the traditional festival celebrated by the monks to recreate the killing of the anti-Buddhist emperor of Tibet Langdarma by the Buddhist monks. The Galdan Namchot is yet another famous festival of the festival of Jammu and Kashmir. Indian Government recently launched the tribal festival to provide artisans, and entrepreneurs the opportunity to promote the tribal culture. The Lathmar Holi of Vrindavan is well known throughout the world. As per the mythology, Lord Krishna visited Barsana during the days proceeding the Holi and ended up teasing the gopis. The Gopis retorted by beating the Krishna with lathis.

Another popular tribal festival is Bhagoria festival celebrated in Jhabua and Khargone district of Madhya Pradesh. This festival is the pre-marriage selection ground where Bhil men and the Bhilala tribe from Madhya Pradesh go spouse hunting. This festival celebrates the elopement of the men and women who later on are accepted as the bride and bride's groom by the society. Thaipaum festival is celebrated in Tamil Nadu by devotees of lord Muruga, and it involves various act of penance such as walking on coal and piercing lips with the spears. During the onset of winter season on night of Dussehra, the Kurnool district of Andhra Pradesh celebrates the Banni festival near Devaragattu temple, where they carry the idols of Siva and Parvati in their hands. They also carry the sticks with which they beat each other. Garuda Thukaoom is another festival celebrated in Kerala. Garuda is believed to be the vehicle of the Lord Vishnu, and as per the legend, Vishnu sent Garuda to goddess Kali to quench her thirst by drinking his blood. During this festival, the people dress up like Garuda, and they hang themselves from their waist with hooks. These days, the hanging is done with tied cloths. The establishment of the Tharu Tribal Museum in Uttar Pradesh, specifically in Tharu Pradhan village and Imila Kodar village of Balarampur district, reflects the government's recognition of the rich cultural heritage of the Tharu tribe. This initiative is essential for preserving and showcasing the traditions, artifacts, and history of the Tharu community and contributing to the conservation and promotion of indigenous cultures in India. This tribe celebrates Deepawali festival as the mourning festival. Federation of Indian Chambers of Commerce and Industry (FICCI) participated in the "Great India Tribal Festival", to be held in InterGift held from September 13 to 17 2023 with the support of Ministry of Commerce and Industry. At the same time, Adi Mahotsav was celebrated in the various states of India.

Palm Conservation by Indigenous Tribes

Mizoram and the states of southern India are well known for their palm conservation efforts. Despite the fact that Mizoram is recognised as the bamboo queen, southern India is famed for its oil business and palm oil conservation. Women in southern coastal districts such as Kozhikode are actively involved in palm conservation. Similarly, in the eastern states, mangrove conservation and restoration has become critical for maintaining ecological balance and sustainable development. Mangrove forests should be preserved in order to supply raw materials for manufacture, and mangrove production and conservation are inextricably linked to the protection of ecology and the environment. Irrigation of mangroves contributes to a more sustainable technique that leads to more diversity and output. Similarly, there can be a lot of tourism developed around the concept of ecological tourism. The Indian government has launched a number of initiatives to conserve the coastal ecology and mangrove plantations. While plantations play an essential role, tribes frequently follow the shifting crops. Many indigenous cultures are increasing land productivity through rotation and shifting farming. However, shifting farming frequently causes forest fires.

Anthropology of Tribes in India

The cultures of both castes and tribes are in constant interaction with each other in Indian civilisation, which is a confluence of so many communities founded on the basis of birth and origin, classed as castes and tribes. The origins of the castes and tribes are extremely difficult to pinpoint on a timeline. Change and modification assimilation is the cause of constant change and progress in tribal society. Numerous historical events have altered the trajectory of these tribal cultures that have flowed through Indian civilisation since time immemorial. The ability of these communities to survive the withers and shocks of cultural shifts is exclusively responsible for their sustainability. The world has recognised the significance of these communities, which have remained strong in the face of numerous waves of change, in conserving the environment and human civilisation's history. Indeed, the beneficial characteristics of these communities include their distinct talents, knowledge and sustainable practices, as well as their close contact with nature, which is expressed through narratives, cultures, stories, festivals and religions.

Members of a tribe are integrated through common cultural practices, which are preserved in the form of services and rituals at various religious places, including temple services at famous temples such as Jaganath Puri, Odisha. Furthermore, occupational homogeneity is the foundation of tribe creation among the diverse tribes. Groups and communities are created based on occupation, and these groups and tribes provide a source of income for the members of the group. Throughout the tribes' history, communities have moved from one place to another in quest of a livelihood and a vocation.

The most common phenomenon among the numerous tribes and their people is migration. This is a very regular occurrence among members of the Santhal culture. Indeed, many social scientists and scholars feel that Hinduization of culture and language plays an important part in tribal propagation. The majority of tribal languages have their roots in the Sanskrit language, which has led to the tribe's progress and well-being. The tribes' anthropological qualities include geographical sovereignty, shared customs and ancestry through birth. The social resilience, territorial attachment, segmental solidarity, economic sovereignty, the centrality of family and the use of rudimentary technology are the key reasons responsible for the social revolution of these tribes. Tribes keep their distance from one another, and various climatic conditions and resources give rise to subsistence economies and communities. There is no agreed definition of tribes, save from a few definitions provided by social scholars. Many Indian epics, including the Mahabharata, Ramayana and Jataka stories, make mention of tribes and diverse cultures. Various sociological processes, such as Sanskritisation and Westernisation, influence societal evolution. The literature emphasises the significance of Westernising the practices and traditions of the disenfranchised lower class in order to enable the transition and advancement of the lower castes into the mainstream. Sanskritisation has so arisen as a fundamental trend of tribal and tribal people social reformation. The second aspect that leads to the upliftment of many tribes and communities through the use of social forces is social mobility. The Kharwar of Palamau in Bihar and Mirzapur as well as the Polia of Dinjapur, Rungpur, Jalpaiguri and Coonch Behar are among the most noteworthy of these social uprisings. Nyishi tribe found in Arunachal Pradesh have staunch belief in the existence of the spirits and spiritual matters.

Over time, the emphasis has been placed on the caste census in order to enumerate the ordering of tribe members in society. One of the key trademarks of tribal social mobility, as demonstrated by the anthropological model, is the lack of fight for power among tribal people to the top class. Anthropology is the field in India that deals with tribes and tribe identification. As previously noted, many studies and researchers have attempted to examine native people or indigenous people from the standpoint of anthropology in order to determine the origins of human civilisation. With the issues that the tribal population encounters, a specific discipline of political studies has evolved to address concerns about the rights of community or tribe members. Thus, tribes members have a sacred bond with nature, which manifests itself through culture, deities, gods and festivals. As a result, these indigenous people hold incredibly unique wisdom that can lead the path for a sustainable civiliaation.

Tribes have segmentary and egalitarian genealogy, and they are not interdependent unlike the other sects and sections of cultures. Much to the fortune of social structures and society, the tribes are more egalitarian, and they work on non-literate ethnic traditions. They sustained by subsistence farming, shifting cultivation and hunting and gathering. They are isolated from the society and form groups with people with same characteristics and nature.

The Anthropological perspective on Indian tribes has several elements. Majumdar (1958) was a functionalist anthropologist who stressed the relevance of disruption in the culture's basis in producing strains and stresses in the culture. According to him, the foundation of any culture is determined by four variables: man, area, resources and cooperation. He emphasised the significance of cultural resilience. Majumdar states that if a culture is robust enough, it can absorb shocks and return to its former form by decomposing or transforming to attain equilibrium. He felt that assimilation of changes throughout time resulted in transformations and positive developments in society. He was also an integrationist because he emphasised the need of assimilation. Majumdar researched several tribes and cultures, notably the Khasa tribes. Sanskritisation, along with Westernisation, aided in the transformation of India's tribal caste society.

The usage of mass media, such as film, has played a critical part in the upliftment of lower castes and communities. The adoption of higher caste rituals and traditions has played a critical part in the upliftment of the lower castes. Prior to the Sanskritisation of tribal culture, society ordering was mostly vertical; but, with the Sanskritisation of tribal society, society ordering has become horizontal, with upward mobility among tribe and community members. Substantification of tribal society has been tremendously significant in tribal society upliftment. The growth of numerous sects, religious practices and locations has caused the fault lines between the top and lower castes to blur. The practice of Sanskritisation involves a cultural transformation in which lower castes and communities adopt the customs, rituals, and practices of the higher castes to elevate their social status.

Tribal Traditions

Indigenous people believe that most knowledge is embedded in their natural surroundings, in the ground, in plants, herbs, shrubs, riverine, mountains. Indigenous people celebrate various customs and traditions where they develop a relationship with the nature and the human and non-human world. They celebrate the afterlife and believe in genealogies and the importance of knowing the origins, which include discovering the roots of human lineage. Thus, genealogies and the afterlife are two important events for the native people. Through this ontology, they develop the epistemology of indigenous lives and native people and their association with the human species.

Tribal Language and Rituals

The tribes have their own social norms, ritual codes and styles of communication. The review of literature highlighted that there are mantra, mudra, dhvani and vyavahariki, which include code of inscriptions. Most indigenous peoples were localised or lived in isolated territory, hence gestures developed in tribal/ indigenous conditions with many local dialects and languages. They spoke one language. Poor transportation kept strangers isolated, so they developed a gesture-based lingua franca. This helped travellers, those lost in the jungle and those who entered another tribe communicate. They then gestured to indicate their intent or clarify their position. Mantras also form an indispensable part of the communication of tribal people and their gest to form a connection with the nature.

There is a famous narrative surrounding the use of mantras by the indigenous tribes. According to belief, Lord Hanuman is said to be now residing in the Kaliyuga era, specifically in the vicinity of the Piduru highlands in Sri Lanka. The Matanga tribes have a mantra that enables one to perceive the visual form of Hanuman. One of the logbook recordings documents the tribes' assistance to Hanuman ji in obtaining honey from a bee hive. As a result, Hanuman ji was pleased and bestowed the tribes with a mantra. These are the documented entries from the log book of the Matanga tribes. Visiting Sri Lanka grants access to the record book, and in 2055, Lord Hanuman may become visible, providing the fortunate with the opportunity to witness his divine presence. Dhvani and use of musical instrument is an important part of spiritual expression of tribes and indigenous people. The major element and structure of literature can be explained with Dhvani. The aesthetic effect (Rasā), the figural mode and devices (Alam-kāra), the stylistic values (Riti) and excellence and defects (Guna-dosa). Dhvani has two elements namely Sphota or the grammar and Vyanjana or the poetics. The famous saying goes that काव्यस्य आत्मा ध्वनि: or ध्वनति इति ध्वनि: – That which sug-gest both word and meaning is Dhvani. The Dhvani theory found its first sys-tematic expression in Ānandvardhan's "Dhvanyāloka". His theory dominated Indian poetics from the 9th to 12th century AD. The narrative of Nachiketa and Yama is a testimony to the staunch belief in afterlife for the native people. They believe that after life, there is another life and the living beings move in circles. The Hinduism has made its vast impact on tribal life. However, some tribal people are fast modernising to adopt Christianity and Buddhism. Tribal people have also undertaken various movements such as Bhagat movements, which include Tana Bhagat movement, the Nemha Bhagat movement, and Bachi Dan Bhagat movement are some movements undertaken by the Bhagat tribe for inclusion. The tribal people have immense contribution to the freedom of India. Hon'ble Birsa Munda movement to free the lands from the control of Zamindars had a great contribution in the independence movement of India. Thus, indige-nous tribes are making extremely novel contribution to the ecology and devel-opment of a territory, and their rights should be protected adequately.

The Oral Traditions of the Tribes and the Tribal People

The folktales and folklores are the creative expressions of the traditions of the society in a rural environment. These traditions include myths, stories, folklore, rituals, dances, riddles and puzzles, and these have been passed on from generation to generation. Many of the European historians and the researchers have shown interest in these folklores and chronicled them in the form of books such as Santal folklores, Sora tribe tale and other such stories.

Tribes and Music

Tribes identify and differentiate themselves by the use of the music, and each of the community has its own form of music. Tribal people make and compose various forms of music which include tribal, plains and folk. The music of the tribes ranges from Carnatic which includes playing clarinets, brass and drums to celebrate the rituals, celebrations. One such example is the use of rhythm, parallel symphonies where by the music is tied and related to the structure of the dance. The dances and the music in tribal life are connected to the nature. The buffalo trumpet in the Kanha district, called as the hakum, is related to the harvest season. This also includes playing of various drums such as mandri, kotoloka and kundir. During the Bhagoria festival near the time of Dussehra, various folk songs are played and celebrated. The girls greet the grooms with the Dadariya songs. Pardhauni and Tertali are other kind of dance forms performed by the tribes in Madhya Pradesh, India. Further, Saila dance is performed by the many other tribes in India. Redcliffe has demarcated two forms of musical strata which include cultivated and uncultivated music which can be categorised as classical and countryside music which includes seasonal, ceremonial, ritual, narrative and love songs. Further, the music can be desi sangit or marga sangit. The marga sangit is the original composition, and the desi sangit is the regional and localised sangit. Yet another folk art form Rammat refers to the traditional arts of Bikaner and Jaisalmer, as well as the deserts of Rajasthan. Originally, Bikaner was known for its heroic songs, most of which were about Rajasthan heroes. There are various other popular forms of art such as Khayal, which have originated in Rajasthan, and it comprises of famous folklore and poetic interpretations such as Dhola and Maru.

Conclusion

Culture of the indigenous groups in terms of their festivals, beliefs and attitudes plays an important role in the success of the entrepreneurial ventures. These indigenous people have skills in various art forms, food, various types of garments and the textiles. Indigenous people are known for their unique traditions that include the songs and dances and the folklores. Most of the important practice in a self-help group is contributed by the traditions, culture of the indigenous clans and people. The United Nations has adopted the goal for the conservation of the traditional practices of the tribal people including the rights to conservation of the towns and villages.

Further Reading

Teltumbde, A. (2016). Dichotomisation of caste and class. *Economic and Political Weekly*, *51*(47), 34–38. http://www.jstor.org/stable/44165876

Fuller, C. J. (2017). Ethnographic inquiry in colonial India: Herbert Risley, William Crooke, and the study of tribes and castes. *The Journal of the Royal Anthropological Institute*, *23*(3), 603–621. ISSN 1359-098.

References

Britannica, T. Editors of Encyclopaedia. (2014, May 14). *Toda*. Encyclopedia Britannica. https://www.britannica.com/topic/Toda-people-India

Chaubey, G., Kadian, A., Bala, S., Rao, V. R. (2015, June 10). Genetic affinity of the Bhil, Kol, and Gond mentioned in Epic Ramayana. *PLoS One*, *10*(6), e0127655. http://doi.org/10.1371/journal.pone.0127655. Erratum in: PLS One. 2015;10(7): e0134200. PMID: 26061398; PMCID: PMC4465503

Davey, G. (2016). Identity and quality of life among Badagas in South India.

Devadasan, P. (2016). A study about the lifestyle of Jenu kuruba tribes working as unorganized laborers.

Fuller, C. (2022). Ethnography and racial theory in the British Raj: The anthropological work of H. H. Risley. In *Bérose - Encyclopédie internationale des histoires de l'anthropologie*. Paris.

Ghosh, S. (2020, May). Mongabay. https://india.mongabay.com/2020/11/climate-change-may-have-pushed-the-toda-community-up-the-nilgiris-3500-years-ago/

Guha, A. (2018). Social anthropology of B.S. Guha: An exploration. *Indian Anthropologist*, *48*(1), 1–12. https://www.jstor.org/stable/26633108

India.gov.in national portal in India. (2024, March). Schemes by the Government of India. India.gov.in national portal in India. https://www.india.gov.in/my-government/schemes

Kivisild, T., Rootsi, S., Metspalu, M., Mastana, S., Kaldma, K., Parik, J., Metspalu, E., Adojaan, M., Tolk, H. V., Stepanov, V., Gölge, M., Usanga, E., Papiha, S. S., Cinnioğlu, C., King, R., Cavalli-Sforza, L., Underhill, P. A., & Villems, R. (2003, February). The genetic heritage of the earliest settlers persists both in Indian tribal and caste populations. *The American Journal of Human Genetics*, *72*(2), 313–332. Epub 2003 Jan 20. PMID: 12536373; PMCID: PMC379225. https://doi.org/10.1086/346068

Majumdar, R. C. (1958). The Indika of Megasthenes. *Journal of the American Oriental Society*, *78*(4), 273–276.

Chapter 2

A Systematic Literature Review Study on the Social Inclusion of the Indigenous People

Abstract

Developing economies like India have adopted the Sustainable Development Goals of sustainable cities and communities and reduced inequalities to achieve inclusive development and growth. Globally, the indigenous communities or tribals seek reparation for conflicts between proclaiming indigenous rights and claiming natural resources. There is little literature on challenges to the social inclusion of the tribes or the indigenous people. This literature review study aimed to (a) introduce the problem of social exclusion of indigenous people, (b) discuss the most researched dimensions of social inclusion of the tribal or indigenous people using relevant theoretical frameworks and (c) to develop conceptual frameworks on the theory of social inclusion of the indigenous people. PRISMA protocol was followed, and various tools were used for bibliographic management and text mining with 58 articles selected from 944 journals indexed in Web of Sciences. The analysis of the literature underscores four pivotal themes namely (1) the cultural identity of indigenous people, (2) the debate on the legitimacy of the rights of indigenous people rights and sustainable development, (3) factors impacting the social inclusion of the indigenous people and (4) coping strategies for the social inclusion of the indigenous people. The literature review highlights urgent needs to socially include indigenous and tribal people. Various factors impact the financial inclusion of the poor, including cognitive and affective factors. It is essential to leverage the skills and expertise of the local indigenous people for forest management and land management to ensure the social inclusion of the poor and tribes.

Keywords: Sustainable development goals; indigenous inclusion; social exclusion; social inclusion; financial inclusion

Sustainable Pathways, 41–69
Copyright © 2024 Nishi Malhotra
Published under exclusive licence by Emerald Publishing Limited
doi:10.1108/978-1-83549-490-520241005

Introduction

Indigenous communities or tribes are the historical communities that have existed for ages along with the mainstream communities. Most of these communities are plagued with land ownership challenges, inhospitable lifestyles, poor health conditions, poverty and social exclusion. The basic premise for their existence is a powerful identity based on cultural factors. Heraclitus and Hume have high-lighted the importance of ethnic and cultural sameness as the prerequisite for the identification of a tribe. These ethnic or indigenous people are different from the mainstream. Thus, although the identity of sameness is important, it is only through the recognition of the differences between the communities that the identity becomes relational (Niezen, 2003). In 2015, the United Nations endorsed the agenda for sustainable development. This goal aims to reduce poverty while achieving social, economic and environmental sustainability (United Nations, 2015) equitably. This goal is to ensure that no one will be left behind.

Under the recent condition of globalisation and modernisation, the indigenous identity arises contextually (Cohen, 1978). In India, the Constitution of India provides for the identification of the indigenous people as scheduled tribes. In the constituent assembly, while framing the Constitution, Jaipal Singh, the tribal representative, favoured the term *Adivasi*. Still, Dr B.R. Ambedkar favoured the use of the term scheduled tribes because, according to him, the scheduled tribes are the people with the mark of identification, i.e. to mark out the people with differences in physical features in religion, physical features, language and custom, (Saksena, 1981; Verma, 1990). In India, there are 705 ethnic indigenous groups officially recognised as 'Scheduled Tribes'. Indian Constitution and several legal provisions, such as the Fifth schedule for central India and the Sixth schedule for several areas of north-eastern India, provide for the self-determination and recognition of the rights of the indigenous people. However, India also voted in favour of the Declaration of Rights of Indigenous People, consenting that after independence, all the Indians were indigenous. But the implementation of these rights is free from being satisfactory. Despite constitutional identity, the tribes have not been included in the mainstream due to the lack of the requisite skills. Through the theoretical lens of the resource-based view, the indigenous people are seeking redressal for the conflicts that arise as they find it difficult to assert their indigenous rights (Ambagudia, 2010). As per the existing literature, the tribal people face various threats to the indigenous land and resources, including the dislocation of indigenous resources from traditional use in the name of environmental conservatism. Besides that, the poverty level is the highest among the indigenous people. Tribes have never been holistically included in the mainstream, but efforts have been made to include them through various policy measures (Xaxa, 2008). Social inclusion of the tribes is a major challenge accentuated by various social, cultural, economic, political and technological factors. These challenges include the inability to participate in social, economic, political and cultural life. It also consists of the distance from mainstream politics, isolation from social mechanisms, poverty, social exclusion and discrimination, problems in cultural assimilation and identification of tribes and lack of a sociopolitical framework to include the poor and indigenous people through various rules and regulations (Panda, 2017). This study aims to wholistically analyse the existing literature in the domain of the problems in the social inclusion of indigenous tribes in the mainstream through relevant theoretical lenses.

Definition of Social Inclusion

Disadvantaged people form the contours and boundaries of the social exclusion problem in India (Poppay, 2010). The concept of social exclusion was originally developed in Europe. But due to adoption by the World Bank, the concept has gained wider acceptance among developmental organisations and institutions (Silver, 1994). Within the extent of literature, social exclusion has been defined as having two dimensions: the *shopping list* approach and the *relational* approach. The shopping list approach describes social exclusion from the perspective of the 'state' experienced by marginalised members of indigenous or tribal groups. From the shopping list approach, the excluded members of the society suffer from exclusion from specific types of experiences due to lack of a livelihood, permanent employment, property, land, housing, minimum consumption levels, education, skills, democratic participation, dominant race, humanity, respect and fulfilment. Thus, social exclusion is not simply the lack of money but refers to various psychological and social experiences.

On a *relational* plane, social exclusion is defined as the exclusion of individuals from a society driven by the unjust distribution of power and the existence of hierarchal power relationships within a social structure. Fig. 1 highlights the various dimensions of the social exclusion problem. Broadly, the social exclusion could be due to a lack of appropriate *conditions* or ecosystem in the form of livelihood, democratic participation and land and housing to ensure *participation*. Secondly, it might be in the form of hierarchal power relations and unjust distribution of resources. This could be a result of a lack of social identity. To ensure social inclusion, there is a need to frame appropriate legislation, protocols and

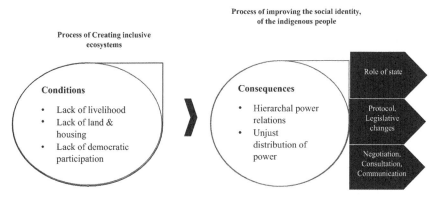

Fig. 1.   Dimensions of Social Exclusion.

legal changes to ensure participation. It also envisages a role for the state in policymaking. Towards this end, there is a need for proper negotiation and consultation to provide a social identity for the indigenous people.

The World Bank has defined social inclusion as improving how individuals participate in society. Social inclusion empowers individuals to take part in society through empowerment. It empowers the poor and marginalised individuals to take advantage of the opportunities. This enables individuals to access financial markets, services and social and public places (World Bank, 2013). Indigenous people or tribal people are excluded from society, as they have unique needs. They need loans much more frequently, in small sizes and at extremely low-interest rates. Social exclusion is defined as the absence of social integration and lack of power. It is an outcome of the lack of social capital, which can be defined as the networks of social relations among people characterised by norms of trust and reciprocity (Stone, 2001). Lack of social inclusion has been defined as lower levels of social trust and lack of reciprocity among the group members (Cameron, 2005). Social exclusion is defined as a group gaining a privileged place for its member at the expense of the other groups. Max Weber, a late 19th- and 20th-century German political economist and sociologist, gave this definition. Also, the members who have been excluded from the insurance system are termed socially excluded (Lenoir, 1974). France was the place of origin of the concept of social exclusion. Most marginalised people were excluded from the social system due to the lack of opportunities in the social and economic spheres. Atkinson (1998) has defined social exclusion from three dimensions: agency, relativity and circumstantial. Social exclusion results from the norms and expectations of the members of the society. This is termed an *agency*. Or this could be an outcome of the act of the individuals and institutions who might want to exclude them by their *decisions*. Social exclusion might also be an outcome of the norms and expectations of society at a specific time, which is termed *relativity*. Burchardt et al. (2002) has emphasised that an individual is socially excluded if they cannot participate in the activities of the society in which they reside. Amartya Sen (2000) has defined social exclusion as the lack of the capabilities required to participate in the social process. There are approximately 476 million indigenous people or tribes world over in approximately 90 nations across the world. These people constitute around 6% of the total global population. These people often lack formal recognition of their land, territories and natural resources (Gracey & King, 2009). They often suffer various social barriers and cannot participate in political and social processes and get access to social justice (The World Bank, 2020). These social and economic conditions lead to low-income people's marginalisation and exclusion from the mainstream. Indigenous people are more likely to suffer from various kinds of exclusion.

Research Problem

Education for sustainable development has been conceptualised to address the various global challenges in preserving ecology and biodiversity. To date, the pedagogy in ecological conservation is mechanistic and does not consider natural and local factors. Indigenous ways of living emphasise the bonding, interconnection and reciprocal stewardship in the natural settings of the world and thus are indispensable for sustainable development. Thus, it is important to realise that Education for sustainable development is encapsulated within the natural laws and indigenous knowledge owned by the natives and the stewards of the forests called indigenous people. We contend that addressing an existential threat from the same epistemological perspective as what generated the issue will not result in the necessary transformation for the sustainability of our biosphere (Jones, 2019). These indigenous people have access to the rarest knowledge about the forests, climate change and the biosphere, to name a few. Based on a set of natural laws, indigenous cultures have a natural awareness of the many interconnections and reciprocity required with our environment (Thaman et al., 2013). This study aims to review the existing literature and themes in conserving the indigenous community knowledge, practices and cultural codes to ensure social inclusion for achieving the UN Sustainable Development Goals (Selaledi et al., 2021).

Methodology

The systematic literature review was adopted for analysis (Thomas & Harden, 2008; Tranfield et al., 2003). The systematic literature review is a scientific process driven by rules to ensure comprehensiveness, transparency and bias-free (Dixon-Woods & Silverman, 2011). Thus, a systematic literature review is a high-level overview of the primary research that identifies, selects, synthesises and apprises all relevant, high-quality research evidence. Based on the quality, certain studies were identified and filtered from the study. The systematic literature review helps to eliminate the bias and answer a few focused questions. In a systematic literature review, several essential components such as prespecified eligibility criteria, systematic search strategy, and assessment of the validity of study findings, assessment of the validity of study's findings, interpretation, and the reference list, are meticulously followed to ensure rigor and reliability. This kind of literature review links the practising research to high-quality evidence and supports evidence-based practice.

The Web of Sciences (WoS) and Scopus databases were used for the literature review. In the initial research, approximately 945 research articles were selected. The key papers were selected using key terms such as the social exclusion of the indigenous people. While shortlisting the papers, the main criterion was the different perspectives on the subject of social exclusion of the indigenous or the tribal people. Ultimately, 50 papers that are most relevant to the study were shortlisted for the study. In this study, the bibliometric analysis and the content analysis of the existing studies in the domain of the social inclusion of indigenous tribes are included for analysis.

To synthesise the literature following our theoretical frameworks, the themes identified were organised around the respective theoretical constructs of *legitimacy theory* to discuss the issue of identity crisis among the members of the indigenous groups and tribals, *social contract* theory to discuss the issue of factors impacting the social inclusion of people with low incomes and *dynamic punctuated equilibrium model* to discuss the coping strategies to mitigate social inclusion among the indigenous groups. The following research questions drive the research:

- What evidence is there in the literature that social exclusion, particularly cultural identity crisis, is a major challenge towards achieving Sustainable Development Goals for indigenous communities?
- What evidence is there in the literature that multiple factors impact the social inclusion of indigenous people?
- What evidence is there in the literature that various coping strategies are adopted by the state and welfare bodies to ensure the social inclusion of indigenous communities?

To conduct the systematic literature review, the following steps as prescribed by EPPI Centre (2007) were followed, and it is illustrated graphically as in Fig. 2.

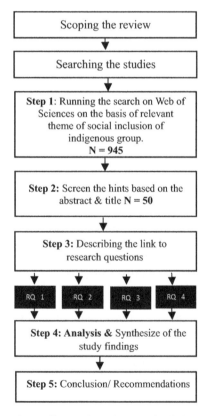

Fig. 2.   Flow Chart Illustrating the Methodology for Systematic Literature Review. *Source:* Adapted from EPPI Centre (2007).

- *Scoping the review*: The explicit criterion was specified to decide which studies will be included in the systematic literature review. The criterion for the inclusion of the articles in the systematic literature review is given in Table 1.

Table 1. Criterion for the Inclusion of Articles in the Systematic Literature Review.

Criterion Type	Inclusion Criteria
Topic	Literature must relate explicitly to the research questions (social exclusion of indigenous people).
Database	Literature must be listed in the Web of Sciences or Scopus.
Geographical spread	Literature must relate to natives and indigenous communities from any place in the world.
Research methodology	Research must be based on qualitative research.
Transparency, reliability and validity	Research must be explicit with well-defined methodology, sample size, instrument, analysis, etc. The findings of the research must be reliable and valid.

The steps for the systematic literature review using the PRISM methodology are given below:

Searching the studies: To select the articles for the research study, only studies listed in Demonstration, Scopus and WoS were selected. The articles that were not available completely were removed from the database. While culling the data, extreme care was taken to extract the data. The data were extracted and saved in the comma-separated values (CSV) and Bibtex format and stored for further use. For the selection of the keywords, the terms social inclusion and indigenous communities were used for analysis. The filtration was limited to the articles in Q1 and Q2 journals indexed in the WoS. The criterion was applied to the qualitative and empirical studies. The free bibliographic software Mendeley was used to compile and manage the documentary databases.

Screening the articles based on abstract and title: The protocol was designed to conduct the systematic literature review. This included screening through the title and abstract. The bibliographic coding was done using the VOSviewer, a software for creating network maps based on network data to screen the articles. These maps help to visualise and explore these maps. A total of 1,602 keywords, the limit was established to 32 keywords. The research paper for the bibliometric analysis was shortlisted using the *Dimension* software. The research questions were conceptualised at this stage, and a linkage was established between the literature review and the research questions.

Research questions development: The study aims to conduct a bibliometric and systematic literature review. The research questions identified are listed above, alongside the justification. A descriptive analysis was undertaken to provide information about the annual citations, performance of the journals and keywords. Trinidad et al. (2021) prescribe this method because it allows the researcher to understand the reliability of the journals and publications. Knowledge about the citations can enable the researcher to understand the journal. The conceptual analysis helps uncover the latest research topics and hotspots in the dataset. The description of each portion of the bibliometric analysis for the journal is given below:

- *Publication analysis:* This step aims to measure the authors' contribution to the indigenous people's social inclusion using the full counting method, which provides 100% weightage to the contributors or the authors.
- *Bibliographic coupling:* Bibliographic coupling occurs when two or more authors cite one or more papers common (Kessler, 1963). This method aims to determine the relatedness of the two publications in terms of bibliographies (Abdullah & Naved Khan, 2021).
- *Citation analysis*: This analysis is used to examine the popularity of an article by measuring the number of times or frequency of an article is cited (Ding & Cronin, 2011).
- *Co-word analysis:* Co-word analysis is used to discover the research hotspots using the keywords and their co-occurrences (Bui et al., 2020).

Analysis and synthesis of the results: The research papers were extracted as articles from the *Demonstration* software. The bibliographic methods explored the information needed to analyse the research questions. *VOSviewer* was developed by Eck and Waltman (2010) and is a widely used software for network mapping of keywords, countries and journals. VOSviewer is used to build network maps to visualise and analyse the relationships between the selected items (Gu et al., 2021), keywords, nations and journals.

Research Findings

Bibliometric Study

The bibliometric analysis utilises the most important studies to identify the most influential patterns and trends in the social inclusion of the indigenous community patterns. Therefore, this section further emphasises the critical results generated via bibliometric analysis.

Descriptive Analysis

The most thorough overview of the publication patterns, trends and citation patterns for the social inclusion study is provided in this paragraph, followed by the most important themes and practices in the research on the social inclusion of indigenous tribes or communities.

Network Visualisation

The network visualisation further portrays the co-words, countries and bibliographic coupling. The network analysis gives the researchers a graphical visualisation of collaboration, co-occurrences and bibliographic coupling. The network visualisation section presents the relations between the selected sections using node size, node colour and connecting lines' thickness (Guleria & Kaur, 1989–2019; Zhang, 2019).

Co-authorship Countries

Bibliographic coupling for the nations is presented in Fig. 3 with network visualisation. A country's minimum number of publications is 5. Of the 131 nations, 59 met the threshold. The number of clusters, links and total strength was calculated

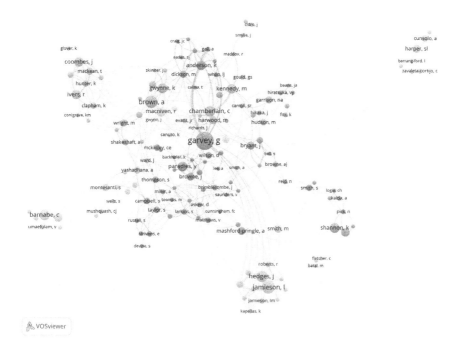

Fig. 3.   Bibliographic Coupling for the Nations (Network
Visualisation).

for all the nations. The number 1 nation was the United States, with 729 documents, 9,219 citations and 170,700 link strength. The other nations were the United Kingdom (355; 5,768; 137,543), Australia (501; 6,067; 121,925), Canada (490; 5,627; 137,543) and Germany (108; 1,313; 55,577). The different colours in the document show the clusters are more frequently linked to each other. It implies that the nations originated from the nations in the same cluster that was more frequently linked with each other. At the biggest cluster are the United States of America, the United Kingdom, Australia, Canada and Germany.

Bibliographic coupling (Kessler, 1963): introduced bibliographic coupling to highlight the similarities between two articles (Freire & Veríssimo, 2020). The bibliographic coupling plays a vital role in determining the relatedness of the selected items such as publications. In this study, the bibliographic coupling of the articles was conducted using the VOSviewer software. Bibliographic coupling is required to understand better the essential theoretical foundation of the 161 publications included in the sample for the analysis. The analysis reveals that there is a set of 151, i.e. 93.78% of the sample. (Jennie Poppay, 2010).

From the list of the 151 articles, the articles with the highest indices of bibliographic coupling are mentioned below:

- Mustonen, T., Harper, S., Pecl, G., Broto, V. C., Lansbury, N., Okem, A., Ayanlade, S., Ayanlade, A., Dawson, J. (2022). The role of Indigenous knowledge and local knowledge in understanding and adapting to climate change.
- Berrang-Ford, L., Dingle, K., Ford, J. D., Lee, C., Lwasa, S., Namanya, D. B., ... Edge, V. (2012). Vulnerability of indigenous health to climate change: A case study of Uganda's Batwa Pygmies. *Social Science & Medicine*, 75(6), 1067–1077.
- Akinola, R., Pereira, L. M., Mabhaudhi, T., de Bruin, F.-M., & Rusch, L. (2020). A review of Indigenous food crops in Africa and the implications for more sustainable and healthy food systems. *Sustainability*, 12(8), 3493. MDPI AG. http://doi.org/10.3390/su12083493
- Kenny, T.-A., Little, M., Lemieux, T., Griffin, P. J., Wesche, S. D., Ota, Y., Batal, M. et al. (2020). The retail food sector and Indigenous peoples in high-income countries: A systematic scoping review. *International Journal of Environmental Research and Public Health*, 17(23), 8818. MDPI AG. http://doi.org/10.3390/ijerph17238818
- Nyboer, E. A., Reid, A. J., Jeanson, A. L. et al. (2023). Goals, challenges, and next steps in transdisciplinary fisheries research perspectives and experiences from early-career researchers. *Reviews in Fish Biology and Fisheries*, 33, 349–374. https://doi.org/10.1007/s11160-022-09719-6

Bibliographic coupling of the publication exists when two publications share the same reference to an article. Alternatively, articles with similar research interests can be identified using the bibliographic coupling of publications. Fig. 4A and B provide details of the network analysis for the bibliographic coupling.

(a)

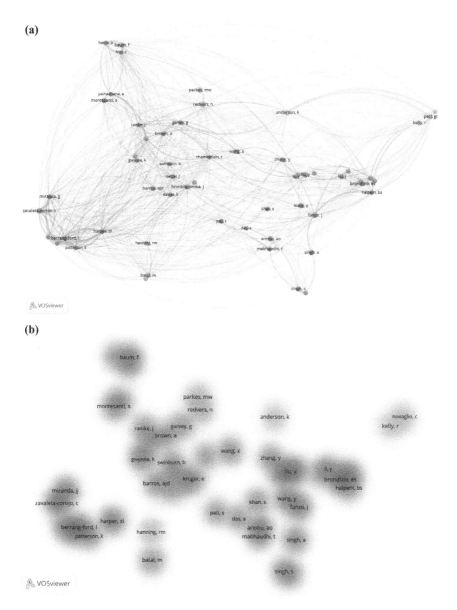

(b)

Fig. 4.   Network Analysis Through Bibliographic Coupling. (a) Visualisation of author wise co-citation analysis. (b) Co-word analysis of keywords: heat map.

Popular Themes in the Literature on the Social Inclusion of Indigenous People

After conducting the bibliographic analysis, a highly rigorous literature analysis was performed to determine the general trends and patterns in the social inclusion of indigenous communities across the globe. The UN Declaration on the Rights of the Indigenous Peoples identifies indigenous people as 'people' with the right to self-determination. *Article 3:* Indigenous people possess the right to self-determination. They can determine their political status and freely pursue economic, social, and cultural rights. *Article 4:* Indigenous people exercise their right to self-determination and have the right to autonomy or self-government in matters relating to their internal and local affairs, as well as ways and means for financing their autonomous functions.

Cultural Identity in the Social Inclusion of the Indigenous Tribes

Indigenous communities have a historical continuity, were invaded and now consider themselves distinct from the mainstream population, per United Nations Department of Economic & Social Affairs (UN-DESA): Indigenous people. Another definition is: 'Peoples in independent countries who are regarded as Indigenous on account of their descent from the populations which inhabited the country, or a geographical region to which the country belongs, at the time of conquest or colonization or the establishment of present state boundaries and who, irrespective of their legal status, retain some or all of their own social, economic, cultural and political institutions' by (ILO) International Labour Organization's Indigenous and Tribal People's Convention. These people have developed a niche for themselves because of their traditional knowledge about the biodiversity passed on orally from generation to generation (Teran, 2018). World Intellectual Property Organization (WIPO) (2018) has defined traditional knowledge of the indigenous tribes as 'The intellectual and intangible cultural heritage, practices, and knowledge systems of traditional communities, including Indigenous and Local Communities (traditional knowledge in a general sense or *lato* sensu).'

Besides the economic reasons such as poverty, the contemporary literature defined social exclusion as a result of the dynamic social processes that lead to the lack of participation of people experiencing poverty in the economic processes and the workings of society (Finer & Smyth, 2004). Thus, the social exclusion of the poor, as experienced by the indigenous tribes and communities, is complex and multidimensional. It cannot be defined as a unidimensional notion of poverty as a lack of economic resources. Most of the existing dimensions lack a basic definition of social exclusion of the poor as a lack of participation in decision-making. Identifying cultural and indigenous rights is most important to ensure the social inclusion of the indigenous people (John, 2008). Towards this end, many researchers argue that maintaining a cultural identity different and diverse from the mainstream can lead to chronic poverty and the foreclosure of various employment and education opportunities for indigenous communities and people. While establishing a direct causal relationship between cultural identity and social exclusion can be complex, it is evident that cultural identity plays a significant role in shaping the experiences of indigenous communities within mainstream society. Thus, the first challenge to the social inclusion of the indigenous tribes and communities is the presence of a powerful cultural identity, which makes them unwilling to take up gainful skills for employment. Further, since they are extremely poor, they are motivated to be connected to their historical identity and culture. This is the first cumulative model of social inclusion of indigenous communities that highlights the disadvantages of cultural identity and the need for modernisation to ensure the social inclusion of the poor. Many social researchers, such as (John, 2008), argue that the economic integration of the indigenous communities is a challenge due to their zeal to stay away from the mainstream to maintain their cultural identity. Thus, there is an increasing role for the state and the Government to ensure the modernisation of these tribes to ensure economic upliftment. But there exists a trade-off between the modernisation of the tribes and their cultural identity (Hunter, 2007). Thus, the social inclusion of the indigenous tribes is a multidimensional problem that cannot be resolved by simple redistribution of resources. Indigenous people are essentially critical also for sustainable development. The right over the land and resources or the property right is one of the most crucial parts of their cultural identity, and they assert that the protection of the jurisdictional protection rights is most important for the economic, social and cultural development of these communities (Jojola, 2008). To analyse the complexity of their assertion of property rights and resources, the theoretical lens of the resource-based view (Prahalad & Hamel, 1990) is used to analyse the dimensions of the problem. Thus, the challenges to the social inclusion of the tribes are the protection of their rights and the state's recognition as an independent cultural entity with a cultural identity (Li, 2000). But ensuring their economic growth and achieving sustainable development involves a mission drift. Thus, for the prosperity of the indigenous communities, the tribal people need to be sensitive to the context in which the audience negotiates. To protect their indigenous rights and cultural identity, these people have to negotiate with the international audience within the contours of the policy frameworks designed by the state legislature and judiciary (Weiner, 2009).

The Paradox of Homogenous Identities Among Indigenous Tribes

As quoted by *Quine*, 'To say of anything that it is identical with itself is trivial, and to say that it is identical with anything else is absurd. What then is the use of identity?'.

Undoubtedly, the cultural identities of indigenous people are essential in the recognition of the indigenous people. And the assertion of these rights is fundamental. However, as far as the current literature in the domain of the cultural identity of the indigenous tribes is concerned, it looks at this issue through the philosophical traditions of *essentialism* and *primordialism* (Sylvain, 2002). The pertinent question is regarding the legitimacy of their identities. The power source in their current identities is mainly the historical precedence imposed above from the patriarchal state and colony and built around the traditional values of God, family and nation. These identities are not shared or social and are driven by a common ancestor and origin. These identities are more exclusionary and lead to the inability to participate effectively in social, cultural and economic community life. To legitimate these identities, there is a need for the bottom-up approach through increased participation in decision-making and making the identities more contextual. There is a need for creating a more diverse identity that goes beyond the identity of origin to the shared and collective identities established through network relations and social relationships with mainstream politics and the state (Bauman, 2007). This sensitivity to the modern context and increasing globalisation will enable the tribes to achieve self-identification. Thus, the literature highlights that identities should be relational and traditional. Through the theoretical lens of the dynamic punctuated equilibrium model (Sabherwal et al., 2001), with the change in the context and environment, there is a need for the indigenous communities to not only exploit its existing resources but to explore new opportunities to facilitate social exchange through social capital. This is because these indigenous groups face extreme poverty, illiteracy and do not have any resources to be used as collateral. Their property rights are dubious and the subject of public policy debate. They need social capital generated only through reciprocal relations and knowledge sharing with society and the state. This social capital will enable them to indulge in social exchange and access finance and resources through negotiation and commerce (Ito, 2003).

Relevance of Cultural Identity of the Indigenous People

In the Indian state, the economic growth of the people across the states is not uniform. Human beings are excluded from the socio–economic development initiatives. The economic growth of the people across the states is not consistent. The existing literature highlights that poverty and social exclusion are due to social and institutional discrimination (Sonowal, 2008). Indeed, many corporates have identified the relevance of the unique knowledge of the local communities (Tata Group, 2023). Tata Group recognises the relevance of the indigenous communities' local knowledge and seeks to develop business models to leverage these models. The existing literature highlights the importance of value creation by the tribal people. It involves leveraging the core competencies of the local people for forest management, displaying the culture through tribal tourism, enhancing handicraft capabilities, which are of national importance to certain economies, and deriving the benefits of being considered part of mainstream society. In this regard, the literature highlights the importance of identifying the cultural differences between the indigenous communities and the mainstream populace. The literature highlights that the other collective or social identities, such as ethnicity and the indigenous identity, arise contextually as part of a series of nested dichotomisations in relation to the social distance between oneself and one's interlocutors (Cohen, 1978).

Further, the literature highlights the importance of cultural pluralism. It highlights the need for cultural assimilation to promote economic development while maintaining the cultural pluralism of tribal communities (Vidyarthi & Rai,

1985). Tribes or religious members have requisite uniqueness in culture and knowledge, but they have never been integrated into mainstream society due to the lack of the requisite skills. The state and welfare communities can play an essential role in the social inclusion of these communities through various policy measures (Xaxa, 2008). The state takes various initiatives to integrate indigenous people into the community through cultural assimilation.

Coping With Cultural Changes and Context: Empowering the Indigenous Communities Through Social Capital

Table 2 provides the conceptual framework for the ownership of natural resources based on the resource view framework. The aboriginals or the indigenous inhabitants are the people who are the owners of the ecological niche in the form of land and forests. These tribals have possession of the social and cultural codes. These tribes are essentially a self-contained system of resources. The tribals use political and ritualistic authorities to manage the resource in the natural settings of the land and forests.

Strategies to Leverage the Competitive Capabilities of Tribal People

The knowledge of these tribal communities can be leveraged for sustainable development. The value creation by the tribal communities comprises of (1) leveraging the core competencies of the tribals for forest management, (2) displaying the culture through tribal tourism, (3) enhancing capabilities in handicrafts, which are of national importance to certain economies and (4) deriving the benefits of being considered part of mainstream society.

Theoretical Framework to Understand the Dynamics of the Cultural Identity

Indigenous communities are distinct social and cultural groups with a shared identity due to the collective ancestral ties to the land and unique social customs

Table 2. Natural Resource Based on the Resource View Framework.

Strategic Capability	Environmental Force	Key Resource	Competitive Advantage
Ownership of an ecological niche	Knowledge of the tribes Driving force – social and cultural codes	Ownership of the land and forests	Self-contained system of resources
Possession of the unique skill and knowledge	Resource management by the political and ritualistic authorities	Cultural identity by control of cultural rights Kinship	Aboriginals or the original inhabitants of the forest

linked to the place where they live. Thus, the natural resources and the land are linked to their identities, culture, livelihoods, spirituality and physical welfare. These groups usually have a spoken language of their own. Most of the communities do not have ownership of the land, and the ownership is under customary ownership. Thus, the basis of their survival is their cultural identity, and they face a threat to cultural survival (World Bank, 2023). This study integrates the theoretical framework of the dynamic punctuated equilibrium and resource-based view to understand the concept of the cultural identity of the indigenous tribes and people.

Table 3 briefly describes the evolution of the indigenous tribes within the boundaries of the state of India. In the pre-colonial period, the tribals were considered the lords of the jungle or the forest dwellers who lived under the kinship of the chieftains. They were unique in terms of the existing customs, language, traditions and practices. They had conflicts with the ruling classes and differed from the mainstream agrarian society. Thus, the pre-colonial period is described as the Evolutionary period, where the tribal people with unique customs and traditions conflicted with kinship. During the colonial intervention, the British colonists started various policy measures for the emancipation of the tribal people, and the Government Act 1935 was passed. The colonists prescribed a very protectionist policy towards these tribals. During this period, the tribal people mainly depended on Government measures, including protectionist measures to promote the welfare of the tribal people. The period after the 20th century is mainly the revolutionary period, during which the Constitution of India recognised the unique jatis and rights of the tribal people. The Constitution of India adopted Article 330 and Article 332 for reserving the seats for the scheduled tribes, providing for the electoral reservation and demarcation of the reserved communities. Despite all the efforts, the existing legislative and legal systems have failed to provide justice to the marginalised sections of society.

Factors Impacting the Social Inclusion of the Indigenous People or Tribals

Indigenous people or tribals are the people who are not participating in the social system due to various affective and cognitive factors. Over the period, there has been a shift in the definition of the indigenous people or the tribals. The definition has shifted from the people who are called indigenous by virtue of origin or are categorised by certain biological factors such as the identity of origin or prejudice against a particular religion or caste. In a group, the identification of the people in the group is based on the perception of oneness of belongingness and collection of the people with the same social identification (Tajfel & Turner, 1979); since the reformation and the revolution, the indigenous people are classified based on the structure. The structure refers to the formal network relations of the same occupation. This is often referred to as Assortative matching, and the group's identity is established based on certain economic or social criteria rather than the common origin (Stiglitz, 1990). Fig. 5 provides the classification for the indigenous tribes.

Table 3. Using the Temporal Strategy, the Description of the Status of the Tribes Through the Theoretical Lens of Dynamic Punctuated Equilibrium.

Evolutionary Period	Noise	Revolutionary Period
Pre-Colonial Period	Colonial Intervention	Post-Independence
Existence of local non-agricultural communities. These communities were dependent on land and forests for their survival. Akbarnama defined tribal people as 'men who go naked living in the wilds, and subsist by their bows and arrows and the game they kill.' The existence of kinship	The British colonial period indeed had a profound impact on the settlement of territories and the delineation of rights in regions with significant indigenous or tribal populations. During the colonial era, the Britishers frequently engaged in negotiations and agreements regarding the demarcation of land and the establishment of territorial boundaries. • The exploitation of the tribals or aboriginals • Certain policy measures • Overall further isolation of the indigenous people • Worsening living conditions of the tribal people • Deterioration in the social status of these people • Assimilation of these tribes or aboriginals by the Congress in their fight for independence	The passing of the Constitution of India Adoption of Article 330 and Article 332 for the scheduled tribe Electoral reservations Demarcation of tribal communities The protection of Civil Rights (Anti-Untouchabilities) Act, 1955; The Bonded Labour (Abolition) Act, 1976; Scheduled Castes and Scheduled Tribes (Prevention of Atrocities) Act, 1989, and rules, 1995; The Panchayat Raj Extension to Scheduled Areas Act, 1996; The Scheduled Tribes and Other

Table 3. (*Continued*)

	Evolutionary Period	Noise	Revolutionary Period
	Pre-Colonial Period	Colonial Intervention	Post-Independence
			Traditional Forest Dwellers (Recognition of Forest Rights) Act, 2006; The Criminal Tribal Act, 1871
	Cultural identity	*Cultural emancipation*	*Lack of cultural assimilation*
	• Resource use determines the cultural identity and survival of the people.	• The passing of the Government Act, 1935	• Lack of progress
	• Conflicts between the ruling empire	• Realisation of the need for the economic emancipation of the aboriginal people	• Lack of policy programmes • Increased inequalities • Classification as 'Backward Hindus'
Environment			
Internal Deep structures			
structures	*Mechanistic structures*	*Centralised*	*Recognition as a clan*
	Presence of chiefs and tribals reporting to the chief	The tribes were dependent on the state or the Government for welfare measures.	Hindu society started recognising the tribes as a separate clan.
	• Tribals such as Gonds, Khakkars and Jats participated in the conflicts of the chieftain's society	*The Government Act of 1935 was passed.*	The cultural clan was identified with a particular occupation.
	• Grouped as a tribe by their occupation – non-sedentary	Formation of a protectorate for the welfare of the tribals	Identification as a separate tribal identity and jati
		Recognition of tribals as a	

occupational characteristics and blood relations

marginalised clan in the Hindu society

Movement by colonial anthropologists like Verrier Elwin for the upliftment of the poor tribes and formation of the partial temporary protectorate

- Social customs and practices
- Categorisation – based on occupational traits as best cultivators, agriculturists
- Forest dwellers and protectors of the jungles

Cultural identity

- Unique language
- Unique social custom
- Traditions
- Unique cultivation practices
- Remote and primitive forest dwellers
- Mainly in cultivation and hunting practices
- Chanda, Bhandara, Byga, Dhaiya, Bewar of hill tribes

Different from the rest of India

- People with unique dance and social customs
- Veterans of agricultural practices with rift from the Hindu society

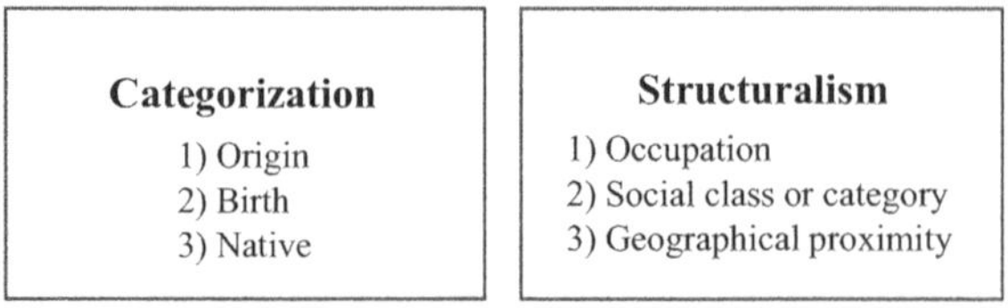

Categorization	Structuralism
1) Origin	1) Occupation
2) Birth	2) Social class or category
3) Native	3) Geographical proximity

Fig. 5.   Evolution of the Theory of Classification of the Indigenous Tribes.

Thus, beyond the illusion of homogeneity of these members in terms of occupation, there is a need for further leveraging the expertise of these tribes to conserve natural resources.

Factors Impacting the Social Inclusion of the Indigenous People or the Tribals

The scheduled tribes in India face the problem of migration and displacement due to industrialisation, debt traps and poverty (Jha & Jhingran, 2002). The geographical isolation of many indigenous communities is a well-documented reality that significantly impacts their access to resources, services, and participation in broader societal activities. This remoteness often results in limited access to infrastructure, healthcare, education, and economic opportunities, further exacerbating the challenges faced by indigenous populations. They are geographically and culturally isolated (Belfer et al., 2019). The studies discuss the lack of resources and social capital to ensure the social inclusion of indigenous people (Claeys & Pugley, 2016). The language barrier and lack of information about the financial creditworthiness of the indigenous people are other factors that impact social inclusion of the indigenous people (Larson et al., 2008). Due to these factors and the lack of literacy, the indigenous people suffer from the lack of work opportunities and livelihood with a low occupational pattern. They also suffer from a lack of health, poverty and increased issues regarding migration (Mukhim, 2013). Scheduled tribes often suffer from forced migration, displacement due to industrialisation and debt traps (Mitra & Singh, 2008). The factors can be expressed as *affective factors and cognitive factors*. The affective factors are described as (1) social biases, (2) gender feudal bias, (3) nomadic lifestyle, (4) extreme poverty and (5) low political representation (Japhet et al., 2015). The cognitive factors impacting the social inclusion of the poor include lack of literacy, digital divide, lack of digital readiness, lack of income and lack of resources, lack of social capital, lack of land rights, existing legislation and unequal distribution of wealth and resources among the indigenous people. The challenges faced by indigenous communities are often compounded by various other factors, including social and state neglect, tacit state denial, social or state violence, customary practices, and social norms. Thus, the affective and cognitive factors

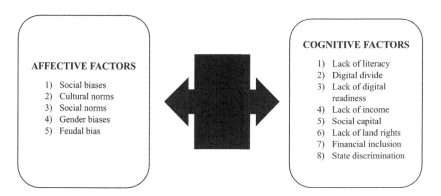

Fig. 6.   Factors Impacting Social Inclusion of Indigenous People and Tribes.

are the critical factors that impact the social inclusion of the poor. Fig. 6 illustrates the various factors that impact the social inclusion of the poor.

Indigenous people have cultural knowledge in the form of the skill of hand and knowledge about artifact making. Incorporating the indigenous knowledge of essential concepts and traditional knowledge should be based on respect, relevance, reciprocity and responsibility as key mechanisms for knowing and learning from them (Kirkness & Barnhardt, 1991). They have certain cultural codes that they do not share with anybody else. For sustainable development, recognising the indigenous knowledge system is significant. Indigenous knowledge is all-encompassing and adopts all external influences (Johnson, 1992). Indigenous knowledge acts as a guide for primitive human societies around the world for achieving sustainable development (Warren, 1991). This knowledge refers to the body of knowledge built by people through generations living in contact with nature. Thus, knowledge about the indigenous people paves the way for sustainable development.

Coping Strategies for the Social Inclusion of the Indigenous People and Tribes

Through the theoretical lens of social theory, the indigenous tribes and people have adopted various coping strategies. In the context of social theory, indigenous tribes, and people have adopted various coping strategies that can be viewed through the theoretical lenses of integration, electoral interventions, and assimilation. An inclusive society, in which all members or individuals have an essential role, is a fundamental aspiration for social equity, cohesion, and well-being. The concept of inclusivity emphasises the importance of creating a community where every individual, regardless of their background, identity, or abilities, can fully participate, contribute, and thrive. This society is based on embracing everything within its ambit and not forcing or coercing anyone. An inclusive community is diverse and uses participatory processes. In an inclusive society, everyone can achieve their full potential without restrictions. Public policy and actions form part of such initiatives.

Organic Integration

Socialisation of the tribes and the indigenous people is essential, as these people suffer from various challenges such as language barriers, social norms, discrimination and social exclusion. The socialisation of the marginalised indigenous people and tribes in the mainstream is influenced by the geographical and political context, including state ideologies. Thus, the state's role is vital in including indigenous people or tribes. In the socialisation of the indigenous people, there is a constant tension between the *identity blind* and the *identity-conscious* socialisation practices for the aboriginal people. Though equality in society can be promoted through the sameness of identity, the lack of similarities in cultural diversity and background can lead to further marginalisation of the indigenous tribes and people. Those practices of socialisation that identify the cultural differences among the members of the indigenous tribes and the people from the mainstream further accentuate the risk of marginalisation (Schwabenland, 2012). According to the literature, indigenous knowledge can play an essential role in achieving sustainable development goals, which include protecting against the decline in biodiversity, loss of ecosystems and climate change. The agrosystem approach, which is part of the indigenous knowledge of the poor tribals, can be adapted to achieve the United Nations Sustainable Development Goals (Shahmohamadloo et al., 2022).

An *integration approach* to social inclusion of the indigenous people includes various initiatives such as (1) dialogue, (2) promoting social integration, (3) creation of an inclusive society (Tu'itahi et al., 2021) The integrative approach to social inclusion is aimed at achieving (1) legal empowerment of the marginalised sections of society, (2) ensuring natural resource management for the poor and (3) relentless communication to ensure the social inclusion of the poor. The literature highlights the need to put indigenous and community-based targets and indicators into their biodiversity frameworks to ensure integrative growth (Fajardo et al., 2021). The literature emphasises the critical importance of establishing key indicators to monitor and assess the well-being and rights of indigenous communities. These indicators include several agreements for legal ownership and indicators of educational biocultural and environmental health. Moreover, the studies highlight the need to engage the communities through negotiations and meetings (Tauli-Corpuz, 2015). Within the integration approach, measures can be taken to recognise and incorporate indigenous people's rights under international law. The literature highlights that several nations have legislations and laws to conserve indigenous rights, but implementation and enforcement are lacking. The protocols should be developed for NGOs, private research companies and government bodies to conserve the rights of the indigenous people. Moreover, a mechanism should be created for implementing a biodiversity knowledge interface. There is a need to create coordination among knowledge systems, capacity building and literacy campaigns to ensure sustainable development (Huntington et al., 2002) The author's measure to improve the organic integration of the tribal community is to put in place strategies to reclaim the ancestral land (Nightingale & Richmond, 2021).

Assimilation is another approach that aims to include people who are not part of the mainstream and are entirely different from the rest of society. Cultural assimilation comes from the perspective that over time, the members of the society left out will adapt to the changing world around them and become homogenous or similar to most people. This assimilation will be achieved by adopting the culture, values and behaviours (Berry, 2011).

Dialectic Analysis of Indigenous Population Socialisation Practices

Macro and organisational contexts: In the first phase, due to the lack of state support and conflicts between the indigenous people and the state, the members of tribal groups have a conflict with their kinships. During the second phase, the indigenous people and the tribal groups generate the social capital with the state agencies as peasants. With reforms, the information flow capability of networks between the tribal groups and the state improves, and the state can exploit indigenous knowledge in the form of forest management and agricultural technology. This was the phase of emancipation of the tribes.

Conceptual Framework of Acculturation and Adaptation Strategies by Indigenous Groups

Social inclusion of the indigenous people is a rigorous exercise that involves various acculturation and adaptation strategies. Acculturation is the result of intercultural contact. These strategies involve cultural changes in both the groups and behavioural and psychological changes (Lebedeva & Ryabichenko, 2016).

From the literature review, using the temporal strategy (Langley, 1999), the analysis is done from the initial phase, where the social context is blind to the identity of the indigenous people. In the pre-colonial era, the tribes were marginalised. These tribes had a conflict with the existing kinship, and they were mainly forest dwellers or farmers. Their land rights were not recognised, and their knowledge was forcibly transferred to the rulers or the kinship. In the existing Hindu society, the indigenous tribes were marginalised. The strategy adopted in this stage was *leveraging dynamic capabilities through exploitation*. Exploitation is where the organisation leverages its capabilities through routines and processes.

The second phase is the stage of identity consciousness in which the caste peasant becomes the basis of cultural identity. It is part of *normative assimilation.* Assimilation refers to an organisational entity's routines and processes that allow it to analyse, understand and interpret the information obtained from external sources (Kim, 1997). Indigenous Knowledge System (IKS) refers to the indigenous people's rigorously tested methods and practices. These practices are the testimony of human intelligence and perseverance. The existing literature highlights the importance of the indigenous people in preserving the indigenous knowledge, which is purported to be superior even to modern knowledge (Negi & Bhatt, 2024). This knowledge is considered traditional and is passed orally from one generation to another through folklore, stories and cultural values. The strand literature highlights the need to engage indigenous communities in conserving forests and natural resources.

Through the lens of social equity, indigenous communities all over the globe act as inherent conservationists asserting their rights to natural resources and their development (Jolly & Thompson-Fawcett, 2021; von der Porten et al., 2019). In this stage, the indigenous people start identifying with the mainstream people and adapting their lifestyles to the majority population or the invaders. They forgo some of their heritage art and cultural practices. This metamorphic phase is marked by the generation of social capital comprising social exchanges and knowledge transfer. These routines and processes facilitate leveraging dynamic capabilities through innovation and knowledge transfer (Zahra & George, 2002). In this phase, the tribals are given a platform to communicate. They uniquely possess local knowledge in terms of agricultural technology, land and forest and communicate through predefined cultural codes and norms. They transfer knowledge through organisational learning and social capital form of partnerships.

In the third phase of identity consciousness, the commitment of the administrative system to the inclusion of the tribals and indigenous community increases manifold. This is the phase of depeasantization with the emergence of a new political framework for ethnic minorities within the constitutional framework. It is *organic integration* as it facilitates the development of the cultural identity and legitimate identification of the indigenous rights of the tribal culture. The integration strategies lead to positive psychological and socio-economic outcomes for the indigenous people (Berry, 1990).

These phases are displayed in Fig. 7.

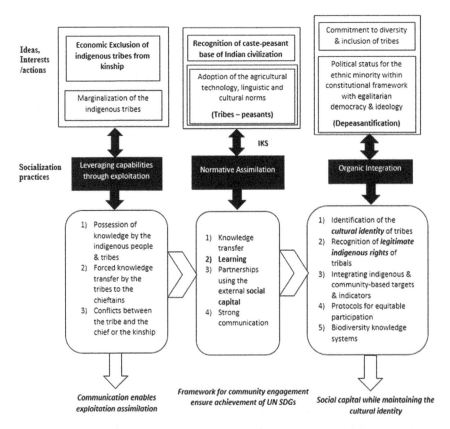

Fig. 7.   Dialectic Pathways in the Socialisation of Indigenous Tribes.

Conclusion

Indigenous people are the original people of the forests and the source of indigenous knowledge and practices. In the dynamic world, the conservation of natural resources has become an important issue. The tribes and the indigenous people can play an important role in preserving the biodiversity. There is a need for making the indigenous people partner in policymaking regarding natural resource management. Their integration into the economic and social system is essential for achieving sustainable goals. The integration of clans and tribes can indeed play a significant role in advancing the UN Sustainable Development Goals (SDGs), particularly in the realms of poverty reduction and community empowerment.

References

Abdullah, S., & Naved Khan, M. (2021). Determining mobile payment adoption: A systematic literature search and bibliometric analysis. *Cogent Business & Management, 8*, 1893245.

Ambagudia, J. (2010). Tribal rights, dispossession and the state in Orissa. *Economic and Political Weekly*, 60–67.

Atkinson, A. B. (1998). Social exclusion, poverty and unemployment. In J. Hills (Ed.), *Exclusion, employment and opportunity*. Centre for Analysis of Social Exclusion (CASE), London School of Economics and Political Science.

Bauman, T. (2007). You mob all agree?' The chronic emergency of culturally competent engaged Indigenous problem solving. *Indigenous Law Bulletin, 6*(29).

Belfer, E., Ford, J. D., Maillet, M., Araos, M., & Flynn, M. (2019). Pursuing an Indigenous platform: Exploring opportunities and constraints for indigenous participation in UNFCCC. *Global Environmental Politics, 19*(1), 12–33.

Berry, J. W. (1990). Psychology of acculturation. In J. Berman (Ed.), *Cross-cultural perspectives* (pp. 201–234). University of Nebraska Press.

Berry, J. W. (2011). Integration and multiculturalism: Ways towards social solidarity. *Papers on Social Representations, 20*(1), 2.1–2.21.

Bui, T. D., Ali, M. H., Tsai, F. M., Iranmanesh, M., Tseng, M. L., & Lim, M. K. (2020). Challenges and trends in sustainable corporate finance. A bibliometric systemmatic review. *Journal of Risk and Financial Management, 13*, 264.

Burchardt, T., Le Grand, J., & Piachaud, D. (2002). Degrees of exclusion: Developing a dynamic, multidimensional measure. In *Understanding social exclusion* (pp. 30–43).

Cameron, H. L. (2005). Social disadvantage and families with young children. *Journal of Family Studies, 11*(2), 297–316.

Claeys, P., & Pugley, D. D. (2016). Peasant and Indigenous transnational, 2019. Adaptation and resilience at the margins: Addressing Indigenous people's marginalization at international climate negotiations. *Environment: Science and Policy for Sustainable Development, 61*(2), 14–30.

Cohen, A. P. (1978). Ethnographic method in the real community. *Sociologia Ruralis, 18*(1), 1–22.

Cohen, G. A. (1978). *Karl Marx's theory of history: A defence.* Oxford University Press.

Ding, Y., & Cronin, B. (2011). Popular or prestigious measures of scholarly esteem. *Information Processing & Management, 47,* 80–96.

Dixon-Woods, M., & Silverman, D. (2011). *Qualitative research.* SAGE.

Evidence for Policy and Practice Information and Co-ordinating Centre. (2007). *EPPI-Centre, social science research unit.* Institute of Education. s.l.:s.n.

Fajardo, P., Beauchesne, D., Carbajal-López, A., Daigle, R. M., Fierro-Arcos, L. D., Goldsmit, J., Zajderman, S., Valdez-Hernández, J. I., Terán Maigua, M. Y., & Christofoletti, R. A. (2021). Aichi target 18 beyond 2020: Mainstreaming traditional biodiversity knowledge in the conservation and sustainable use of marine and coastal ecosystem. *Peer Journal, 9,* e9616.

Finer, C. J., & Smyth, P. (2004). *Social policy and the commonwealth prospects for social inclusion.* Palgrave Macmilian.

Freire, R. R., & Veríssimo, J. M. C. (2020). Mapping co-creation and co-destruction in tourism: A bibliographic coupling analysis. *Anatolia, 32*(2), 207–217.

Gracey, M., & King, M. (2009). Indigenous health part 1: Determinants and disease patterns. *Lancet,* 65–75.

Gu, Z., Meng, F., & Farrukh, M. (2021). Mapping the research on knowledge transfer: A scienctometrics approach. *IEEE Access, 9,* 34647–34649.

Guleria, D., & Kaur, G. (1989–2019).. *Library Hi Tech, 39*(4), 1001–1024.

Hunter, B. H. (2007). Conspicious compassiona and wicked problem: The Howard government's national emergency in Indigenous affairs. *Agenda, 14*(3), 35–54.

Huntington, H. P., Brown-Schwalenberg, P. K., Frost, K. J., Fernandez-Gimenez, M. E., Norton, D. W., & Rosenberg, D. H. (2002). Observations on the workshop as a means of improving communication between holders of traditional and scientific knowledge. *Environmental Management, 30*(6), 778–792.

Ito, S. (2003). Microfinance and social capital: Does social capital help create good practice? *Development in Practice, 13*(4), 322–332.

Japhet, S., Balagurumurthy, & Diwakar, G. D. (2015). De-notified tribes and criminal stigma in Karnataka. *Journal of social inclusion studies, 1*(2), 108–125.

Jha, J., & Jhingran, D. (2002). *Elementary education for the poorest and other deprived groups.* Centre for Policy Research.

John, G. (2008). The Northern territory intervention in Aboriginal affairs: Wicked problem or wicked policy. *Agenda, 14*(3), 65–84.

Johnson, M. (1992). *Capturing traditional environment knowledge, dene cultural institute.* Dene Cultural Institute & International Development Research Centre.

Jojola, T. (2008). Indigenous planning—An emerging context. *Canadian Journal of Urban Research, 17*(1), 37–47.

Jolly, D., & Thompson-Fawcett, M. (2021). Enhancing Indigenous impact assessment: Lessons from Indigenous planning theory. *Environmental Impact Assessment Review, 87.*

Jones, R. (2019). Climate change and Indigenous health promotions. *Global health promotion, 26*(3), 73–81.

Kessler, M. M. (1963). Bibliographic coupling between scientific papers. *American Documentation, 14*(1), 10–25.

Kim, L. (1997). *From imitation to innovation: The dynamics of Korea's technological learning.* Harvard Business School Press.

Kirkness, V. J., & Barnhardt, R. (1991). First nations and higher education: The four R's–respect, relevance, reciprocity, responsibility. *Journal of American Indian Education, 30*(3), 1–15.

Langley, A. (1999). Strategies for theorizing from process data. *Academy of Management Review, 24*(4), 691–710.

Larson, E., Johnson, Z., & Murphy, M. (2008). Merging Indigenous governance: Ainu rights at the intersection of global norms and domestic institutions. *Alternatives: Global, Local, Political, 33*(1), 53–82.

Lebedeva, N. M., & Ryabichenko, T. A. (2016). Assimilation or integration: Similarities and differences between acculturation attitudes of migrants from Central Asia and Russians in Central Russia. *Psychology in Russia*, 98–111.

Lenoir, R. (1974). *Les exclus: Un français sur dix*. Seuil. s.n.

Li, T. M. (2000). Articulating indigenous identity in Indonesia: Resource politics and the tribal slot. *Comparative Studies in Society and History, 42*(1), 149–179.

Mitra, A., & Singh, P. (2008). Trends in literacy rates and schooling among the scheduled tribe women in India. *International Journal of Social Economics, 35*(1), 99–110.

Mukhim, P. (2013). Social inclusion and its significance among indigenous populations. *Indian Journal of Human Development, 7*(2), 330–332.

Negi, V., & Bhatt, I. (2024). Climate change in the Himalayas. Current scenario & prospects.

Niezen, R. (2003). *The origins of Indigenism: Human rights and the politics of identity* (1st ed.). University of California Press.

Nightingale, E., & Richmond, C. A. M. (2021). Reclaiming mountain lake: Applying environmental repossession in Biigtigong Nishnaabeg territory, Canada. *Social Science & Medicine, 272*(C). ONLINE.

Panda, P. K. (2017). Inclusion and economic empowerment of rural-tribal women in lac value chain and market: A case study of Udyogi. *Journal of Social and Economic Development, 19*, 25–41.

Poppay, J. (2010). Understanding and tackling social exclusion. *Journal of Research in Nursing*, 295–297.

Prahalad, C. K., & Hamel, G. (1990). The core competence of the corporation. *Harvard Business Review*, 79–91.

Sabherwal, R., Hirschheim, R., & Goles, T. (2001). The dynamics of alignment: Insights from a punctuated equilibrium model. *Organization Science, 12*(2), 179–197.

Saksena, H. S. (1981). *Safeguards for scheduled castes and tribes: Founding fathers view*. Uppal Publishing House.

Schwabenland, C. (2012). *Metaphor and dialectic in managing diversity*. Springer. s.l.

Selaledi, L., Hassan, Z., Manyelo, T. G., & Mabelebele, M. (2021). Insects' production, consumption, policy, and sustainability: What have we learned from the Indigenous. *Insects, 12*(5), 432.

Sen, A. (2000). *Social exclusion: Concept, application and scrutiny*. Office of Environment and Social Development Asian Development Bank.

Shahmohamadloo, R. S., Febria, C. M., Fraser, E. D. G., & Sibley, P. K. (2022). The sustainable agriculture imperative: A perspective on the need for an agro system approach to meet the United Nations sustainable development goals by 2030. *Integrated Environmental Assessment and Management, 18*(5), 1199–1205.

Silver, H. (1994). Social exclusion and social solidarity: Three paradigms of social exclusion. *International Labor Review, 133*, 531–578.

Sonowal, C. J. (2008). Indian tribes and issue of social inclusion and exclusion. *Studies of Tribes and Tribals, 6*, 123–134.

Stiglitz, J. E. (1990). Peer monitoring and credit markets. *The World Bank Economic Review, 4*(3), 351–366.

Stone, W. (2001). *Measuring social capital: Towards a theoretically informed measurement framework for researching social capital in family and community life.* Australian Institute of Family Studies. s.l.

Sylvain, R. (2002). Land, water, and truth: San identity and global Indigenism. *American Anthropologist, 104*(4), 1074–1085.

Tajfel, H., & Turner, J. C. (1979). An integrative theory of intergroup conflict. In W. G. Austin & S. Worchel (Eds.), *The social psychology of intergroup relations* (pp. 33–37).

Tata Group. (2023). *We dream of a better world: The Tata group and the sustainable development goals.* Tata Group.

Tauli-Corpuz. (2015). *Tauli-Corpuz V. Rights of indigenous women and girls.* Report of the Special Rapporteur on the rights of indigenous peoples A/HRC/30/41.

Teran, M. Y. (2018). *Cultural foundations for developing a Kichwa language program.* Jutaprint.

Thaman, R., Lyver, P., Mpande, R., Perez, E., Cariño, J., & Takeuchi, K. (2013). *The contribution of Indigenous and local knowledge systems to IPBES: building synergies with science.* UNESCO. s.n.

The World Bank. (2020). *Indigenous peoples overview.* The World Bank. s.l.

The World Bank. (2023). *Understanding poverty – The Indigenous people.* [Online]. https://www.worldbank.org/en/topic/indigenouspeoples

Thomas, J., & Harden, A. (2008). Methods for the thematical synthesis of qualitative research in systematic reviews. *British Medical Council (BMC) Medical Research Methodology, 8*, 45.

Tranfield, D., Denyer, D., & Smart, P. (2003). Towards a methodology for developing evidence-informed management knowledge by means of systematic review. *British Journal of Management, 14*(3), 207–222.

Trinidad, M., Ruiz, M., & Caledron, A. (2021). A bibilometric analysis of gamification research. *IEEE Access, 9*, 46505–46544.

Tu'itahi, S., Watson, H., Egan, R., Parkes, M. W., & Waiora, H. T. (2021). The importance of Indigenous worldviews and spirituality to inspire and inform planetary health promotion in the anthropocene. *Global Health Promotions, 28*(4), 73–82.

United Nations. (2015). *Transforming our world: The 2030 agenda for sustainable development.* United Nations.

van Eck, N. J., & Waltman, L. (2010). Software survey: VOSviewer, a computer program for bibliometric mapping. *Scientometrics, 84*, 523–538.

Verma, R. C. (1990). *Indian tribes through the ages.* Publications Division, Ministry of Information and Broadcasting, Government of India.

Vidyarthi, L. P., & Rai, B. K. (1985). *The tribal culture of India.* Concept Publishing Company.

von der Porten, S., Ota, Y., Cisneros-Montemayor, A., & Pictou, S. (2019). The role of indigenous resurgence in marine conservation. *Coastal Manage, 47*(6), 527–547.

Warren, D. M. (1991). *The role of Indigenous knowledge in facilitating the agricultural extension process.* Paper presented at International Workshop on Agricultural Knowledge Systems and the Role of Extension.

Weiner, M. (2009). *Japan's minorities: The illusion of homogeneity.* Taylor n Francis. s.l.

World Bank. (2013). *Inclusion matters: The foundation for shared prosperity.* World Bank. s.l..

World Intellectual Property Organization (WIPO). (2018). *World intellectual property organization.* [Online]. https://www.wipo.int/tk/en/

Xaxa, V. (2008). *State, society and tribes: Issues in post-colonial India.* Pearson Education.

Zahra, A. Z., & George, G. (2002). Absorptive capacity: A review, reconceptualization and extension. *Academy of Management Review, 27*(2), 185–203.

Zhang, G., Kang, L., Dongxiao, G., Wang, X., Yang, X., Zhu, K., & Liang, G. (2019). Visualizing knowledge evolution and hotspots of rural environment and health: A systematic review and research direction. *IEEE Access, 7,* 72538–72550.

Chapter 3

Introduction to Tribes of India: How the Guild System Led to Emergence of Tribal System in India?

Abstract

Despite the Vedic texts and Puranas mentioning the emergence of Varnas and caste classification system, the origin of caste based on occupation and how they became powerful is not yet clearly known. However, the guild system that existed in the past did have a positive impact on the origination of the castes and tribes. This chapter aims to study the powerful guild system to understand the origins of Varnas and castes in the ancient India.

Keywords: Guild system; Varnas; tribes; ancient India; societal legacy

There is a popular saying that 'The strength of the tribe is the unity of the members'. These members of the tribal groups have been staying together for ages. The homogenous group of artisans pursuing the Dhokra art stay together and live at the outskirts of the village in Orissa. The artisan's place of abode is known by peculiar names such Kumbarara beedi for the street of carpenters and Kammara-Gaamo as village of ironsmiths. They migrate from place to place and live a nomadic life. They survive on nothing but the skill of the hand, and they occupy a position of pride in the mosaic of the world heritage. They pursue nothing but their heritage art.

Introduction

Community organisations are no new concept but the people who followed the same occupation and crafts, who stayed in the same place, organised themselves and formed guilds. The literature does not have much evidence about the existence of the guild organisations, and historians are divided about the existence of economic organisations, as there is no evidence about the same. The guild

Sustainable Pathways, 71–93
Copyright © 2024 Nishi Malhotra
Published under exclusive licence by Emerald Publishing Limited
doi:10.1108/978-1-83549-490-520241008

organisation was based on the Varna system, which depicted the division of labour. The Varna system comprised of the Brahmanical society, the Vaishyas and the Shudras. The lower economic class of the traders and artisans also organised themselves in the form of guilds. With the passage of time, agriculture, cattle farming, trade emerged as occupations pursued by the Vaishyas who developed into a separate economic group. Shudras took up the menial crafts and emerged as artisans and the traders. These artisans organised themselves into guilds. Thus, to understand the emergence of the artisan class and craftsmen and their economic system, it is extremely important to understand the guild system that existed in India. This chapter discusses the history of guild system in India. A brief review of the ancient texts such as *Brihaspati Smriti, Dharam Sutras, Kautilya's Arthshastra, Manu Smriti* provide an extremely lucid account of the economic system that existed in the Vedic and Mauryan period in India. These texts provide a brief account of various business corporations in the form of guilds, which facilitated free and fair commerce, justice and also carried out the works of charity and religious upliftment. This research paper is divided into various parts, and each part discusses a definite subject matter. Analysis of the economic regulations and developments through the guild system has been done through discussion of a brief history of the Neolithic man and eventual human development as Indus Valley civilisation. In this context, the research paper discusses the historical genesis of guild system through the lens of various historians and writers such as Kautilya, Panini and Medatithi. The research paper aims at studying the meaning of guild system and what was their relevance during the ancient and mediaeval period. Of particular interest is the commentary of Kautilya and Brihaspati Smriti on nature, reason for the existence of the guilds and validity of various evidences found in form of inscriptions and engravings. A major part of the paper is concerned with describing two major kind of guild systems, i.e. the *Srenis* (Art and Craft Guilds) and *Nigam* (Merchant and Commerce Guilds). In the second phase, the paper describes the governance structure of the guild system. Not only the Northern Guild, which was the strongest guild in the mediaeval period, started declining after seventh century, but also the temples in the South emerged as the centre of powers. While discussing the reasons for decline of the Northern Guild, the research paper discusses the uprising of the temples as banks. Neolithic age that marks the development of agriculture and use of stone weaponry led to the emergence of the sophisticated and advanced markets and market systems. During the Neolithic age, the man started producing agriculture products, and the massive land revolution took place around 8000 BC. Domestication of cattle and use of advanced tools and animals for agriculture started around this time. From an empiricist perspective, various archaeological sites in India such as Burzahom, Kashmir, Srinagar, India, Mehrangarh are the largest and the oldest agricultural settlement in India subcontinent. From the observable artifacts and excavations, the first period of Mehrangarh complex is marked with polished tools, microliths and bone tools. During this period, the subsistence economy consisted of combination of hunting, stock breeding and plant cultivation. The second period marked the existence of pottery making (Red and Black pottery). It was in the third and fourth period that the commercial transactions started. This period is historically extremely relevant, as most of the markets and the trade and commerce started developing during this period. *Stonehenge* is the most important turning point in the Neolithic Era and is marked with the development of largest homes and housing structure. During this period, man became the food producer, and hence, the new markets started developing. The Chalcolithic age artifacts found in Southern India, particularly in Palghat, Kerala, and Bainapalli in North Arcot, represent a significant turning point in the history of India. In the 2nd millennium, the persistent droughts led to the destruction of the Indus Empire and led to the flourishing of the *Janapads and Mahajanapads.* Jainism and Buddhism religion started developing with the birth of ascetic saints like Gautama Buddha and Mahavir Jain. In all these phases of human development, cooperation has played the most important role in the development of human civilisation. Modern age is the by-product of the various sophisticated governance structures and systems, which owe their existence to the glorious past. Ancient India had some of the most sophisticated systems in the form *Gana (Political Systems)* and *Sreni (guild system).* The major turning point in the history of Indian civilisation was the emergence of the Maurya Dynasty under the rule of mighty Chandra Gupta Maurya and his close associate Chanakya or Kautilya. Kautilya wrote the famous book – *Arthashastra.* In this book, the author has a given an elaborate description of Old guild system. These old markets were known as the *Cooperative Guilds (Sámutthãyiká-danyassamayánubandhah).* These market systems are not a new entity, in fact the guild system in the form of *Sreni (Guilds)* a unique system existed during ancient India, around fourth century and seamlessly made its way into the Maurya Dynasty. Arthashastra emphasised the maintenance of balance between state management and people's welfare. An account of the economic systems and prevailing practices in the ancient India is provided by the following texts in chronological order. In the *second century, Arthashastra by Kautilya,* fourth to sixth century BC, the *Dharamsutras, third century AD Manu Smriti and Vishnu Smriti, fourth century, Yajnavalkya,* 500 AD *Narada Smriti* and *sixth or seventh century Brahaspati Smriti.* Buddhist texts like *Vinaya and Sutta Patikas* make a reference to the economic Guilds during the reign of the Chandragupta Maurya.

Objectives

This study is aimed at exploring the unique economic system that existed in ancient India, fourth to sixth century BC under the kinship of Vikramditya Gupta and his aide Kautilya. The study is also aimed at studying the Arthashastra for identifying the various policies suggested to guard against market failure, such as guild system and taxes. The research paper aims at studying the basic economic structure that allowed the trade and commerce to take place and set the pace for modern day trade and commerce system. Voyages for trade did not take place because of individual but because of the corporates and associations called 'Guilds'. Guild system was very powerful, and the objective of this research paper is to study the structure of the guilds in ancient India. The research paper also aims at studying the role of guilds as banks and financiers in Southern India and explores the relationship between temples and guilds in South India.

Methodology

In this study, the qualitative research approach has been followed. Under this methodology, I have carried out extensive literature review of the available documents on guild system that existed during the ancient period. Under the document review are included draft inscriptions and epigraphs about the guild system of the Mauryan period. From different sources, I have collated the interpretation of the inscriptions found from the pre-historic and historic times.

Guild System in India

Guild in the historic times referred to the association of people following the same occupations and crafts, living at one place and cooperating with each other for a common purpose. Majumdar has defined the Guild or Sreni as a union of merchants. Dandekar has defined the Guild as the corporation of businessmen who came together and bound themselves by specific rules and regulations with a view to carry out trade on cooperative basis. Indian ancient literature mentions many economic structures such as 'Ganasahs', 'Sreni', 'Sangh', *Vrāta* and 'Nigam'. For the purpose of research, this paper maintains only 'Economic Guilds' as the subject of research. There is lack of written evidence to conclusively presume that the Guilds existed in ancient India. Though the ancient Vedas such as *Chhandogya Upanishad* and *Brihadaranyaka Upanishad* show the existence of guilds, still there is a debate among the researchers about the validity of existence of guild system such as Kula, Puga and Varna. *Brihadaranyaka Upanishad* provides a lucid commentary on sixth century on analogy of Varna system which makes a mention to *Ganasah*, probably a reference to the existence of economic guilds. Though Harappa civilisation thrived on art, craft and commerce, yet no conclusive evidence of guilds have been found. One of the missing link could be the inability to decipher the script mentioned on local seals and inscriptions excavated from the sites. Not only are the scholars divided on the issue of existence of the guilds, but they also argue that the Vedic civilisation was nomadic and were constantly on war with each other. Despite all the arguments, the terms Sreni and Nigam have been mentioned in number of credible resources such as *Kautilya's Arthashastra, Panini's writing, Megalith's assertions* as the body association of people for a common purpose. However, a particular clan of researchers do argue that the existence of the terms such as Sreni, Puga and Varna did indeed refer to the existence of the guild. Since the script of the Harappa seals cannot be deciphered, we can conclude for the purpose of research that except for Sreni and Nigam, other forms of association such as Puga, Varna and Kula might not have been guild system. *Jataka* tales mention the international trade of India with *Tamarpani (Sri Lanka), Suvarnabhumi (Sumatra)* and *Baveru (Babylonia),* etc. *Fifth century* BC mentions that the artisans, agriculturists, traders and moneylenders had the authority to lay down the rules. *Kautilya's Arthashastra*, sixth century BC, categorically mentioned the guilds as corporations, which were the centre of power. Mauryan Empire, ruled by Chandragupta Maurya, had better maintained highways and increased mobility of men and merchandise. Much akin to the modern day markets, a separate place of carrying trade was allocated to the guilds by the state. The state also participated in the agricultural and industrial production. Another mention of the guild system is made in the *Pattadakal inscription.* From the Basarh site, Basarh fort situated in Vaishali, Bihar, India, during excavations in one of the trenches, a square room containing large number of inscribed seals and sealings of the early Gupta kings have been found. Particularly of interest is the excavation of 273 seals, *with legion Kulika (artisan or merchant), Shresthi (banker) and Sarthavaha (Caravan trader). This establishes the existence of large corporations.* The language of the inscription is Sanskrit, in fourth century Brahmi lipi. One of the seals mentions shresthi-kulika-nigama (the guild of bankers, artisan and merchants) and another referred to the Shresthi-Sarthavaha-Kulika-Nigam (the guild of bankers, caravan, traders and artisan and merchants).

Sources of Study of Guilds: Harappa Culture

The excavations at Harappa have exhibited magnificent cities, but there is no evidence of guilds. If there have been guilds, these would have been guilds of artisans, pottery makers, to name a few. This subject, whether guilds existed during the Vedic period is a subject of great controversy due to the inability to decipher the Harappa culture.

Vedic Culture

However, in Vedic literature, there is mention of '*Shresthi*' and '*Shreni*'; there is no way to decipher whether Shresthi means chief of merchants or it means noble. Historians believe that Vedic mention of 'Shreni' refers to the line and not guild. Despite excavations and discovery of artifacts, the Indian historians are not sure about when the guild system started in India. There is a debate among the scholars, whether the guild system started in the Vedic period or afterwards. Many different forms of guild structures such as Sreni, Puga Gana and Vrāta find mention in the Vedic literature. Guild system originated because of the division of labour under Varna system. Many of the economic occupations such as agriculture, cattle farming and trade developed as a separate group. Vaishyas started pursuing the trade and commerce, and Shudras undertook crafts and art making. Interlinking of the kingdoms by emergence of trade and commerce between the various kingdoms led to the emergence of the organised guilds. During the sixth century, the growth of the states and towns and increasing use of irons led to the emergence of guilds. During the Vedic period, many texts make a mention of the *Gana* or corporate organisation, only in case of *Vaishyas.* In ancient India, the corporates of various kinds existed. These corporates were at perennial threat from the robbers and hostile tribes, while travelling through the highways and the dense forests. A mention of existence of dangers of this kind is made in the *Jataka stories.* The Jataka stories make a mention to the village of 500 robbers with an elder at the head. *Rig Veda* makes a mention to trade by barter, through terms such as *Pan and Pani,* which has been interpreted as *Barter* by various scholars such as *Zimmer and Ludwig.* Of all the business guilds that existed during the Vedic period, the sole evidence to the existence of the guilds exists in the usage of the words such as *Shresthi* and *Gana.* Ancient literature of both *Buddhist and Brahamanical* literature makes a mention of the economic systems called as *Guilds.* In the ancient guild, there is a mention of the Guilds of wood workers, workers in metal, workers in stone, leather works, ivory works, hydraulic engine workers, bamboo workers, braziers, jewellers, weavers, potters, oil millers (*Tilapishaka*), rush workers, dyers, painters, corn dealers (*Dhamnika*), cultivators, fisher folks, butchers, barbers and shampooers, garland makers and flower sellers, mariners, herdsmen, caravan traders, robbers and freebooters, forest police and moneylenders.

Chhandogya Upanishad

The first definite evidence of the existence of the Guilds system in ancient India is found in the *Chhandogya Upanishad,* which belongs to sixth century (approximately fourth to sixth BC). Then there are Smritis – Manu Smriti, Vishnu Smriti, Yagyavalkya Smriti, Brahaspati Smriti and Narad Smriti – and these literature have lot of mention of Guilds, rules and regulations and penalties. The Brahaspati Smriti mentions the metal workers working with gold and silver. Narada Smriti refers to the money gained through usury and black money.

Nature of the Guild was based on the occupation and nature of activity. *Sreni* referred to the guild that was formed to pursue the local art n craft. On the other hand, *Nigam* was a guild formed primarily for the purpose of trade and commerce. Merchant Guilds were of two types, one was stationary and other was moving. The *moving guilds*, i.e. the *Nigam*, were the *Caravans*, which carried the intermediary and raw materials from one place to another, sell it to barter. Then there were few Guilds, where number of guilds joined to form a corporation. Many researchers believe that the Varna or caste system of the period defined the nature of guild system. In pre-Vedic period, the society was divided into four categories – Brahmans, Kshatriyas, Vaishyas and Shudras. Whereas the Vaishyas as a class of people were engaged in trade and commerce, Shudras were involved in art n metal craft. Still, the guild system helped to dilute the sinister caste system and feudal divide in the society. It was above the rites and rituals associated with the birth and was based on nature of vocation and volition of the member. The further stage in the development of the Guild comprised of the next phase of evolution. *Srenis,* which are referred to as the guild of artisans and traders, started making their own laws and legal rules. Jetthakya, who is referred to as the head of the Guild, became an important person in the management of the guild and started representing the guild in the *Royale Court.* Guild system helped in promoting trade, by facilitating procurement of raw materials from the neighbouring cities and states. With the coming of the small kingdoms and royalties, the markets across the country got interlinked. Guild system, which was a centralised corporation of might, could leverage its power to source raw material and skill set of artisans from the distant places. This led to the major migration of the artisans and craftsmen. Before the dawn of the Buddhism and Jainism, till sixth century BC, writing had been discovered. Writing facilitated the formation of Guilds based on *Lekhakriya (Written Codes)* and facilitated trade based on written terms and conditions. During sixth century BC with the coming up of Jainism and Buddhism, which were more egalitarian in nature, the guild system flourished. Buddhism was more tolerant of the people from diverse sects and religions and was not vary of mixing up with people from the lower caste for the purpose of trade. Unlike the Brahmins who sacrificed the animals, the Buddhists and Jains preserved the natural flora and fauna for the purpose of trade and commerce.

Guilds as Court of Justice

Post-Buddhist Era, i.e. during the Mauryan Empire and post-Mauryan Era (320–200 BC), the guild system called Sreni was extremely strong. The North Guild that existed during the Gupta Era was the strongest guild system. The Guilds were democratic governments, which have multifaceted features. These guilds were also trading union, court of justice and technological innovation. *Vinaya – Pitaka* mentions that the guild was entitled to *arbitrate* on various occasions. In matter of Justice, Guilds shared power with the king of the state. '*Raja Nama, yattha raja anusasati raja apaloketabbo, son nama, yattha sem anusasati seni apaloketabbo*', when translated says '*Where the king rules, his consent will have to be obtained; here the guild rules its consent will have to be obtained*'. During the Chalcolithic age, the procurement of raw materials for manufacturing and the control of the quality of goods manufactured were integral aspects of the technological and economic advancements of the time. According to Romila Thapaar, the guild system or Sreni system started during the Buddhist Era, i.e. around the sixth century. The guild system played a pivotal role in organizing and regulating various aspects of economic and occupational activities during ancient and medieval times. Moreover, the idea of the Guild leader or Jetthakya was accepted.

Kautilya

Kautilya, the advisor to Chandra Gupta I was a Professor at the University of Taxila (Now in Pakistan). He was an expert in commerce, warfare, and economics. At that time, Taxila developed into a world class centre for education. Kautilya is suggested the world's first Strategy and Management Guru.

Kautilya Economy

Arthashastra describes the economy as a self-sustaining economy, which was based on indigenous ways of production, distribution and trade. The book also describes the modus operandi, through setting up of the policymaking bodies and structures. The state had a unique Indian Civil service system, accounts revenue, mines, arsenals, taxation and trade and navigation system. During the Maurya Era, the state controlled the markets and also entered the markets to sell the commodities. This research paper aims at studying the Sreni guild system and its historical relevance in development of the modern market system in India. The guild system played an extremely important role, in the socio-economic progress of the economy. The merchants and traders participated in the markets through the Guilds. Although Guilds were working to protect the welfare of the traders, the State Trading body was present to protect the interests of traders and selling the Crown stock.

Importance of Punishment and Profit

Kautilya emphasised the importance of punishment and profit, in promoting the civil welfare. He believed that every state should be made responsible for earning the adequate profits and protecting its financial interest. During his administration, he introduced the wealth test, pleasure test and fear test for the appointment of the ministers.

Financial Audit System

Indian state had a close and controlled financial accounting system. The state had an orderly financial system and the Chancellor had the responsibility of collecting the revenue, preparing the budget and keeping a detailed account of revenues and expenditures. A stock register was maintained by the manufacturing establishments. All the manufacturing concerns were responsible for maintaining the records and followed an annual book closure mechanism.

Financial Governance System

Kautilya in Arthashastra identified governance, human exertion, physical capital, land and knowledge as the symbol of prosperity. Some of the famous quotes from Arthashastra are 'The root of wealth is economic activity and lack of it brings material distress. In the absence of fruitful economic activity, both current prosperity and future growth are in danger of destruction'. Kautilya has also suggested various measures for preservation of the wealth. His other famous quote is

> In the interests of the prosperity of the country, a king should be diligent in foreseeing the possibility of calamities, try to avert them before they arise, overcome those which happen, remove all obstructions to economic activity and prevent loss of revenue to the state.

Tax Revenue

Arthashastra describes the importance of tax revenue. Kautilya believed that all the state activities depended on collection of the revenues, which depended on income generation. This epic claims that anybody who follows the tax revenue policy will suffer depression. Further, the book mentions the measures to increase the taxation base and not the tax rate to increase the revenue. Kautilya emphasised the need for promoting the welfare of the states and also extending the subsidies for the welfare of the people. Hymn 24 of Book IV of the Rig Veda invokes basic demand and supply forces, where buyer and seller bargain for a price (Joyce, 1886). Here is the paraphrased narration of the bargain:

> A customer is trying to buy wine (soma) and fried barley from a priest as sacrificial offerings to seek Indra's favour. Customer bids low price and the offerings remain unsold, for priest is not ready to accept low price. The offerings just cannot be sold for a mere price of ten cows. The needy buyer and shrewd seller both milk out the udder (i.e., bargain hard for the price).

Division of Labour

Rig Veda and Jataka tales make mention about the division of labour and specialisation. In Hymns 4.13 and 18.41 to 18.44, one finds the following description, where Krishna, the speaker, says: 'I created the four divisions of human society based on aptitude and vocation. The division of human labour is based on the qualities inherent in peoples' nature or their make-up.'

Method of Labour Regulation and Private Sector

Kautilya suggested the methods for the regulation of the wages and the settlement of the disputes between the employers and workers. Kautilya mentions about the private sector enterprises to undertake the relevant economic activities with the state.

Pricing of the Merchandise

Ancient thinkers also substantiate the need to undertake the valuation of the commodity not only according to the time and place. The book introduces the concept of utility, in case of the goods and merchandise.

Market Failure and Cartels

Arthashastra mentions the poverty as the sole cause of market failure. In the modern period, market failures can manifest due to various reasons, including the accumulation of wealth in the hands of a few individuals. This scenario often leads to several market inefficiencies, exacerbating inequality and distorting economic outcomes. Kautilya's Arthashastra mentions the relevance of Free Trade Agreements and the need for the preferential trade partners.

Markets in Gupta Period

Markets (Samsthadhyaks) were supposed to protect the welfare of the people. The just prices in the markets were ensured by the *Panyadhyaks – Superintendent of the Trade*, who penalised the entities in event deviation from the trade. Yagyavalkya states that the prices in the markets were announced by the State. The prices for the commodities were decided on the basis of the production supply, investment, transportation cost, duties, interest, risk, rent and demand. The Arthashastra shows an understanding of supply–demand forces but treats them as a problem to be solved, or contained within tolerable limits, by royal action. Due to reasonable amount of foreign trade, Arthashastra provides for various imports and exports controls and talks about *spardha fair competition.*

Role of Intermediaries

The book mentions about the role of various intermediaries such as transporters and the warehouses in ensuring the just price. The trade is mentioned not as the sale of the commodities in the market but as the transportation of commodities.

Manipulation of Prices

The merchants were feared to be able to manipulate the prices in the market and also responsible for tax theft. In this regard, the kingdom had the provision for taxing the transactions and penalising the deviations. Kautilya makes an interesting observation about the manipulation of the prices. It is quite possible that the traders might join together and raise or lower the prices. The book mentions that successful cartels can generate the profit of approximately 10,000 units. Kautilya introduced severe penalties to prevent cartel formation. 'For artisans and artists who by conspiring together bring about a deterioration in the quality of a work or (increase in) profit or hindrance to purchase or sale, the fine is one thousand panas. (IV.2.18, emphasis added)'. 'For traders, too, who by conspiring together hold back wares or sell them at a high price, the fine is one thousand panas. (IV.2.19, emphasis added)'. The book makes an attempt to distinguish between usury, hoarding and the manipulation of the prices by the economic agents.

Use of Secret Agents

Kautilya does not specifically mention the method to detect the cartels. However, he does mention the use of the secret agents to keep an eye on the traders.

Lack of empirical evidence regarding methods of detection of the cartels and collusions has attracted the attention of many scholars. Many of the renowned researchers such as Trautmann have given a very comprehensive analysis of this problem.

Kautilya's Arthashastra

Kautilya's Arthashastra makes a mention about the '*Superintendent of Accounts'*, who were responsible for the regular maintenance of the records relating to customs, professions and transactions of the cooperation. Moreover, three *commissioners* were appointed. These *commissioners* were responsible for the collection of the deposits, which has to be deposited for the lifetime. During the period of *Chandragupta Maurya, the Guilds* held the place of extreme importance. The places were reserved for the houses and domicile of the Guild members. Kings many a time exploited the guilds for his own benefits. The text makes a mention, that if a '*king finds himself in a great himself in the financial trouble and needs money, he can employ a Spy, who would borrow from the corporations gold coins and allowed him to be robbed of it of the same night*'. Kautilya's Arthashastra makes a mention to the guilds as a great military power. In the Book IX, Chapter II, Kautilya addresses the Guild's Army as '*Sreni Wala'. Arthashastra* also refers to the special type of Guilds that survived on both trade and war. '*Kamboja-Surashtra-kshatriya-srenyadayo Vartta-Sastropajivinah*' refers to the kind of economic guilds that survived on both war and commerce. Mahabharata makes a mention of '*Sayodhya Sreni*' and in *Narada Smriti,* in reference to guilds a mention is made that the *Confederacy in secret, resort to arms* without due causes and mutual attack. *Kshatriyas Srenis,* mentioned by Kautilya, existed for a long time in South India. *Velaikkaras* of the 10th and 11th AD refers to the various trading and working classes such as Idangai and Valangai, which are mentioned in the Tanjore inscriptions of the Chola kings, Rajaraja I and Rajendra Chola I. Both *Medhatithi* and *Kullukbhatta* make a mention to Trade Guilds as '*Desa Sangha'*. After the Christian Era, the guild had developed themselves as the most important factor in the *state politics.*

In the post Mauryan BC (between 200 and 300 BC), as the Mauryan Empire was declining, this led to the lessening of the state control over the guilds. This augmented the growth of the guilds. Various documentary evidences found at Bharuct, Sanchi, Mathura and Bodhgaya make a mention of the donation by different traders and craftsmen. Victory of Chandragupta Maurya over the Roman Seleuchus Nictor helped expand the barriers of Indian Empire and also gave an impetus to international trade. Even after the decline of the Mauryan Empire, the trade with Roman Empire flourished on account of powerful Indian state, in South under Satvanhana ruler and in North under Kushans. As the demand for the luxury goods in Rome increased, trade with India rose. The excavations at Arikamedu, near Pondicherry, have provided valuable insights into the historical trade relations between India and Rome. Arikamedu, an ancient port city, was a significant trading hub during the Sangam period in Tamil

Nadu. Wine containers known as amphorae discovered from excavations confirm trade between West Asia and India. From various sites in South India and Western India, Arrctinc ware (known as Arezzo from Italy) have been excavated. The discovery of Roulette wares at archaeological sites, particularly those not manufactured in India, underscores the extent of ancient trade networks and the cultural exchange that took place during historic periods. Chronicles discuss about the brisk trade between Rome and India and arrival of Yavana ships from Rome to India. Moreover, in additions to Pliny's assertions about the drain of imperial wealth, number of hoards of Roman coins have been excavated from Vindhyas in South India. The *Periplus of Erythraei Sea,* an account of earlier trade between India and Rome, makes innumerable references to the trade between India and Rome. The Periplus was written by an anonymous writer and provides a holistic picture of the various trading centres in India. There are mentions of the majestic port of Barygaza, known as modern day Bharuch, India. The book mentions God's own country Kerala as 'Ccrobothra'. Just as India imported various commodities from outside, India also imported butter, ghee, ivory, spices, cotton, muslin, silk, horns, coloured lac, pearl, pearl oysters, purple, rhinoceros to different part of world. Much alike Periplus, Pliny mentions various items of trade such as ebony (the plant), turpentine tree, pepper plant, olive tree, clove tree, unicorn, elephants, dolphin birds and various precious stones and gems including, crystals, opal, diamonds, gold, pearl, to name a few. As per the historical texts, Augustus Empire had the major trade relations with India. The major trade routes were sea routes from Black Sea across the Caspian Sea from Bactria to China, from Syria to Euphrates and from Red Sea and Indian Ocean. Though there are ample evidences about the presence of the guild, there are no guild coins from the Gupta Era. The Deccan region, located in south-central India, has a rich historical and cultural heritage. The mention of the insignia and seal in the ancient Deccan inscriptions signifies the importance and significance of these symbols during that time. The famous *Deccan inscription* has mention of the insignia and the seal. Ayyavole guild has its own banners. *Shikarpur inscription of Trailokyamala Deva* 1054 AD describes the guild as one of the most powerful guilds. It lauds the distinguished clan of members and further elucidates that this clan used the canopy in the form of white umbrellas and carried spearheaded rods. The insignia of the guild is described as the banner bearing the device of the Mount Kailash. Similarly, the *Belur inscription* of Hoysala ruler Narsimha – I, 1167 AD – mentions that the guild of Vira Banjigas had the Visuddha gudda flag. There are also mentions of members of Mummuri guild holding special staff in their hands, in the *Belgaum inscription* of *Kartavirya IV, 1024 AD.* Though the king seldom had the say in the functioning of the Guilds, he shared a relationship of trust and faith with the guild. The Dambal record of Vikramaditya VI, dated 1095 AD, provides valuable historical insights into the governance and administrative practices of that time. The mention of King Jagadekamalla Deva granting the use of umbrellas, chauris, and charters to a guild using flags with the insignia of a hill signifies the importance of symbols and regalia in the administrative and societal framework of that era. Own coins and flags added to the prestige of the guild.

Mauryan Period (300 BC to 200 BC). Cullakāliṅga-Jātaka, Book IV – 301 (Catukkanipata) has a reference to the Dantapura (Palur) the port which was linked to the city of Assaka through various means of transport. Moreover, both the cities engaged in trade with each other. Mamsa Jatakas, Volume III – 301 – this story mentions the City of Banaras under the king Braham Dutta and clearly mentions the existence of trade links between the different part of the world and Banaras in the old days. Kosambi Jatakas, Volume III – 301 – mentions the exchange between Kosala and city of Kasi.

Coins and Coinage

The Gupta kingdom was famous for its numismatic coinage and coins. Hoards of gold coins, silver coins, which are known as *Dinars*, have been found from various places in Kalighat, modern day Calcutta, India. The first gold coin was issued under the reign of famous Vikramditya, Chandragupta I. Then came Samudragupta, under whose reign the Mauryan economy flourished. The depiction of rulers on coins is a significant aspect of ancient numismatics, providing valuable insights into their reign, attributes, and symbolism. In the case of Kumar Gupta I, the coins showcasing him riding an elephant, or lion, or holding a veena signify various symbolic representations and attributes associated with the ruler and his reign. Samudragupta I and Kumargupta issued various coins depicting the rituals such as 'Ashvamedha'. This can be established from vast treasure of gold coins circulated during the reign of this ruler. These coins carried the image of the king and the image of deity on obverse. The coins narrating the rituals and rites such as 'Ashvamedha' were issued by the Gupta Empire. Many of these coins were present in the British Museum, London, England. The famous Chief Controller of the coins certified the genuineness of the coins.

Chinchani Plates of the Rashrakutas King Krishna III, 1000 AD

Regarding the use of coins, the *Chinchani plates of the Rashrakutas king Krishna III*, 1000 AD refer to the use of coins, minted by the *Sreshthin Gambhuvaka*. During the Rashtrakuta dynasty's reign, the merchant *Sreshthin Gambhuvaka* from *Samyana* held the authority for minting coins under the royal lineage. Not only Rashrakutas but also the Chalukyan ruler *Somesvara III*, 1126 AD, mentions the use of the *Gadyana* type coins, called 'Vartakka Lokki Gadyana' minted by merchant. From the various evidences gathered about the use of various insignia, flags and symbols by the guild, it can be concluded that the guilds enjoyed special status in the society and even the state recognised this and gave autonomy to the guilds.

The single plate measures 17.5 inches in length, 8.8 inches in breadth, and 0.1 inches in thickness. It weighs 130 Tolas and lacks a seal engraved on one side. This plate, with its precise measurements, 50 lines of writing, and weight, presents a simple and elegant design suitable for various purposes. The plate is written in *Sanskrit* language. The inscription starts with the Pranava, which is the adoration of the Mother Goddess. After this line, all the imperial kings of the Rashrakutas Dynasty are mentioned in the correct order, starting from Dantidurga (742–56 AD), his successor Krishnaraja (Krishna I 756–75AD), Govindraja (Govinda II, 775–80 AD), successor of Krishnaraja, Nirupama (Dhruva, 780–94 AD), Jagat-tunga (Govind III 794–814 AD), Amorghavarsha (Amorghavarsha I, 814–840 AD) and Amoghavarsha's son Akalavarsha (Krishna II, 879–915 AD) who succeeded Indra Raja. Verse 6 mentions Govindraja (Govind IV, 929–34 AD) surnamed Suvaranavarsha and verse 7 Amorghavarsha (Amorghavarsha III, 934–39 AD). The following four stanzas describe the reign of the king Krishnaraja (Krishna III – 939–67 AD), son of Amorghavarsha.

Verse 10 speaks about the reigning monarch Krishna III, who is stated to have conquered certain enemies, when he was a crown prince. Verses 12–14 speak of the god Bhillmaladeva, who is known as Madhusudana (Vishnu) worshipped at unspecified place at the time of charter. Verses 15–19 state that, at the same place, there was another *maṭhikā*, i.e. monastery or temple, which had been constructed by Kautuka and at the gate of which the goddess called Bhagavatī had been installed for worship. The inscription mentions the word *Dīp-ōtsava,* which is nothing else but the festival of lights or Deepavali. Of interest is the use of the word *Dramma,* which refers to the coin of copper or silver, and the inscription seems to specify the payment in coins minted by trader named *Sreshthin Gambhuvaka.*

Vedic Guild System

Many of the scholars perceive that the Aryan society was preoccupied with war, and they could not produce surplus food grains and spent time in making crafts.

Corporations: Evidence of Corporation Form of Guilds

The mention of guilds in various Buddhist texts, such as *Jataka stories*, *Maha-vastu*, and *Milindapāñha*, provides valuable insights into the social and economic structures of ancient India. Kautilya's Arthashastra and Panini Asthdhyaya also make a mention of the guild system. The research paper is a descriptive study, based on Kautilya's Arthashastra, Panini Asthdhyaya, of the Guilds that existed in ancient India.

Difficulties in deciphering the meaning of the Guild – Avoid the Pathetic Fallacy: Researchers while reviewing the literature regarding the presence of the integrated bodies of members, or cooperative associations that facilitated trade, are faced with the difficulty to derive meanings from the original text, where these bodies are referred to as Kula, Gana, Sreni to name a few. To avoid the Pathetic Fallacy of making a contextual error, this study presents some logic that has been used to associate these terms with the local bodies regulating commerce.

Sreni

- Medhatithi has explained the term Sreni mentioned in Manu III, as the guild of merchants, artisans and bankers.
- Panini uses the word Sreni, which has been explained by Tattvabodhini and Kayyala as an assembly of people pursuing common craft or trading in commodity.
- One of the researchers has defined the Sreni in Narada I, as 'Guild of Merchants and Actor'.
- Kautilya has used the word *Sreni*, in two meanings – as guild of workmen, but in VII, the word has a political reference, which means Military clan.
- The Mahabharata mentions the word *Sreni* as Guild of merchants

Kula

- *Kula,* in Narada I, has been mentioned an assemblage of few persons and others as a family meaning.
- *Yagyavalkya* makes a mention of the term *Kula,* which has been explained by *Mitakshara* as assemblage of kinsmen, relations and friends.
- *Kula* term has been used by *Kautilya* to mean council of regency or oligarchy, the rule of which is preferable to that of the unsuitable king.

Sangha

- The 'Kasika', authored by Vamana and Jayaditya, is highly regarded as the primary commentary on Paninian Grammar. The term 'Sangha' is utilised in various contexts within the text, showcasing its significance in discussing Buddhist ethics and as a representation of the fundamental principles guiding Buddhist communication. Additionally, in general usage, Kasika defines 'Sangha' as an assembly of people or corporations, categorizing it into varieties like Puga and Vrāta.
- Kautilya confines the use of the word Sangha, to mean political corporations.

Why Guild Existed?

In ancient India, the status of the individual and his social class depended on his Varna, caste, sect and guild. Unlike the caste and Varna, which were hereditary, the guild system was social. Similarly, the caste system was permanent, but the Guild could be changed. Guild enjoyed lot of autonomy and say among the Royale clan. The king respected the guild laws, which were based on the customs, traditions and usages. Guilds emerged due to the need for the Guilds, Customs and Traditions. In the words of Manu, a king should frame his own rules after taking into consideration the rules of the Guilds.

Characteristics of the Guild System

- Each guild system should have its own professional codes.
- It has its own working arrangements.
- Duties and obligations – the guild system ensured adherence to the religious systems.
- Promotion of the local craft and craftsmanship through the guild system.
- Guilds had their own insignia and flags.

Governance Structure of the Guild

As per the *Narada and Brahaspati Smriti,* guilds have a three tier structure comprised of General Assembly, Body of Executive Officers and the Head of the Guild. The State respected the working of most of the Guilds and Guild laws. Guilds enjoyed the autonomy in their working, and the king upheld the laws, customs and rules of the Guilds, unless and until the working of the Guild is against the social welfare of the people. The responsibility for fostering a supportive environment for the Guilds' functioning was vested in the governing administrative authority, the king himself. Brahaspati Smriti mentions about the number of members in an economic guild to be 2, 3 and 5. In addition to this, the inscription of *Ayyavole Guild* mentioned the number of coins as 'Five Hundred' or more or less. Beside this record, there are no records of number of members in an economic guild. *Yajnavalkyasmriti* refers to the various qualifications for the executive officers of the guild, the powers of the executive officers and their qualifications and powers. If an individual was willing to join the guild, he could do so, without consideration to his caste. Though the nature of the Guild depended on vocation and the particular sect specialised in a particular kind of vocation, yet an individual had discretion to pursue a particular vocation. Despite the freedom of choice, the individual had to seek the permission of his parents. Deccan Society was home to number of different guilds comprising of Weavers Guild, Potteries Guild, Jewellers and Goldsmith Guild. The concept of *specialisation* of labour existed during the guild system in ancient period.

Three Tiers of the Guild

Fig. 8 demonstrates the 'Three Tiers of the Guild.'

Fig. 8.   Governance Structure: Guild System.

Functions of Guild System

- The guild system in ancient societies encompassed a wide array of functions, including administrative, economic, charitable, and banking activities.
- Alleviation of distress and undertook works of piety and charity.

Economic Function

- Guilds provided financial loans and finances to the artisans.
- Guild functioned as a bank, semi-bank, as the members made investment on permanent basis. This was called as Akshayanevi. On the basis of terms agreed upon by the depositors and the Guild, the money was to be utilised for the pious acts such as feeding monks, lighting the lamps in Viharas, etc. The interest of the deposit, i.e. monthly interest, is to be used for these activities.
- Guilds provided for the life of the family members of the members, in case of eventuality.
- Judicial Power – Guild heads and Executive Officers acted as Courts for the Public in matter of economic nature (Exceptions – Some Civil Matters).

    - Copper plate inscriptions discovered from Bengal (Damodarpur), Shresthi, Kulika and Kayas has helped the District Administrative officers to settle civil matters
    - Yagyavalkya mentions Sreni as one type of Court of Justice

Membership of Guild

General Qualifications to Become Member of Guild. Anyone who became member of the Guild became the member of the General Assembly. To become the member, the individual had three options.

(1) *Lekhakriya*: If the person is literate, he can sign the form and can become the member of the Guild.
(2) *Madhyastha:* If the person knows someone, he can get the reference.
(3) *Kosha:* As described by Narada – individual has to face the ordeal – an image of the deity is bathed, and from that water, the person who wants to become the member of the Guild is given water to drink. If within a fortnight a person does not fall ill, he is accepted as the member of the Guild.

Exit From the Guild (Mitra Mishra and Chandeshwar)

The process of leaving a guild in ancient societies varied in terms of protocol. Some sources indicate that a member needed to seek permission from the head of the guild before departing, while others suggest that informing the guild of one's decision to leave was sufficient. It's interesting to note that in the guild system, all members shared the assets and liabilities equally. This equitable practice likely fostered a sense of fairness, unity, and solidarity within the guild.

Asset and Liability Sharing

The members of the Guild shared equally between all the members of the Guild. Guilds provided deposits and loans to the members against the payment of interest. Shreni was defined as the 'association of one Jati for many Jatis'. However, the nature of the guilds differed according to the nature of work. Guild was a democratic set up, and the decisions were taken by the majority. As per the Brahaspati Smriti, the part of the profits of the Guild is to be used for the maintenance of the roads, water and highways.

Executive Officers

The Brahaspati Smriti specifies that the number of members in an economic guild can be 2, 3, or 5, detailing the acceptable group sizes within such organisational structures. Brahaspati Smriti mentions that every guild had 2, 3 or 5 – these members were to look after the guild and to help the headman to look after the Guild. The Executive Officers were the real managers of the guild. Heads of the Guild were involved in representing the guild in the Royal Court. The Executive Officers also had supreme power to punish the guilty members.

However, injustices by the Executive Court could be referred to the Head of the Guild or the Government Court.

• The members of the Guild had the right to free speech and expression.
• The members should be from the noble family – Brahaspati Vedas.
• The members should be well versed in Vedas – Brahaspati Vedas.
• The members of the Guild will have to seek the permission of the Guild to become an Ascetic or to marry.

Head Man or the Chairman of Guild

Literature does not provide any information about how the Head of the Shreni was selected. Head of the Shreni was selected by majority. He was involved in representing Guild in the Royale Court. In case of failure to perform the duties, the Head of the Guild can be removed from the office. He was known as the 'Pamukkha' or 'Jetthakya'. Depending on the occupation of the head of the Guild, he was known as 'Malakara Jetthakya', i.e. garland maker or Veddhaki Jetthakya, if he was a carpenter and so on. There was no information about the mode of payment and his tenure in the office. The guild system was shaped by the vocation and specialisation of different sects, yet individuals retained the discretion to pursue their preferred vocation within this framework. In many of the literature, the term 'Setthi' has been used to refer to the head of the guild. In the Hindu and Telegu inscriptions, the Chiefs of the guilds were referred to as

'Pattansvami'. *Balgamve inscription* of Vikramditya 1098 AD refers to the *Pattansvami* (Head of the Guild) at Balgamve.

Head Man as Part of Royale Court

For the formation of the Guild, the permission of the king was required. Only rich merchants could become the head of the Guilds. The head was generally part of the Royale Court. Anathpindi, a contemporary of Gautama Buddha, is known for constructing numerous Viharas to accommodate traveling caravans. His contribution to building these structures facilitated the lodging and support of travelers during that era.

Lord Rama and Guild System

Similarly, when Bharat goes to meet Lord Rama in Chitrakut, Bharat invites all the Guild heads to join him. When Lord Rama comes back to Ayodhya, after exile, all guild heads come and join to receive him, and at the time of coronation of Lord Rama, Guild heads were requested to sprinkle water at the time of *Abhishek*.

King Bimbasara and Guild System

King Bimbasara while visiting Gautam Buddha invited all the members of the Guild to join him. King of Avadh requested the king Magadha for *Sethi or Shresthi* to manage financial affairs at Saket.

Krishna Balram Theatrical Performance and Guild

Harivanshpuran provides when Krishna and Balram were taken on Kans in the wrestling bout, separate pavilions were given for the Guilds.
  Duties of the Headman were as follows:

- To make provision for food and water for the members of Caravan.
- To procure the raw materials.
- To oversee the manufacturing facility.
- To provide for the food for the animals.
- *To provide security and provide militia to save the life of the guild member*: In Jatakas, there is a mention that the persons travelling through the forests were attacked by the robbers. A good head was responsible for protecting the merchandise.
- *To ensure terms of Barter* – Value of Merchandise, Markets and demand.
- To protect the interest of the members of the Guild and protect the interest of the members.
- *Kautilya's Arthashastra: Shresthi:* He was the head of the Merchant Guild. To protect the interest of the merchants, he was part of king's Court. Prior to the

emergence of the prominent Mahajanapads like Kosala, Vatsa (or Vamsa), Avanti, and Magadha, there existed smaller kingdoms such as the Sakya kingdom. These early smaller kingdoms played a foundational role in the political landscape of ancient India before the rise of the larger and more influential Mahajanapads. In these kingdoms, the kings were rich lords who tried to loot the Guild. Kautilya's Arthashastra has mention of the spies of king who rob the Guilds of the borrowed capital from the kingdom, leading to excessive exploitation of the Guilds. In this situation, the *Shresthi* tried to protect the interest of the Guilds.

- *Sarthavaha* – he is mentioned as the head of the Caravan. He was responsible for directing the Caravan and maintaining the rules of 'Barter'.
- King can interfere with rule of the guilds, only if it offends the rule of the king or the Morality.

Migration of Guilds

Guild system can migrate from one place to another place. Mandasore inscription by Padsavati mentions the migration of guild from Gujarat area between Narmada and Tapi, Laata and Khandesh to Mandasore, Madhya Pradesh. One of the reasons for migration was brisk trade between India and Roman Empire. In coastal India, hundreds and thousands of first and second century BC coins from the Roman Empire have been found in Madhya Pradesh. The migration of the Guild took place during the reign of Kumargupta, 436 AD. It was during the third century that the trade links between Rome and India declined. Trade commodities included muslin, the spices, etc. Pliny, the member of Rome Senate, has made various mentions of the commentary on trade terms between India and Rome. Bharuch was one of the most important ports for trade between India and Rome.

Description of the Inscription

The inscription starts with three verses of *Mangala,* the Sun, the first and third of which invoke the divinity's blessings, and the second and middle one of which mentions *Lata* or Gujarat to *Dasapura* or *Mandasor (Verses 6–13)*. There is a mention of *Dasapura* in the form of a word picture, its lake and its edifices. After this, there is a graphic description of the Guild and various hobbies pursued by various members *(Verses 14–20)*. *Verse 21* describes in detail the pre-eminence of the silk cloth manufactured by them and the desire of the Guild to become some religious benefaction.

Indore Copper Plate Inscription

There is a mention of a Guild member making a promise to supply the oil to light the lamp in the temple. This inscription belongs to the Skandgupta Era.

Description of the Indore Plate

During the illustrious and triumphal rule of the esteemed *Paramabhattaraka* and *Maharajadhiraja*, the magnificent *Skanda Gupta*, the kingdom experienced immense growth. This prosperous expansion coincided with the month of Phalguna, enhancing the overall prosperity and enjoyment *in the land of Antravedi*, governed by the revered *Vishyaputi Sharvanga*, who was esteemed and favored by his governing prowess. *Line (5 to 8)* The Brahman *Deva Vishnu*, who belongs to the community of *Chaturvedins of Padma* of the town of Chandrapura – who is the son of *Deva* (and) son's son of *Haritrata* and the son son's of *Dudika*, who always recites the hymns of *aghnihotra – sacrifice*, who belongs to Ranayaniya (*Shakha*) and who is of *Varsangha* gotra – for increase of his own fame gives an endowment *(of which interest is)* is to be applied to *(maintenance)* the divine lamp for the divine Sun, which has been established *(in a temple)* by the *Kshatriya Achalavarman and Bhrukunthasinha*, merchants of the town of *Indirapuram*, on the east of settlement *(and)* actually touching the city of *Indirapuram (Line – 8)*. This gift of a Brâhman's endowment of (the temple of) the Sun, (is) the perpetual property of the guild of oil men, of which *Jîvanta* is the head, residing at the town of Indrapura, as long as it continues in complete unity, (even) in moving away from this settlement. The ancient text discusses a gift given by a Brahman to a guild of oil men, led by Jivanta, in the town of Indrapura. The gift, valued as a perpetual property, is given in exchange for the provision of two palas of oil to the Brahman for the duration of the sun and moon's existence. The endowment is dependent on the condition that the guild maintains unity, even if they relocate from Indrapura (Indore).

Guild System – Sarthavaha (Caravan Trade System): The Caravan Trade system or Sarthavaha was expected to know the availability of water, good roads and methodological provision for the food for the cattle. The head of the Caravan, known as the Sarthavaha, had the duty of guaranteeing the provision of food for the travelers. Shresthi or the Banker used to interact and coordinate with the kingdom, to ensure of the economic interests of the kingdom. It's fascinating to note that in ancient India, the sixteen Mahajanapads held crucial roles in the socio-political landscape. Among these, the Mahajanapads of Kosala were indeed responsible for protecting and preserving the interests of the Guilds within its territory. This highlights the intricate relationships and responsibilities that existed within the governance structures of the Mahajanapads during that era.

Kingdom of Kalinga: *Loot of the Guild*: Kautilya's Arthashastra refers to the decline of the Guilds, at the behest of the spies of the king.

Indian Guild in Burma

11th-century to 12th-century inscriptions found in Burma make a mention of Indian guild system and claims that the Pagan Temple was made by the Indian South Indian Guild.

whatisindia.com/inscriptions/earlyguptakings/theguptainscriptions120.html.

Decline of the Guilds: The North Guild declined after the attacks from the Huns and Malik Kafur. During the period of 600–1200 AD, the guilds, which had been the focal point of power, began to decline. This was a significant transition in the organisational and economic structures of the time, marking a shift in power dynamics and influence within societal systems. The north-eastern Indian guilds started degenerating due to the weak successors of Gupta Empire. Many chronicles substantiate that the power of the guilds was integrated for a brief period under the rule of Harsabardhana, but it led to the unification of entire North India. There was a sudden increase in number of conflicts after this period, and the condition was further worsened by the conquest from Huns and Ghazni after that. 6th century BC was marked with the upheaval of the Samantas over Nigmas and Srenis. The *'Dudhapani'* rock inscription, dating back to the eighth century, provides insights into the lives of three merchants in the Hazaribagh district of Magadha.

Description of 'Dudhapani Inscription': It is inscribed on a rock hill close to the village of Dudhapani, district Hazaribagh. The inscription consists of 13 lines of writing, mentioned over an area of 1.83 metres broad and 37 centimetres high. The inscription starts with an invocation to the goddess of fortune, king of Magadha, Adisimha, ruler of 3 villages, Chhingala, Nabhutisandaka, Bhramarasalamali. The story starts by narrating how three brothers Udayamana, Sridhantamana and Ajintamana, originally merchants went to business from Ayodhya to Tamralipti, and after making lot of money, while going back home, they tarried at one of the three villages, apparently Bhramarasalamali (as mentioned in verses 4 and 5). During that time, the king Adisimha came to the forest near the village on hunting expedition and ordered him to give back Avalaga. On behest of the villagers, the eldest brother did send an Avalagana and became the favourite of the king. Pleased at this, the king not only bestowed a Sriptta on him but also on Udayamana's solicitation assured the people of Bhramarasalamali of his royal favour. On return to the village, the inhabitants, with the king's approval, requested him to become their Raja. The literature highlights Udayamana's long and vigorous life (Verses 17–19) and his decision to send his brothers, Sridhantamana and Ajitamana, to govern himself, Nabhuti Sandaka, and Chinngal in response to the request from another village. The inscription also describes that the ruling family at Bhramarasalamali owes its exis-tence and greatness to the rule of Udayamana. The inscription ends with the prayer for the uninterrupted continuance of rule of prince Udayamana.

Guilds in South India. However, in South India, the Guilds flourished as these regions were protected from the Northern invasions. During this time, the South Indian Temples and Guilds flourished. Of this, one worth mentioning is Nana-deshi, which implies that their forefathers came from Akshetra. Manikgramam is another guild, which mentions the visit by foreign traders for the trade purpose. An inscription found at Singhal (South East Asia) makes a mention of the international activities of the Guild including the construction activities.

Increasing Importance of the Temples

Temples became extremely important for trade. As these temples became extremely rich, these temples started lending money for trade. Eighty villages were donated by Harsha to the Nalanda Monastery. Unlike the Guilds, the temples were not looted. As per various copper plate inscriptions found, cite the contract between the Guilds and the temples. These temples functioned as the financiers, and these temples had contracts with many of the Art and Merchant Guilds in India and abroad.

Conclusion

Guild system played an extremely important role in the development of art and commerce in India. Not only the guild system helped in promoting commerce, but also it helped in eradication of the caste system. With the coming up of the Guilds, individuals gained a lot of economic power. They also derived the power to do justice and pass judgements. These guilds played an extremely important function in the modern-day economic development. Present-day corporation structure owes its existence to the guild system of ancient India.

References

Joyce, R. B. (1886). Griffith, Sir Samuel Walker (1845–1920), Australian Dictionary of Biography, National Centreof Biography, Australian National University. https://adb.anu.edu.au/biography/griffith-sir-samuel-walker-445/text11119, published first in hardcopy 1983. Accessed on April 7, 2006.

Chapter 4

Introduction to Tribes in India: Factors Affecting the Inclusion of Tribes

Abstract

Indian tribes have existed for time immemorial, and the tribals and indigenous people are extremely important for saving and getting command over the natural resources. There are various cognitive and affective factors that impact the existence of the tribes and the tribal people. There is not much information about what factors impact the inclusion of these tribes in the mainstream. The indigenous people are extremely important for the existence of the human kind, and this paper aims to explore the factors impacting the inclusion of the tribes.

Keywords: Inclusion; tribes; factors; social exclusion; cultural legacy

Introduction

Standing on the shores of the river Saraswati, of what remains of that river, unknowingly the modern Indians are reminded of their glorious past, and it intrigues all of us to inquisitively try to decipher our antecedents and the past. The present date pinnacle of civilisation has been passed on to all of us by our ancestors and past generations. When life began on the Earth, man evolved by passing through various stages of development and evolution that include Palaeolithic-Mesolithic-Neolithic cultural evolution before moving into the stage of civilised human existence. The role of tribal societies, particularly that of hunters and explorers, in navigating the evolution of Earth and nature is paramount. It has deeply influenced the journey of our ancestors and contributed significantly to the development of civilised humans. The tribals have remained in deep integrity and harmony with the nature and have helped preserve the world. However, the tribes and the indigenous people have enabled us to preserve the past traditions and experiences. Undoubtedly in the Vedic past under the rule of the Mauryan Empire, the state existed with the varna system. This is the time

Sustainable Pathways, 95–105

Copyright © 2024 Nishi Malhotra

Published under exclusive licence by Emerald Publishing Limited

doi:10.1108/978-1-83549-490-520241010

period in which Jana pada existed, and the dwellers paid higher obeisance to the Jan pada than the varna. As the time passed by, new foreign influences accultured with the existing clans leading to formation of tribes. Rig Veda teaches us about our ancient civilisation and the ancient Hindu civilisation, and at the same time, the scriptures and holy Rig Veda teaches us about the non-Aryans and the tribes. Who were those people who resided in far lands, and besides the occupational diversities, they crossed the mountains and rivers to make inroads and flourish with the Aryans. Indeed, acculturation was a great force that impacted the fabric of the Indian tribal culture. Rig Veda talks about the power of the new entrants that brought the foreign influence. The Rig Veda discusses about the tribe of Pakthas in Afghanistan that are also called as Pakthun and Gandharis, Panis and Dasa. The Greek cultural milieu had a great impact on the race and ethnicity of the people in Indian subcontinent. In Central Asia, tribal unrest led to vast tribal migration. The Battle of 10 Kings or dasa rajna talks about the strifes and conflicts between the Dasas and Aryans. The Vedic scriptures make a mention of the Bharata tribe to which the famous kings belonged to. Thus Purus, Tritsu and Bharaths are the Indo-Aryan tribes that have existed for long time now. Thus, since time immemorial, men have realised the importance of native people, the aboriginals, that stay in harmony with the land. The Arthshastra delves into the allocation of fort-guarding responsibilities to chiefs such as Chandales and Vagurikas. Additionally, Kautilya emphasises the significance of employing spies who disguise themselves as hermits to conduct forest reconnaissance. Thus, in order to control the natural resources, the aboriginals and natives are extremely important.

The Indian population is around 1.4 billion people, with approximately 105 million tribal people, 50% of whom are women and 50% of whom are men. The population of scheduled tribe people is rapidly expanding. This demographic accounts for about 15% of the entire population, with 90% living in rural areas. The recognition of tribal groups as such in Schedule V by the President of India is a significant step towards acknowledging the unique socio-cultural, economic, and political challenges faced by these communities. In India, 75 highly suscep-tible tribal communities have been identified, with the majority residing in Andhra Pradesh, Assam, Jharkhand, Gujarat, Chhattisgarh, Orissa, Rajasthan and West Bengal. Tribes in India are collectivist in nature and are insulated from the interactionist institutional process. They have their own distinct culture, as well as a distinct social and cultural identity. They were once thought to be people having unique ancestors. Following British imperialism, the idea of tribe became associated with primitiveness in an anthropological framework. When the British seized and annexed lands in India, they understood that tribes were extremely different from the mainstream, and that these collectivist institutions had their own culture, with their own language and beliefs. Sociologists refined the concept of tribe as a stage in human development. Indian society was founded on castes, division of work and prejudice. These collectivist institutional frameworks were extremely egalitarian and lived in kinship. These tribes may be nomadic or unnotified. According to the timeline, some tribes would make their way through movements, and many were identified as criminal tribes and denotified in the process. Nomadic tribes are continuously on the move from one location to another. Tribes are a homogeneous group of people within the group in the Indian culture, and they do differ from one another. They are classified according to their size, occupation and cultural contact. They are at various phases of development in a kinship-based culture. The tribals have the highest rate of illiteracy, and they are the most marginalised group in society. After colonisation, tribes were defined, and tribal group restoration became extremely difficult. These tribes began to lose the right to use their land and were burdened with debt. The passage of India's constitution gave them with the necessary autonomy and flexibility to integrate and mix with the mainstream population.

Problems and Challenges Faced by Tribes in India

Tribal identification involves the application of four key criteria: biogenetic, linguistic, economic, and geographic. The tribes are dispersed throughout India. Madhya Pradesh has the highest percentage of tribes, followed by the Andaman and Nicobar Islands. Tribal problems are exacerbated by urbanisation policies, resistance to change and industrialisation, which causes a variety of social problems. These factors contribute to a higher level of tribal movement. Conversion to other religions such as Christianity or Buddhism in order to benefit from the scholarship is a major issue for Indian tribes. Furthermore, tribals, who were once autonomous collectivist institutional structures, are losing their land rights, and the state is aware of this and has already launched several measures to use these people's wisdom for national development. Financial exclusion is one of the most serious issues that tribes confront, and there is an urgent need to overcome their inhabitation and isolation through favourable policies. Malnutrition, poverty, illiteracy, rehabilitation, land alienation and inadequate compensation are among the difficulties confronting the tribes. The indigenous people's increasing reliance on informal sources of finance such as stores and money-lenders is a significant concern. Poverty is widespread among tribals, and tribals are experiencing an identity crisis. They lack adequate skills and medical prudence, and their life expectancy is decreased as a result of a lack of medical literacy. It is exceedingly difficult to integrate these individuals in the development process due to a lack of legislation, and there is a need to promote participation, literacy, organising public opinion, financial inclusion and scholarship among people. Indian tribes face a lack of access to healthcare since they rely mostly on their beliefs and customs. The tribes' difficulties can be classed as (1) cognitive factors and (2) affective variables (see Fig. 9).

Cognitive Factors

The access to medical services presents a number of issues for aboriginal people. The cognitive aspects mostly involve a lack of understanding about health services and opinions about traditional practices. The tribes' health literacy levels are quite low, and they score very low in terms of sanitation and hygiene. They adhere to

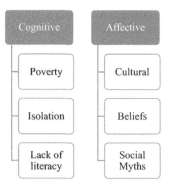

Fig. 9.   Factors to Identify the Tribes.

antiquated conventional health practices based on their beliefs, making them more vulnerable to health pandemics. These factors include the tribal population's high level of poverty, isolation and separation from the mainstream, a lack of education, female illiteracy and health difficulties. These cognitive processes are mostly to blame for tribal cultures and people's underdevelopment.

Affective Factors

The affective factors refer to the beliefs and attitudes of the people towards medicine and health. The tribes in India are in the possession of the rare traditional knowledge regarding the herbs and traditional medicinal practices. The affective factors include the cultural factors, which include the social myths, mindset and attitudes and cultural beliefs about the development. The factors that influence the well-being of tribal communities are outlined as follows:

(1) extreme poverty and poverty levels among the tribals;
(2) poor literacy levels and education levels among the poor;
(3) malnutrition and disease;
(4) migration and displacement;

- Sabka sath sabka vikas sabka prayas;
- Insurance coverage;
- Pushan Abhiyaan;
- Jandhan Aadhar and Mobile (JAM).

The Ancient Medical Practices and National Policy of Medicinal Pluralism

Tribal communities live in hamlets surrounded by natural wonders. They have a complex relationship with Mother Earth. Folklore and customs have a significant impact on their well-being and health. Around 25,000 pharmaceutical compositions are owned by Indian tribes. Traditional knowledge about health, plants and medicines is an important part of these tribes' lives. Western medical systems made inroads into the Indian economy as a result of colonisation. The struggle for cultural predominance between the mainstream and the tribal people continues. Despite the usefulness of indigenous tribal medicines in curing many diseases, there is a need to preserve this medical system in order to promote the Indian way of life. India has emphasised the need of preserving Ayurvedic and archaic medicinal systems through literature, scriptures and home medicines. India has recently set the groundwork for the creation of a traditional medicine facility in Jamnagar, Gujarat. By blending historic traditional treatments and medicinal practices with modern healthcare procedures, India has created a national strategy on medicinal pluralism. The term medical pluralism was coined in the 1970s by the social sciences literature to refer to the adoption of diverse medical policies and practices. The National Rural Health Mission (NRHM) plans to incorporate Ayurveda, Yoga, Unani, Siddha and Homoeopathy in 2005. Professionalisation of the traditional medicinal system is a significant difficulty because these medical systems have no written documentation. Local healthcare traditions have emerged as a key issue of study and debate in the research community. Home remedies and folklore are abbreviated as LHT. Article 24 of the United Nations Declaration on the Rights of Indigenous Peoples recognises the need for healthcare and tribal medicine. Despite the prevalence of positivist paradigms in medicine, traditional healthcare methods promote the relevance of socially constructed beliefs and traditions. Traditional medicinal practices are widely accepted for a variety of reasons, including belief in efficacy, cultural affinity, trust and ease of access. However, despite easy availability, local medicine is often underappreciated due to a disconnect with policy implementation, a lack of policy support, myths and disbeliefs. With the adoption of Ayurveda, Yoga, Naturopathy, Unani, Siddha and Homeopathy (AYUSH) by India, things are rapidly changing. The Indian government is attempting to educate people about the importance of emotional and mental well-being in promoting healthy life. Holism or a contented mind and a joyful soul are prerequisites for good existence. The AYUSH medical revolution emphasises the importance of societal change and self-acceptance. It is critical for holistic health to learn from age-old traditional methods and to foster collaboration between traditional medicines and the modern-day healthcare system. This statement emphasises the importance of integrating efficient modern systems with ancient medicinal techniques within the ecological system approach to promote a healthy life. It highlights the value of combining traditional wisdom with contemporary innovations to support overall well-being. If you have specific aspects of this approach that you would like to further explore or discuss, feel free to share them, and I can provide a detailed analysis. The integrated system will almost certainly be more self-sustaining and reciprocal. Furthermore, social change is required to overcome the barriers given by limited rationality and myths and beliefs about the negative effects of traditional medicine. India has a diverse range of flora and wildlife. India is a cradle of medicines and ancient medicinal practices, with tall Himalayan peaks wrapped with thick biological forests rich in medicine and herbs in the north, followed by middle and lower Himalayas or Shivalik to

Nilgiris hills in the south. India is attempting to educate the general public about the benefits of traditional medicines and lifestyle practices like Yoga and Panchakarma, to mention a few. Thus, from a resource standpoint, India is abundant in flora and fauna, and Indian medical healers possess a rich natural history and medicinal techniques. The incorporation of Vedic practices and local health traditions has had a transforming impact on the local population's and people's quality of life. The orientalist culture is well known around the world, and the World Health Organization (WHO) has adapted age-old traditional techniques such as Malaria programmes in Ghana, Mali and Nigeria, where 60% of people suffer from fever.

AYUSH

The Indian government is attempting to educate people about the importance of emotional and mental well-being in promoting healthy life. Holism, or mental contentment and happiness, is a requirement for good existence. The necessity for social change and self-acceptance is emphasised in AYUSH medicine reform. It is critical for holistic health to learn from age-old traditional methods and to foster collaboration between traditional medicines and the modern-day healthcare system. The Indian pharmaceutical system is founded on the philosophy of the spirit, mind and body. The ecological systems theory promotes the ongoing interplay between ecology and the environment. The system is self-sustaining and reciprocal, with each actor influencing and being influenced by it. Through the theoretical lens of the resource-based view, land and its treasures are precious resources, and old customs are nothing more than punctuated equilibrium. The incorporation of these Vedic practices with local health traditions has a transforming effect on one's quality of life. Lifestyle of health and sustainability (LOHAS), as it is commonly known, has a comprehensive impact on people's lives. Traditional healers and remedies have long been recognised in orientalist society. Traditional remedies and plant drugs are used by 80% of the poor world's population. Many tribal medicines have been scientifically proven, and further awareness is needed. The WHO has just endorsed the concept of health for all, and traditional medicine must be adopted. To ensure that the benefits of traditional medicinal systems are fully realised, it is necessary to develop a policy, give access through affordable primary healthcare systems and provide suitable direction. The tribal medicine system is founded on an inductive and empirical method based on trial and error and empirical evidence. It has evolved over time and has been passed down from generation to generation. Caution is required against orthodox practices, which are practised by healers and are part of our society. According to Siegrist, every civilisation, including India, has its own medicinal civilisation. Traditional medicinal techniques predominated in India prior to the introduction of modern health practices. The Indian government is attempting to educate the public about the relevance of traditional medicines in ensuring people's health. AYUSH medical reform emphasises the need of societal change and acceptance. It is critical for holistic acceptance to learn from traditional techniques and to foster collaboration between traditional practices and the modern-day healthcare system. The ongoing interplay between ecology and environment is propagated by ecological systems theory. The system is self-sustaining and reciprocal, with each other influencing and being influenced by it.

Upliftment of Tribals

The Aryans who lived in India formed a Vedic culture and gave rise to natural healing and philosophy as early as 2500 BC during the Indus Valley civilisation. Traditional medicine is mentioned in our holy Vedic writings of Rig Veda, Sama Veda, Yajur Veda and Athar Veda. Athar Veda has references to medicinal topics such as disease, medication and treatment and did not support witch doctors throughout the period of naturalism. The Rig Vedas mention Atreya, Dhanwanti, who revitalised medicine around 1500 BC. Folk practices and magical practices were mentioned in 1552 BC, and the old testament also included herb irrigation. Traditional medicine accounts for 40% of our medicine. Aspirin is made from willow bark, which is an important example. It was used as a pain reliever and anti-inflammatory in a Bayer formulation. Madagascar, periwinkle, foxglove and Mexican yam all played a role in the medical breakthrough. Today's immunisation is based on Turkish folklore practices among Greek and Armenian women.

The policy adopted for the upliftment of the tribals can be classified as (1) Policy of Assimilation and (2) Policy of Isolation.

Policy of Isolation: The isolationist method was developed by Verrier Elwin, who advocated for tribals to be left alone and segregated from the mainstream population. Many indigenous peoples and local tribes were marginalised and denied their cultural rights during the colonial British Raj. Overall, the British Empire followed a policy of non-interference in tribal peoples' rights and existence. The underlying notion was to allow the tribes to live independently and apart from the mainstream. In the early nineteenth century, the British took an isolationist stance to tribal peoples, and most British officials sought to destroy the aboriginal and native populations. Many British citizens considered exterminating, killing or capturing the tribals through patrols. Though the British authorities considered exterminating the aboriginal population, they soon changed their minds and pursued an assimilation approach. The majority of tribal history literature in India cites Brigadier General Cummins' involvement in dismissing the idea of isolating and capturing tribals as ludicrous and instead deciding to incorporate tribals into the mainstream. This includes subduing the tribes, cultivating them by including them and forcing them to stay in the camps, feeding them with native cuisine and also showering them with presents and gifts to assure their absorption into the mainstream. But after having a bad encounter with the Sentinelese tribe, they decided to abandon the tribes and isolate them. Verrier Elwin, a British citizen who visited India in 1927, supported the idea of permanent isolation of tribes and the use of isolationism as a development method. He suggested that because the tribals' manner of life is so different from the mainstream, they should be separated from the rest of the community. The concept of promoting a healthy life through the ecological system approach underscores the importance of blending efficient modern systems with the time-tested healing practices of ancient medicinal techniques. Aside from that, anthropological considerations were the other causes for these tribes' seclusion. The anthropological approach to tribal inclusion in the mainstream was primarily focused on treating tribal people as specimens and improving social conditions. Elwin believed that the tribals should not be allowed to communicate with the outside world. He also advocated for the establishment of a national park to safeguard the tribes from exploitation. He also emphasised the importance of meticulous planning and growth.

Policy of Assimilation: Late G.S. Ghurye is considered to be the originator of the approach of the assimilation towards the inclusion of the tribes in the mainstream. The father of nation Bapu, Mahatma Gandhi, G.S.Ghurye and M.N. Srinivasan refuted the isolationist. They argued that the Britishers were trying to divide the Hindus and tribal people, and they argued that this isolationism will be detrimental to the growth and development plans of the nation. Rather, the Indian policymakers promoted the idea of including the tribal communities in mainstream, without tinkering with their belief system and value systems. Pt Jawaharlal Nehru promoted the idea of inclusion of the tribals through the principle of Panchsheel. With policy and political reforms, the idea of inclusion of tribals in mainstream matured from assimilation to inclusion and integration. The main idea for assimilation of the tribals in the mainstream was to inculcate positive changes in the life of the tribal people. Many such initiatives were taken to include the tribals in mainstream that include rehabilitation of the refugees from Bengal in Koraput region in Orissa with tribal people. The objective was to enable the tribal people to experience the mainstream life and coexist with mainstream population. The five principles of Panchsheel have been adopted for the upliftment of the tribals, and these principles include:

(1) Tribals should be allowed to develop on their own.
(2) Tribal development should be achieved without impacting their ethos and value systems.
(3) Index should be developed for the upliftment of the poor.
(4) Rights of tribal people should be respected.

Policy of integration: Pandit Jawaharlal Nehru was considered the architect of the policy of integration. The integrationist approach refers to the adoption of the policy of integration of the tribals with the mainstream. It includes creating the policy with emphasis on achieving equality, upward mobility, economic viability and proximity to national mainstream. This approach emphasises two sets of measures: (1) Protective and (2) promotional measures to ensure the inclusion of the poor tribals in the mainstream. As far as the protective measures are concerned, these measures include the administrative and legal mechanism to ensure inclusion of the local communities in their social and cultural milieu. While as isolationists, many of the policymakers were of the view that the local community's integration might disturb the well-being of the mainstream, and thus, emphasis was on integration of the tribals in the mainstream. At the same time, India recognised the importance of integration of the poor people in tribes. Through the process of acculturation and integration of the tribes into the mainstream, the tribal people have aimed to achieve equality, upward mobility and economic feasibility for the tribal people.

After the coming up of the Constitution of India, the tribal people have got their representation in the society. Indigenous culture is the reflection of the age-old traditions and customs. Earlier, the tribes were termed as savage; however with the democratic institutionalisation of the society, the scheduled tribes are being given adequate importance and their skills are being recognised by India. To promote tribes, India has undertaken various programmes and policy initiatives which include the promotion of the handicrafts through various micro-finance schemes. The tribal growth in India is mediated through various social interactions, including predispositions, attitudes, interests, and self-categorisation of individuals and groups. The concept of tribal identity is facing various challenges from the powerful upper class lobby and is leading to trouble for the people among the lower castes and tribes. The integration of efficient modern systems with ancient medicinal techniques has implications for the marginalisation of impoverished and tribal communities.

Tribals and the Preservation of Languages

Identity of the tribal people is an extremely precarious issue, and regarding this, the tribals feel that the preservation of language is an extremely important issue for the preservation of the identity. The Sanskritisation and Conversions are two important changes that are taking place among the tribal groups and their identity. Sanskritisation is the process through which low-class Hindu or tribal groups are changing their customs, rituals and ideology. Many of the researchers such as G.S. Ghurye have defined the separation between the tribes and the caste as the artificial divide and not the actual fault lines. India has undertaken various social and nation-building activities which include.

Sanskritisation of the Indigenous Tribes

As per the literature, the tribes in India are undergoing massive transformations. One among those transformations is the migration from the caste into tribes. Tribal identity is a concept that originated after the independence of the nation, with the formulation of the Constitution. Tribes are the communities that have followed the primitive culture, and they pursue the primitive style of living. These people are undergoing the phase of Sanskritisation to overcome the psychological threats of the people from the communities. There are intuitively, as per the researchers, no antecedents to the philosophical origins of the tribes in India. Despite the lack of a paradigm, the tribal identities are based upon the Sanskritisation model and the assimilation of the communities into Hinduism through the process of transformation and adoption of the practices of the people at the tribal people. The case in point is the assimilation of the various tribes such as Gond into the fabric of the Indian culture. Sanskritisation refers to the even higher level of purification of the tribal people through the imitation of the cults and practices of the Hindu people. Through the process of acculturation and mixing up of the races, the tribals are interacting with the higher caste groups through the more intimate interaction between the lower caste and the lower caste celebrating the festivals and the occasions of the higher castes with the rituals in order to get the acceptance from the Kshatriya samaj and the upper caste. The process of assimilation of lower castes into the mainstream is slow, but the phenomenon of Sanskritisation is leading to increased discrimination and unjust treatment of the poor and tribal communities at the hands of the well-off. Since time immemorial, the tribals are worshipping the Hindu Gods such as Pashupati Maharaj, Navagraha's, Ganesha, Surya God.

Empowerment of Tribal 'Sabka Sath Sabka Vikas'

Unity in the face of diversity is among the most remarkable features of India. India is home to the second largest tribal population in the globe. The 2011 Census indicates that 8.9% of the total population of India is categorised as tribal. The nation's indigenous population possesses unique lifestyles, customs and an extensive heritage, in addition to their own traditions and cultures. India's history and independence struggle have been profoundly influenced by tribal movements. Such peoples consist of the Khasi-Garo, Mizo and Kol, among others. The nation will perpetually bear in mind the heroic deeds of Rani Kamalapati and the altruistic nature of Gond Maharani Veer Durgavati. The struggle of Veer Maharana Pratap is inconceivable without the valiant Bhils who risked their lives alongside him in battle. There are numerous Adivasis. India particularly celebrates Bhagwan Birsa Munda, as Janjatiya Gaurav Divas India has launched the *Pradhan Mantri Janjati Adivasi Nyaya Maha Abhiyan (PM JANMAN)*, with a budget of around Rs. 24,000 crore for the overall development of Particularly Vulnerable Tribal Groups (PVTGs). To empower the tribal communities, the Government has undertaken various initiatives such as educational empowerment through Eklavya Model residential School, economic empowerment through Pradhan Mantri Vanbandhu Vikas Yojana, *improved infastructure and ilivelihood opportunities under the Pradhan Mantri Adi Adarsh Gram Yojana (PMAAGY)*. The government has taken initiatives to improve the health of tribal communities, including the Nikshay Mitra initiative, which provides additional support for tribal groups on tuberculosis treatment, including diagnostic, nutritional, and vocational support.

Conclusion

The tribes are extremely important for the sustenance of the ecology and the sustainable environment. Indian Government has undertaken various initiatives for the upliftment of the tribes and the tribals. In this regard, various schemes have been undertaken by the Government. And undoubtedly, there is need for inclusion and providing the resolution to the problems faced by the tribes and tribal people. The present Government in India has followed a highly positive and balanced approach towards the integration of tribes with the mainstream, while also providing representation to tribes in the country's economic and social structures. This approach has been critical in preserving the natural resources of the country.

Further Reading

Majumdar, K., & Chatterjee, D. (2022). Eco literacy among Tribals in Eastern India. *South Asia Research*, *42*(1), 76–92. https://doi.org/10.1177/02627280211056838

Subba, T. B. (2020). Verrier Elwin and his fieldwork method. *Journal of the Anthropological Survey of India*, *69*(1), 7–14. https://doi.org/10.1177/2277436X20905924

References

Ghurye, G. S. (1969). *Govind Sadashiv, 1893–1983*.

Chapter 5

Financial Inclusion of Native Tribes in India and Challenges

Abstract

Financial inclusion implies providing the access to finance for the people at the bottom of the pyramid. The financial inclusion of the rural people remains the challenge because the poor people, especially the tribal people, do not have knowledge and are financially illiterate. They cannot also bank and require specialised support to access financial capabilities. The marginalised people do not have access to finance, and the social collateral or the social capital enables the marginalised members to get access to finance.

Keywords: Financial inclusion; financial literacy; social collateral; marginalised societies; knowledge sharing

Introduction

The tribes in India and world over suffer from various challenges including financial exclusion. This implies that they do not have access to financial resources as they do not have collateral, and the banks do not have information about them. There are demand and supply factors that impact the inclusion of the marginalised native tribes in the financial system. The community programmes such as self-help group linkage programme are a unique initiative started by the National Agricultural Rural Development Bank (NABARD) under aegis of Deen Dayal Antodaya Yojana National Rural Livelihoods Mission (DAY NRLM) to support the marginalised women from the native communities, especially to get financially included through group lending from banks based on the social capital. This chapter will present various case studies and experiences of the indigenous tribes and communities of having loans from the bank under the self-help group linkage programme and how it has helped them to improve their lives. On the demand side, this scheme discusses the impact of financial literacy programmes run by India on the well-being of the poor natives. Woes of tribal and native people are well recognised and even United

Sustainable Pathways, 107–126
Copyright © 2024 Nishi Malhotra
Published under exclusive licence by Emerald Publishing Limited
doi:10.1108/978-1-83549-490-520241012

Nations highlights the need for the financial inclusion of the natives and tribal people through access to financial resources in the form of Sustainable Development Goals (SDGs) to achieve equality and poverty reduction. Towards this end, India has undertaken an initiative named 'Sabka Sath Sabka Vikas'. This programme is aimed at overall empowerment and development of all the marginalised and tribal communities. There are 370 million indigenous people across India. The scheduled tribes and other particularly vulnerable tribal groups have a dwindling population, and there is a need to protect their culture, art and traditions. There are 197 tribal languages, and the languages of these tribal people are dwindling. There is a need for preserving the language of these people and to include these people in the mainstream. The tribal art and culture is the foundation of our rich Indian heritage, but the very same tribal people struggle to find employment and livelihood. The data show that literacy levels and the employment rates are extremely low among the tribal population. Besides low savings and asset ownership, these people also do not have access to finance. Due to lack of collateral, they are unable to get bank loans and bank credit. The creditworthiness of these low micro borrowers or tribal people in the microfinance industry is unknown to most conventional financial institutions. This is commonly referred to as the problem of knowledge asymmetry in the context of Moral Hazard and Adverse Selection (Stiglitz, 1991). Due to information asymmetry, market failure exhibits higher transaction costs. The problem of information asymmetry has been analysed through the theoretical lens of agency theory (Jensen & Meckling, 1976), transaction costs (Williamson, 1975), resource-based approach (Barney, 1991), institutional theory (Di Maggio & Powell, 1991), resource dependence theory (Benson et al., 1978) and signalling theory (Spence, 1973). According to numerous research, the importance of social norms, trust and relationships in enabling growth with equity and development is highlighted in this study. The Self-Help Group Bank linkage is a microfinance organisation that emphasises empowerment via participation. This essay examines the concept of social capital via the viewpoint of horizontal and vertical interactions (Ito, 2003). Social capital emphasises the importance of mutual ties between members in the form of flat social structures and vertical links in the form of lender–borrower interactions in the context of a self-help organisation. This study aims to evaluate the impact of self-help groups in the 20 villages of the Ajeevika, NRLM project.

Research Problem

The poor people do not have access to financial resources, due to which they find it extremely difficult to find a livelihood for themselves. The lack of access to financial resources is the main reason for the financial exclusion of the poor. This study aims to identify the *how* and *why* the natives and indigenous people in India are unable to access the financial loans in India. The challenges faced by the native people in accessing finance are not a well-researched area. For this study, within the qualitative methodology, the grounded theory method has been used. The *semi-structured interviews* have been conducted with the heads of the self-help promoting institutions (SHPIs) set up by India, to gather some insights about the challenges faced by the native and indigenous people in getting access to finance. Despite the existence of the conceptual research, existing literature does not provide adequate empirical evidence regarding the challenges faced by the tribal people in accessing finance. This study will identify the various factors that impact the financial viability of the members of the self-help groups formed by the native people.

Theoretical Lens

There are two kinds of approaches available to analyse the lack of sustainability of the self-help groups. As per Robinson (2001), there are two different approaches to microfinance in India, the old paradigm that refers to the *donor-based subsidised* model and the newer paradigm, which refers to *sustainable finance*. The author argues that this approach can be referred to as the poverty lending approach and financial system approach. As per the article, the *financial systems* approach emphasises *commercial and financial intermediation*, which works on the principle of sustainable finance, and the *poverty alleviation* approach works on the principle of *social welfare and reduction of poverty*. This approach prefers the social objectives over and above the financial objectives or the Return on Investment. Since 1999, in the wake of liberalisation, India has adopted the sustainable finance approach. The thrust is on denying the *donor-based subsidy* to the people at the bottom of the pyramid and emphasising the need for financial independence among the poor including the native tribals.

Conceptual Frameworks: Ontology of the Social Groups

Most of the literature adopts a structuralist ontology towards the social groups, which are based on some sort of social structures and institutions that are governed by the social norms and regulations. The literature highlights that the social being is obviously connected to society and to human social behaviour. At the same time, the existing research hypothesises that the social relationships might or might not be cooperative. The social relationships or lattice of relations might be non-cooperative. The structures in theory are defined as relations of grounding or fundamentality that provide some boundaries to the social relationships. Further, the famous sociologist Katherine Ritchie highlights the relations of fundamentality, and these relations are the outcome of human actions and behaviours. Moreover, he highlights that the relationships are not naturally occurring phenomenon. As per the researcher, the social relationships are social phenomena that include the social institutions, social practices and conventions, social roles, social hierarchies, social locations or geographies. The paper defines social structure as aggregation of behaviour regulated through legal regularities, relationships and roles, systems and resource, as shown in Fig. 10.

The literature highlights that the relations that hold between nodes can be symmetric or asymmetric. They can be hierarchical or non-hierarchical. Authority, privilege, subordination and other power relations are hierarchical. The lattice of relations among the members of a community differing by the level

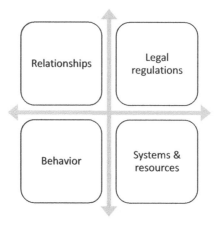

Fig. 10.   Four Dimensions of Configuration of Social Structure.
Source: Katherine Ritche.

of complexity leads to group dynamics or the forces which when bound into a social contract can be used for governance and for moulding the financial attitudes and bringing about desired financial behaviour among the members of the group. Social structures are not simply structures that relate social things. A social structure is a structure that is dependent on social factors. Most of the researchers in the field of sociology of group dynamics have adopted a structuralist approach to the group formation. According to researchers, the process of selecting objects and arranging them into a structure can be referred to as the configuration of the group or arrangement of the group, depending on the criteria used to select the objects. Further, the research highlights that there are various factors and forces that impact the formation of the group. These forces include factors like social practices, habits, beliefs, intentions, arrangements and patterns of action. Social groups are structured entities and internally structured, and these groups as a social structure are intentionally created and structured to meet desired objective. In this theoretical framework of social structure theory, this chapter aims to analyse the groups formed under self-help group bank linkage programme and the various factors that impact the functioning of these groups. Indeed, the objective of the group is to facilitate the financial inclusion of the natives and indigenous people who are artisans and who have pursued some form of art. The groups formed under the aegis of DAY aim to provide access to finance to a set of artisans belonging to the tribal community and then helping them to inculcate good financial habits and attitudes. The objective is to make it possible for the natives and tribal people to meet their financial needs and get included in the formal financial system through regular savings and repayment of loans taken through livelihood and the earning capability. This chapter mainly aims to discuss the role of relationships, behaviours and regulations in a group in impacting the financial behaviours and outcomes in a group.

Methodology and Interviews

To achieve the financial inclusion of the poor and the tribal people, around 10–20 semi-structured interviews were conducted with the members of the self-help groups and the various agencies or SHPIs hand holding the natives to achieve financial sustainability through the self-help groups. The excerpts of the interviews conducted with the heads of the tribal communities are represented below in quotes and as table transcripts (Tables 4–7).

The first interview was conducted with the set of indigenous people, all women who had come together to form a self-help group. Self-help group linkage is a novel programme that is initiated by the NABARD.

Interview 1

Interviewer: How many people are there in your group?

Respondent: There are 10 people in the group.

Interviewer: Is your group linked to SBLP?

Respondent: Yes, we are linked to the SBLP (self-help group bank linkage).

Interviewer: How do you select the members in your group?

Respondent: All the members are extremely old and if new members are to be selected, they are selected randomly from various fields. They all from different backgrounds and different vocations. But they all know each other as they are from the same village. And this facilitates us to take bank loans. We have taken a loan of Rs. 10 Lakhs from the bank.

Interviewer: What is the reason for high repayment of the self-help group?

Respondent: Bank is wary to lend to borrowers who do not have collateral. But in a group, the repayment rates are high. This is because on 10th month of every member contribute the savings and by the 15th of the month the book keeping is completed for the group.

Interviewer: What is the solution to repayment default by the member?

Respondent: In case of default, we take over the physical asset of the defaulter (Land and Building). In case of group there is no collateral.

Interviewer: Who is the leader and how he is selected?

Respondent: Yes, there is a leader.

Interviewer: What happens if the member is not able to repay the bank loan?

Respondent: If the member is unable to repay the bank loan, then other members are responsible to make the payment to bank on behalf of the member. Till this date there has been no instance of default in our village. All the members in our group repay the loan in time.

Interviewer: Do member peer monitor each other?

Table 4. Open Coding – Transcript Table.

Line-by-Line Analysis	In Vivo Coding	Open Coding	
		Descriptive Coding	Analytical Coding
1) If new members are to be selected, they are *selected randomly* from *various fields*.	Random selection from various fields	Criteria of selection	Non-homogenous matching
2) All from *different backgrounds* and *different vocations*.	Different vocation and social background	Like-mindedness and vocational membership	Homogeneity of profession and business correlation
3) But they *all know each other* as they are *from the same village*.	Selection criteria – same neighbourhood of people who know each other	Geographic proximity and peer information	Social ties, peer information and common domicile or neighbourhood
4) *Bank is wary* to lend to borrowers who do not have collateral.	Apprehension in microfinancing by formal institution – lack of collateral	Diagnosing problem/issue in microfinancing	Creditworthiness issue in microfinancing
5) But in a group, the repayment rates are high.	Impact of group lending	Individual vs group borrowing	Rationalising group lending
This is because, on the 10th month of every year, each member of the group contributes their savings towards the collective arrangement of objects in a predetermined structure, following a predetermined criterion.	Saving regularly	Rationalising higher repayments in group	Higher repayments due to higher savings/thrifts

7) By the 15th of the month, the book keeping is completed for the group.	Regular record keeping and book keeping	Rationalising higher repayments in group	Higher repayments due to regular record keeping
8) Interviewer .... *Is there a leader in the group?*		Prompt	Fact finding
9) Yes, there is a leader.	Agree	Agreement	Affirmative
10) If the member is unable to repay the bank loan, then other members are responsible to make the payment to bank on behalf of the member.	Paying on behalf of each other in case of individual default	Mutual sharing of individual liability	Joint liability and peer support
11) Members discuss their problems and financial matters with each other.	Information sharing among members	Information sharing	Peer learning
12) The entire society monitors and builds pressure.	Peer to peer monitoring	Social monitoring and pressure	Peer pressure and peer monitoring
13) If a person has taken a loan of Rs. 1 lakh, the members inquire about the repayment of the loan from the members.	Inquiring/tracking utilisation of money by peers	Peer monitoring	Peer monitoring
14) There are six members who are educated. Some members make leather bags, some are artisans and all of them are experts.	Group size and membership of group – artisans and craftsmen	Group size/vocation	Description of group size and vocation

(Continued)

Table 4. (*Continued*)

Line-by-Line Analysis	In Vivo Coding	Open Coding	
		Descriptive Coding	Analytical Coding
15) All of them are experts.	Homogeneity of skills and craftsmanship	Expertise of craftsmanship	Homogeneity of expertise/mastery of skill
16) SHG is 6 KM from the bank, and the bank is within the Mandal.	Distance from bank and proximity to Mandal	Proximity to bank and access to finance	Proximity to financial services
17) In the monthly meeting, the Sarpanch, bank representative, counsels the defaulting member.	Problem of defaulting member and resolution by counselling by bankers and village community	Social pressure and counselling to resolve issue of defaulting member	Social pressure and counselling/debt behaviour
18) All groups are linked to the SHG federations. The interest rate of group is decided by the group and approved by the leader.	Clustering and linking to SHG federation/debt covenants and norming	Debt covenants/group norming	Clustering/debt covenants/group norming
19) After formation of the group, there is lot of improvement in the standard of living.	Benefits of group lending/social welfare	Social welfare/group lending	Social welfare/group lending
20) In her Mandal, Panchayat and DRDI, the members are commanding lot of respect in the society.	Social welfare due to group lending	Improved societal position due to group lending	Improved social respect/group lending

Table 5. Open Coding – Transcript Table.

Line-by-Line Analysis	In Vivo Coding	Descriptive Coding	Analytical Coding
1) Coming from a family with a long history of involvement in this profession, dating back to his grandfather's time, he has been exposed to the bunker industry since a young age.	Lineage and family vocation	Craftsmanship and ancestral art and profession	Lineage/family vocation/ expertise in profession
2) As per the respondent, since all the members of the group are from the same profession, this helps in reducing the rate of loan default.	Low interest rate due to same profession		Homogeneity of business/ reduced cost/interest rate
3) The members are selected as per the type of profession.	Selection criteria – homogeneity of profession	Criteria of selection of members	Homogeneity of business – criteria of selection of member
4) Though members do not generally default, but if the members default, then the entire group which stays nearby counsels the member.	Financial discipline through peer pressure and counselling	Peer pressure/ counselling	Peer pressure

(Continued)

Table 5. (*Continued*)

Line-by-Line Analysis	In Vivo Coding	Descriptive Coding	Analytical Coding
5) Even in monthly meetings, the member is counselled.	Peer pressure/frequency of meetings	Peer pressure/ frequency of meetings	Peer control/peer pressure/ frequency of meetings
6) All the fingers in a hand are not the same and some 10% people always default.	Difference in risk propensity of borrower	Diverse borrower's risk type	Default rate linked to borrower risk type
9) The members are all in same profession, and through monitoring, it is ensured that they do not misuse the funds.	Peer monitoring reduces the misuse of funds	Peer monitoring/ misuse of funds	Misuse of funds/peer monitoring
10) If they do, they are warned and mostly they are able to repay their loan bank.	Better repayment due to peer pressure and mitigation of misuse of funds	Higher repayment – peer pressure/ counselling	Peer pressure/better repayment

Table 6. Open Coding – Transcript Table.

Line-by-Line Analysis	In Vivo Coding	Descriptive Coding	Analytical Coding
1) Whether your group is linked to bank under SBLP?	Inquiring about the group linkage	Question about the credit linkage of bank?	Questioning about the fact of case?
2) No, we are thinking of taking loan.	Negation and intention to take loan	Credit needs/borrowing requirement	Group credit needs
3) There are 10 members in the group.	Size of loan	Group loan	Size of the group
4) How your group select the members in the group?	Group selection criterion	Selection criterion	Group selection criterion
5) There is a criterion. In a village, the members solicit cooperation and membership from the villagers.	Affirmative. Peer selection through social ties and network	Peer selection criterion. Social ties	Peer selection criterion. Social ties
6) Do members know each other?	Knowledge of members	Peer information	Peer information
7) Yes, absolutely.	Agreement	Affirmative	Assertion and affirmation
8) How it helps in case of a group?	Questioning the usefulness if group lending	Group lending vs individual lending	Benefits of group lending

Table 7. Open Coding – Transcript Table.

Line-by-Line Analysis	In Vivo Coding	Descriptive Coding	Analytical Coding
What is the reason for the success of the group?	Questioning for insights	Questioning the state of things	Questioning the state of reality
There are 11 members in the group.	Constitution of group	Size of group	Characteristics of group – size
Have you taken a loan under SBLP?	Questioning to get information?	Questioning capital structure of group	Source of capital
Yes.	Affirmation	Agreement	Affirming – credit as source of capital
These are the women from the same profession, and all of them are involved in making bedsheets.	Homogeneity of profession as criteria of selection	Criteria of selection/screening – homogeneity of profession	Criterion of selection
Profit earned from the profession is equally distributed to all the members.	Distribution of profits	Income sharing	Criterion for income sharing
This is the financial discipline and behaviour of the group that leads to better repayments and better loan performance.	Financial sustainability due to financial discipline	Financial sustainability – cause and effect between financial discipline and behaviour	Organisational commitment leads to financial sustainability.
Members regularly conduct meetings at least 4–5 times in a month.	Cause of financial sustainability – regular meetings	Institutional structure/meetings linked to financial sustainability	Institutional structure/processes

In a group, all members have joint liability, and since our members never default and repayments are made in time.	Good credit behaviour/ regular repayments in a joint liability set up	Credit behaviour- regular repayments/no default in joint liability	Organisational commitment leads to good credit behaviour.
Financial discipline, cooperation of the members, cohesion in the group and linkages, informal network and sharing of information among the members lead to better financial performance.	Cause of financial sustainability – informal network/social capital/social cohesion	Informal network/social capital leads to financial sustainability	Informal organisation structure/communication leads to financial sustainability
A group leader is appointed, and he is responsible for maintenance of books of account.	Book keeping by leader	Group role – leaders prepare records of finance	Group roles, leadership and institutional responsibilities
Bank is at a distance of 0.5 km, and we all members are in neighbour and at a distance of 100 m.	Nearness from the bank and close proximity of members	Geographical proximity of financial resource and members	Geographical proximity/ access to resources and social network
Peer monitoring is one of the major factors for the success of the group.	Relationship between process of peer monitoring and group efficiency	Informal structure/process of peer monitoring leads to group effectiveness	Social culture of peer monitoring leads to group effectiveness/better control and efficiency.
Group lending has far reached social impacts	Intralending, rotation of savings lead to self-sufficiency	Social control/collaborative financial resource view/equity	Resource dependency theory/ symbiotic interdependencies/

(Continued)

Table 7. (*Continued*)

Line-by-Line Analysis	In Vivo Coding	Descriptive Coding	Analytical Coding
including the better standard of living, better income.	of group and individual development	in distribution of financial resources lead to social impact	sharing of resources/equity in distribution resources lead to group welfare.
Common vocation and since all women make bedsheets on a common khadi and handloom, the members are able to better peer monitor each other.	*Common ground –* Composition of group, homogeneity of vocation, business correlation leads peer monitoring	Business correlation leads to peer monitoring	Theory-driven group formation facilitates social learning (theory of group dynamics) and through agency leads to interaction; *Group Norms/Control:* Group norms lead to better control through peer monitoring.
Transparency in reporting sales, income, and loans enables the sustainability of the group by providing a clear understanding of the group's financial performance and enabling informed decision-making.	Book keeping leads to group sustainability	Institutional processes – adherence to group norms, book keeping leads to financial sustainability.	Institutional sustainability leads to financial sustainability.
Bank also has a very positive attitude towards our self-help groups, and this has enabled us to get a loan of additional Rs. 8 lakhs.	Lender (Principal) has positive disposition towards the group.	Lattice of relations – vertical relationship between borrower and lender is harmonious	Positive power relations/ vertical relationship between bank and borrower due to institutional and financial sustainability

Respondent: Members discuss their problems and financial matters with each other. As all the villagers know each other. They discuss their financial matters as and when they meet in the village. The entire society monitors and builds pressure. Family members, members of SHG ask and monitor the utilization of loan amount. For e.g. If a person has taken a loan of Rs. 1 Lakh, the members inquire about the repayment of the loan from the members.

Interviewer: Why your SHG is successful?

Respondent: There are six members who are educated. Some member makes leather bags, some are artisans and all of them are experts. During COVID-19 there was no collection but we used Google pay. Bank has supported us.

Interviewer: How far is your SHG from the bank?

Respondent: Our SHG is 6 KM from the bank and the bank is within the Mandal. If somebody does not make the payment, there is a counselling at Panchayat level. In the monthly meeting, the Sarpanch, bank representative counsels the defaulting member. All groups are linked to the SHG Federations. The interest rate of group is decided by the group and approved by the leader.

Interviewer: Do you think there is a positive impact of SHG membership on standard of living of the members?

Respondent: After formation of the group there is lot of improvement in the standard of living of the people in terms of use of funds, savings, social welfare. In her Mandal, Panchayat and DRDI the members are commanding lot of respect in the society.

The open coding of the interview revealed that the groups are formed by the SHPIs on the basis of the homogeneity of profession or on the basis of the social ties. Thus, from the interview, it became apparent that the members of the groups use the homogeneity and acquaintance due to geographical proximity and profession as the criterion for the selection of the members of the group. This group formation has helped the members get access to the finance and loan. It has enabled them to achieve higher financial sustainability and inclusion. The members of the group are artisans who are following the same art, and they are a priori aware about the credibility and creditworthiness of the members. The social contract with social capital motivates them to peer monitor each other. The bank provides them the loan on the condition that they will return back the money and no one will default on payment. This further motivates them to maintain proper books of accounts and, if somebody defaults on payment, to apply peer pressure and discipline him. This enables them to achieve the financial sustainability. In yet another interview with the self-help group run by the women who pursue the same art, the ethos of group feeling and camaraderie came across as the main factors behind the motivation to work together to achieve financial self-sufficiency. Here are the excerpts from the interview.

Interview 2

Interviewer: How many members are there in your group?
Respondent: 25 members.
Interviewer: Have you taken loan from bank under SBLP?
Respondent: Group has not got loan under the self-help group bank linkage programme.
Interviewer: How you choose members in the group?
Respondent: The leader of the group selects members with the necessary skill set and provides them with livelihood, attaching them to the group. All the members in the group are acquaintance. The bank loan is cheap in terms of the interest rate. The process of providing loan is tedious and bank officials are wary of lending to the members. They are very arrogant and we do not know them.

The member of the self-help group who was interviewed shared his experience of group formation and his inducement to join group to avail bank loan at lesser rate of interests. However, he shared that the bank officials are arrogant, and they are not very enthused to provide loans to poor micro borrowers or artisans from the self-help groups. This brought to light the lack of acceptance of the native artisans into the formal financial system and the bad attitude of the bankers towards the members of the self-help groups.

Many interviews were conducted with the artisan community. One such interview was conducted with the bunker community, and the respondent highlighted the challenges in the administration and management of the group. Given below are the excerpts from the interview and the coding. Respondents told that they are coming from the family of bunkers, and they have been in this profession since the times of his grandfathers. Our group has taken the loan under the self-help group linkage from the bank. Earlier, it was Swarn Jayanti Rozgar Yojana, and now it is DAY. As per the respondent, since all the members of the group are from the same profession, this helps in reducing the rate of loan default. This group according to the member is extremely old and members came together since the implementation of the self-help group bank linkage programme. The members are selected as per the type of profession. Though members do not generally default, but if the members default, then the entire group which stays nearby counsels the member. Even in monthly meetings, the member is counselled. He drew an analogy that just as all the fingers on a hand are not the same, some members of the group may have a default tendency, with approximately 10% defaulting. The members are all in same profession, and through monitoring, it is ensured that they do not misuse the funds. If they do, they are warned and mostly they are able to repay their loan bank.

Financial indiscipline through the use of the funds for non-productive purposes came across as the major problem behind the financial unsustainability of the groups. The member emphasises the use of the peer pressure and extreme measures such as penalising the defaulters. Not only this, the members highlighted that there are cases of misuse of the loan amount for the non-productive purposes, and there is need for hand holding and counselling. Counselling of the members in a group of homogenous members from the same profession is quite easy as per the respondent, since they are from the same profession and locality. Thus, group overall is an effective mechanism to achieve financial sustainability and financial growth. The success of the self-help group programme can be gauged from the excerpts of the interview given below:

Interview 3

Interviewer: Whether your group is linked to bank under SBLP?

Respondent: No, we are thinking of taking loan.

Interviewer: In your group there are how many members?

Respondent: There are 10 members in the group.

Interviewer: How your group select the members in the group?

Respondent: There is a criterion. In a village the members solicit cooperation and membership from the villagers.

Interviewer: Do members know each other?

Member: Yes absolutely.

Interviewer: How it helps in case of a group?

Member: Absolutely, members of a group are trusted by the bank and if an individual member approaches the bank from the group the bank remains sceptical that they might not pay. Banks are further motivated by the regular monthly meetings. Our group conducts weekly meeting in which we decide the amount of loan to be taken and the savings amount to be collected. One member in the meeting is selected as the leader of the group. In our group there are no instances of loan default. If the member does not pay, he is expelled from the group. Peer monitoring and social sanction help in reinforcement and better repayment of loans. As all the members take the loan for productive activities and are aware of the joint liability, they peer monitor and individually member know that they might need the loan and in case of default might be expelled from the group. So, they work sincerely for the success of the group. Since members are from the same society and village, they discuss the financial problems with each other. From the savings of all the members, loan is given to the needy person. By virtue of social network and relationship, member peer monitors each other. If member takes the loan and use it for non-productive purpose, we call the meeting and advise the leader to penalise the member.

The interview with the group members of a Khadi Handloom run by natives from bunker community highlighted the unique characteristics of the social innovation called as self-help group bank linkage programme started by NABARD and the India under the aegis of DAY NRLM. The members praised the selection criterion of the self-help group bank linkage programme. They believe that having members who stay within the distance of 0.5 kms or in proximity helps to peer monitor and communicate with each other.

Interview 4

Interviewer: What is the reason for the success of the group?

Respondent: The reason for the success of the group is the forward and backward linkages of the group.

Interviewer: How many members are there in your group?

Respondent: There are 11 members in the group.

Interviewer: Have you taken a loan under SBLP?

Respondent: Yes.

Interviewer: What are the criteria for the selection of the members of the group?

Respondent: These are the women from the same profession and all of them are involved in making bedsheets. Profits earned from the profession is equally distributed to all the members.

Interviewer: How group enables the members to get better loans?

Respondent: This is the financial discipline and behaviour of the group that leads to better repayments and better loan performance.

Interviewer: Who takes care of the institutional sustainability and structures of the group?

Respondent: Members regularly conduct meetings at least 4–5 times in a month. In a group all members have joint liability, and since our members never default and repayments are made in time. Bank loans are paid in time. Financial discipline, cooperation of the members, cohesion in the group and linkages, informal network and sharing of information among the members lead to better financial performance. A group leader is appointed and he is responsible for maintenance of books of account. Bank is at a distance of 0.5 Km and we all members are in neighbour and at distance of 100 m. peer monitoring is one of the major factors for the success of the group. Group lending has far reached social impacts including the better standard of living, better income. Common vocation and since all women make bedsheets on a common khadi and handloom, the members are able to better peer monitor each other. Transparency of operations regarding sales generated, income, loan enables the sustainability of the group. Bank also has a very positive attitude towards our self-help groups and this has enabled us to get a loan of additional Rs 8 Lakhs.

The interview was analysed line by line, and in vivo coding was done to derive the descriptive and analytical codes.

The analysis of interview highlighted that the relationships among the groups are intricate and very informal as the members know each other a priori, and these relationships are the social capital of the group that facilitate the access to financial capital in the form of loans from the banks. This informality is displayed in Fig. 11. The bank might be wary of lending to the individual member, but the banks find it easy to lend money to the collective groups because of their social capital. The peer selection and peer monitoring emerging from the joint liability social contract facilitates the financial sustainability and repayment of loans with ease leading to financial inclusion of the members of the group. The mechanism penalises the defaulting members and rewards the good members by providing them higher amount of loans.

Thus, indeed the Government initiatives to financially include the jobless and unemployed tribal people are seeing the light of the day. There is on ground a new entity, the semi-formal sector emerging in the form of micro borrowers from the marginalised community, who are getting access to the financial loans from the formal sector based on their creditworthiness and financial sustainability. The groups are formed based on the social capital and the relationships among the homogenous set of people. This force enables the poor and marginalised people to access finance. It also enables them to peer monitor each other for achieving financial sustainability. The members preselect each other on the basis of access to prior information about the creditworthiness of the other members. The members know about other members of the group, and through a social contract, they all agree to govern each other and monitor each other through group mechanism like meetings. If an individual defaults within the group, he is penalised and is asked to repay the loan, and thus, peer pressure plays an extremely important role in the financial sustainability of the group.

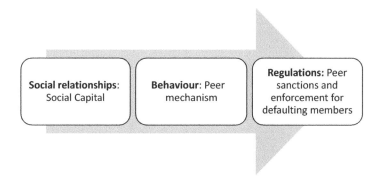

Fig. 11.   Factors Impacting the Success of Self-Help Group Bank Linkage Programme.

Conclusion

Groups as a structure are formal mechanism to enable the members to leverage their social capital through the enforcement and adherence to norms driven by existing social norms and customs or beliefs. The groups are governed by the internal mechanism which comprises of relationships, regulations, systems and behaviours. These forces help the members to achieve financial sustainability and financial prudence.

References

Andrews, A. O. (1993). In W. W. Powell & P. J. DiMaggio (Eds.), Review of the new institutionalism in organizational analysis. *Administrative Science Quarterly*, *38*(4), 691–693. https://doi.org/10.2307/2393344

Barney, J. (1991). Firm resources and sustained competitive advantage. *Journal of Management*, *17*, 99–120. http://doi.org/10.1177/014920639101700108

Benson, J. K., Pfeffer, J., & Salancik, G. R. (1978). The external control of organizations. *Administrative Science Quarterly*, *23*, 358.

Ito, S. (2003, August). Microfinance and social capital: Does social capital help create good practice? *Development in Practice*, *13*(4), 322–332. Taylor & Francis Journals.

Jensen, M. C., & Meckling, W. H. (1976, October). Theory of the firm: Managerial behavior, agency costs and ownership structure. *Journal of Financial Economics*, *3*(4), 305–360. Elsevier.

Robinson, M. S. (2001). *The microfinance revolution: Sustainable finance for the poor.* World Bank. http://hdl.handle.net/10986/28956. License:CC BY 3.0 IGO.

Spence, M. (1973). Job market signaling. *The Quarterly Journal of Economics*, *87*(3), 355–374. Oxford University Press.

Stiglitz, J. E. (1991). *The invisible hand and modern welfare economics.* NBER Working Papers 3641. National Bureau of Economic Research, Inc.

Williamson, O. E. (1975). *Markets and hierarchies: Analysis and antitrust implications: A study in the economics of internal organization.* Free Press.

Chapter 6

Right of the Indigenous People and Works Done by the Indian Government

Abstract

The marginalised people at the bottom of the pyramid are unable to access finance due to the lack of collateral and physical property. The self-help group linkage programme enables the people at the bottom of the pyramid to finance through their social capital and social relationship. In a group, the liability for each of the members is limited, and the group assumes joint liability for loans taken by the members of group.

Keywords: Government schemes; state interventions; self-help group linkage programme; community initiatives; group dynamics in a self-help group or group dynamics

Introduction

Self-help group bank linkage programme (SBLP) has emerged as the tool for ensuring access to finance for the people at the bottom of the pyramid. The members of the groups do not have collateral, and thus, banks are wary to lend to them. But the social norms and social capital existing in the group enable the indigenous people who are the members of the group to achieve financial sustainability and institutional sustainability leading. The foundation of a group is the social contract that is entered into by the members of the group by virtue of their existing relationships with the other members of the group, who are from the same profession or stay in geographical proximity to the other members of the group. The groups work based on the social beliefs and relationships, which include rules and understandings. All the members enter social contract with joint liability, where if even one of the members defaults, then all the other members get together to provide required financial help and handholding to the members of the group. Thus, counselling and regulation through a limited liability contract plays an extremely important role in the governance of the group. This chapter

Sustainable Pathways, 127–160
Copyright © 2024 Nishi Malhotra
Published under exclusive licence by Emerald Publishing Limited
doi:10.1108/978-1-83549-490-520241014

aims to explore the importance of the limited liability and regulations in ensuring the financial sustainability groups.

Objective

The previous chapter highlighted the importance of group formation and the criterion of homogeneity of the members in ensuring financial sustainability group. This chapter aims to explore the role of the enforcement and punitive norms and actions in ensuring the financial sustainability of the group.

Research Problem

The indigenous groups and native people are an important part of the financial ecosystem. There are more than 705 ethnic communities in India and 476 million people across more than 90 nations across the globe. These people possess the skills in their hand and possess unique knowledge about the natural resources, and they represent more than 5,000 cultures across the globe. One of the most pressing problems that these people face is that more than 18% of these indigenous people are living in abject poverty. Generally, as part of policy towards social inclusion, the states and the Government across the world have adopted a policy of not funding but promoting the finance for the values and value creation by these communities. These communities have a strong culture, and they carry out various developmental activities for the welfare of the people at the bottom of the pyramid. These natives have been endowed with the ancestral values that have been entrusted to them. Since 1999, the Government has adopted the financial system and sustainable finance approach to strengthen the financial sustainability of the community-based lending groups. This chapter aims to explore the various factors that impact the strength of the organisational processes of a community lending group, to ensure sustainability and financial efficiency of these institutions. The self-help groups (SHGs) are mainly aimed at promoting the financial wellness of the micro borrowers at the bottom of the pyramid. The SHG is a unique organisation that builds financial resilience by harnessing the knowledge and cultural values to build the relationships with the banks and financial institutions. This chapter aims to explore the various factors and the forces in a community organisation like SHGs that help to achieve the financial resilience.

Theoretical Lens

Community initiatives bring participation and decentralisation. Community is a small spatial unit, homogenous, comprised of the same type of members, governed by common ground or norms. These initiatives are aimed at development and impact number of actors. It is comprised of the external and internal institutions. The researchers have observed a transformation in groups from being kinship-based to being contractual and based on individual rights. The literature highlights that prior to the emergence of the sustainable finance, most of researchers earlier depended on the donor-based subsidy as they did not have access to formal finance due to lack of information about their creditworthiness and the lack of collateral. But soon after that came the phase of financialisation of these community groups through financial inclusion, training and workshop to ensure that the members of the groups become financially disciplined to return their loans to the lenders in time. Thus, in the form of SHGs, social organisations have replaced the community initiatives. Traditional structures have been replaced by rational and scientific temper. Social changes have replaced the old world of coercive principles. Social changes have replaced the old world of coercive principles and the social groups where communities are homogenous entities in terms of endowment of resources (RBV), which include the social capital, financial resources and human capital. Communities play a vital role in fostering common interests, identification, and internalised norms, which are utilised to operationalise peer mechanisms in ensuring timely repayment of loans and credit. Further, the communities are social structures, and their outcomes are impacted by the multiple interests of members, processes of interaction, institutional arrangements and structures. Following the ontology of Durkheim, Spencer and Mark, this chapter propagates that the modern social changes based on equity and participative principles have replaced the traditional structures. These changes are made visible in the form of democratic governance processes and financialisation programmes such as the dynamics of the **SBLP** that aim to achieve the financial inclusion of the people at the bottom of the pyramid. This chapter argues that communities are homogenous in terms of endowment of resources (RBV), which implies that communities comprise of members who come from the same background, such as same locality or geographical proximity and same profession, which leads to better financial inclusion. From institutional theory perspective, communities are social structures, and their outcomes are impacted by the multiple interests of members, processes of interaction, institutional arrangements and structures. Social contracts and obligations of joint liability define the contours of the borrowing within a joint liability group framework. Communities run smoothly on the basis of common agreed rules. The members in the group negotiate for the fixation of norms and rules to share common resources. The semi-formal institutions such as SHGs encompass a combination of formal and informal norms. These rules and norms govern the interactions among the actor. In sociology, institutions are essential for enabling social interactions by facilitating social exchange through social influence and social control. Self-help groups, as structured organisations, involve three primary components: (1) creating rules, (2) enforcing the rules, and (3) resolving disputes. The community-based groups of native artisans depend on size, composition, resource dependence and norms. Institutional arrangements comprise of the processes of decision-making and enforcement. Thus, community-based organisations have an important role to play in the conservation of the natural resources (Agarwal and Gibson). The natives and indigenous tribes have an important role to play in the conservation of the natural resources through sustainable farming and agricultural practices and protection of the heritage art and culture.

Research Methodology

The United Nations has highlighted the need for empowering the people at the bottom of the pyramid and particularly the vulnerable groups including the indigenous people. India has adopted the innovative approach of *sabka sath and sabka vikas* through *mahila sashatikaran* through the SHGs for the women artisans and the handicraft makers. This social innovation, known as Self-Help Groups (SHGs), possesses distinctive features. This study aims to explore these unique institutional processes that are designed to promote the financial inclusion of indigenous tribes. Specifically, it focuses on group lending initiatives under the Deen Dayal Antyodaya Yojana (DAY) within the National Rural Livelihoods Mission (NRLM). There are not many studies on how the groups ensure the financial inclusion of the poor vulnerable tribes, and this study aims to explore the unique features of SHGs that lead to financial inclusion by using the grounded theory approach.

Discussion and Findings

An interview was conducted with the members from the SHG and the heads of the Self-help promotion institution (SHPI) to understand the various challenges faced by the members of the SHGs formed by the women from the tribal communities and indigenous communities. The excerpts of the interview are given below:

Interviewer: What are the challenges faced by the banks in monitoring, selection and sanctioning?

Respondent: RBI has mandated the linkage of the SHG of banks without any collateral. There is no need for the collateral and documents. Groups are graded after 6 months, when the group become eligible for the bank loan on basis of the Panchsutras. On basis of this Rs 1 Lakh is given to the group.

Interviewer: Does bank sanction the groups? And how do the group perform and how are they monitored?

Respondent: The groups are mature and they have very high repayment but there is some problem regarding the utilization of the money. They misuse the funds for consumption purpose. Women members are very capable but they should be given more financial literacy. Definitely after we provide them CCL, the bankers should be trained as they scare the women. Besides that, members in the group are from the common background in same vocation and village due to which they have information about each other. The members are able to peer monitor each other. Block officers maintain a personal relationship with the borrowers and the officers cooperate with the borrowers. In the monthly meeting, the community resource person is deployed to collect information and provide this information to the banks. On a personal level the relationship is maintained with the members and also there is a book keeper and they work voluntarily to audit the workings, savings and borrowings of the members. This leads to the better repayment of the loans. This has helped to enhance self-efficacy of the borrowers and there is minimal need for default. In the initial years the members are not proficient but in the later years they become proficient in maintaining and paying the loan amount. No women default in our block and *social relationship, social ties and peer monitoring is extremely successful.* (See Table 8 for line-by-line analysis of the first interview).

This interview highlights that the institutional processes which comprise of the monitoring by a three-tier body comprised of the block, district and state level bodies in ensuring the financial inclusion of the poor indigenous people. Besides this, the grading of the SHGs, book keeping, peer monitoring and the community resource persons help to achieve financial sustainability of the groups and timely repayment of loans of the SHGs.

The next interview highlights the various challenges to financial inclusion in India, including physical barriers in access to the basic banking services, branch penetration, lengthy documentation, high cost of debt and various challenges to travel and work in India. The authors highlighted the impact of various initiatives such as Swabhiman Campaign, Business Correspondence Model, Pradhan Mantri Jan Dhan Yojana, Pradhan Mantri Fasal Bima Yojana and Pradhan Mantri Jeevan Jyoti to name a few. The next interview was conducted with the indigenous tribes that pursue the Madhubani art and paintings, and they stay in communities in the Madhubani region in Bihar and Jharkhand. The excerpts from the interview are mentioned below:

Interviewer: Can you tell me something about your SHG? How many people are there in the group?

Respondent: SHG is linked to Ajeevika NRLM and is involved in the manufacturing of the Mahbubani paintings. There are 15 members in my group and all do Mahbubani painting. There are more than 40 members, who are part of the Kala Kriti SHG. And all of us are involved in Madhu Bani painting and we do exhibition in various states such as Kerala, Mumbai, Karnataka and Patna. Not all but few women members are selected who can talk to the people outside the SHG. We make paintings and this painting style commands great price and involves lot of hard work and labour.

Interviewer: How the members are selected in your group?

Respondent: The India has started the Ajeevika programme, under which the members initially join the group to earn livelihood. Then the members from the Ajeevika group, who are self-selected

Table 8. Line-By-Line Analysis and Coding for Interview I.

Line-by-Line Analysis	In Vivo Coding	Descriptive Coding	Analytical Coding
RBI has mandated the linkage of the SHG of banks without any collateral.	Mandatory linkage of SHG with banks without collateral	SBLP credit linkage as per NABARD linkage	Group lending with social collateral eliminates need for physical collateral
Groups are graded after 6 months, when the group becomes eligible for the bank loan on basis of the Panchsutras.	Grading for performance assessment of groups	Credit risk assessment of groups on basis of adherence to Panchsutras	Credit risk assessment on basis of adherence to Panchsutras
On basis of this, Rs. 1 lakh is given to the group.	Credit disbursement on basis of grading	Credit allocation on basis of borrower risk type assessment	SBLP credit allocation criteria as per borrower risk type
The groups are mature, and they have very high repayment, but there is some problem regarding the utilisation of the money.	High repayment but misutilisation of funds in group	Misutilisation of funds with higher repayment	Moral hazard
Women members are very capable, but they should be given more financial literacy.	Gender focussed financial literacy training	Financial literacy training for women as they are capable	Gender equity through social intermediation
Besides that, members in the group are from the common background in the same vocation and village due to which they have information about each other.	Composition of groups – homogeneity of group and common domicile leads to perfect information	Composition of group – homogenous in terms of village and vocation reduces information asymmetry	Role of group cohesion and homogeneity to reduce information asymmetry

The members are able to peer monitor each other.	Peer monitoring among homogenous group	Homogeneity leads to associative effects and interactions	Peer monitoring due to associative interactions and group homogeneity
Block officers maintain a personal relationship with the borrowers, and the officers cooperate with the borrowers.	Block officers from NRLM as lynchpin to facilitate financial inclusion	Intermediation by Ajeevika block officers	Relationship management and intermediation by NRLM Ajeevika block officers
In the monthly meeting, the community resource person is deployed to collect information and provide this information to the banks. On a personal level, the relationship is maintained with the members and also there is a book keeper.	Intermediation, between bank and lender by CRP. Intermediation by the book keeper	Intermediation and support under Ajeevika NRLM by CRP & book keeper	Intermediation by Ajeevika NRLM
They work voluntarily to audit the workings, savings and borrowings of the members. This leads to the better repayment of the loans. This has helped to enhance self-efficacy of the borrowers, and there is minimal need for default.	Group norms – audit by intermediaries lead to better repayment	External audit leads to better repayment	Enforcement and legal regulations lead to better repayment

join the self-help group. We have not taken the bank loan, but we have taken the loan under CLF Ajeevika programme. We do not face any kind difficulties in making the payments or savings amounts.

Interviewer: How do members maintain the performance of the group?

Respondent: Our members are aligned to households and are not part of any organization. Our members are extremely versatile in Madhu Bani painting and this is an ancestral art form. It is a heritage art and is passed on from generations to generation. My mother, grandmother and great grand mother use to pursue this art form and we have become proficient in this. Ajeevika has given a push to this and our group deposits Rs 10 per member per month and then we became eligible for loan. And our women members are definitely very proactive. In our group, the CM or the Chief (Kosh Adhyaksh) maintains the books of accounts. Members of the group are not literate and they are made aware by the Kosh Adhyaksh. All the members are not literate and illiterate members are apprised of their savings and outstanding loan amount by the chief accountant. Our group members are extremely hard working and they collectively work extremely hard from 11 p.m. till 4 a.m. in the morning. None of the members have received any kind of help from any of the members. Ajeevika NRLM block officers do come and they assist the members in making the loan repayment.

Interviewer: What are your thoughts on SHG formation?

Respondent: We classify the members who approach for joining the group on the basis of the vocation. Some people are interested in block printing, some are interested in Dye painting and so on. Then we help them open their bank accounts. Then we provide them the passbooks, accounts book and meeting book. Every month the members have to submit the savings amount and update it to the bank. These members get loan provide loan from the bank without any collateral. The bank manager provides the loan on basis of application to the members of the group. There is also subsidy provided to the members of the group. At the stage of formation, the members are grouped together on the basis of the like mindedness of the members. The members of the group make the regular payments and maintain the books of accounts. There is a tally application for updating the loan amount. Members of the group monitor each other. Every month there is a meeting for the discussion around financial transactions. They monitor each other and NRLM also monitor these groups.

In handicraft and textile sector, the small groups are monitored. These groups face challenges in terms of the marketing of the products. The solution to these challenges is in terms of training and are able to meet the challenges in existing society. Financial literacy programme helps increase their financial sustainability. These self-help groups also enable the groups to become self-reliant. (See Table 9 for line-by-line analysis of interview 2).

In yet another interview, the artisans from the Madhubani village highlighted that the members of the SHGs peer select each other using some criterion such as homogeneity of the members based on the profession and geographical proximity.

Interviewer: How many members are there in your group?
Respondent: There are 12 members in our group and 2 members died.

We do Sikki handicraft work. We are from Madhubani village, and we train the members on Sikki art. As an apprentice, new members slowly and slowly observe the senior members and thus become proficient in this art form. We have not taken any loan from the bank, but we have been supported by the Jio loan. To convert our old house into a workshop, we secured a loan of Rs 328,000 from the corporation. One lakh rupee was used for purchase of furniture, one lakh for purchase of the raw material and Rs. 128,000 was used for the repair of the house. This house was used as the workshop for making the handicraft. Four Self-Help Groups have united to form an SHG Federation. This includes Jawala, Bhagwati, Bhairav and Ganesh. All the 4 SHGs combined, 35 members are working together. Tula Mohalla comprises of Jawala and Bhagwati. Bhairav and Ganesh are far off, and we find it difficult to reach them. There is no loan repayment problem in the group. If there is a problem in repayment, then the Adhyaksh counsels the defaulters to repay the loan. And sensitise them of the joint liability, in which they are told of the problem of free riding. Defaulting member is told to repay the loans to facilitate the rotation of savings and progressive funding by the banks. NRLM also plays an important role in conducting the weekly meetings. During COVID-19, frequency of meetings has increased to 5 months. There are few members who do not come due to personal reason such as visiting the parent home town. Group creates a peer mechanism through which people who lack collateral by virtue of their social capital can access the capital to carry out the entrepreneurship venture. The members of NRLM assisted and trained us to save Rs. 1 monthly. We have also made internal rules of governance such as commission agent rate for manufacturer, gifts and donations and bonus. This is discussed regularly in the meeting of the group. It is only through cooperation and counselling in a group scenario the leader of the group motivates and pressurises the members to repay. There is an instance, one of the Didi who died use to make goods and at the end she was making goods that were not that fine and intricate in quality. Still her goods were cold in the mela, and she was never able to procure

Table 9. Line-By-Line Analysis and Coding for Interview II.

Line-by-Line Coding	In Vivo Coding	Descriptive Coding	Analytical Coding
We classify the members who approach for joining the group on the basis of the vocation. Some people are interested in block printing; some are interested in Dye painting and so on.	Selection criterion – homogeneity of profession	Selection criterion – homogeneity of profession, business correlation	Criterion for group formation
Then we help them open their bank accounts. Then we provide them the passbooks, accounts book and meeting book.	Group norms and regulations regarding book keeping and meeting	Group formation – record keeping and book keeping	Group formation – group norms and regulations
Every month, the members have to submit the savings amount and update it to the bank.	Group norms – regular savings	Group formation and group norms	Group norms and financial sustainability
These members receive loans from banks without requiring collateral. The bank manager sanctions loans based on the group members' applications. Additionally, subsidies are extended to the group members.	Group loan from bank without collateral; role of loan officer as liaison	Access to credit without physical collateral	Credit linkage without capital

At the stage of formation, the members are grouped together on the basis of the like mindedness of the members.	Criterion – group selection on basis of homogeneity of members	Group selection criterion on homogeneity of group members	Criterion of group selection – common ground, homogeneity
The members of the group make the regular payments and maintain the books of accounts. There is a tally application for updating the loan amount. Members of the group monitor each other. Every month, there is a meeting for the discussion around financial transactions.	Group norms – regular payment and maintenance of books of accounts, peer monitoring and meetings	Strong institutional structures including the processes of book keeping, record keeping, peer monitoring	Adherence to group norms; group behaviour is impacted by the external factors such as activities, interactions, sentiments (attitudes, beliefs) of a person – group norms impact behaviour Hawthorne effect – (group norms) peer monitoring and adherence to group rules impact the outcomes of group
NRLM also monitors these groups. In handicraft and textile sector, the small groups are monitored.	Monitoring of group performance by NRLM	Enforcement of group norms by NRLM	Delegated monitoring by NRLM officers, enforcement of group norms
These groups face challenges in terms of the marketing of the products.	Lack of market linkages	Challenges faced by self-help group under self-help group bank linkage	Challenges faced by SHGs
Financial literacy programme helps increase their financial sustainability. These self-help groups also enable the groups to become self-reliant.	Financial literacy to improve financial sustainability of groups	Importance of financial literacy on financial sustainability of groups	Theory of planned behaviour – financial literacy to improve financial behaviour and ensure sustainability of group

orders for fulfilment. It was only once that she got the order. To cater to the clients, the other member Didi took the savings from the member and helped her. Many of the young girls have also joined the group in handicraft making. Our group is like a family which comprises of 4 different households and there have been instances of counselling and difference of opinion, but it helps us to ensure better repayment of loans. I participated in the Ajeevika Mela in 2017 and 2019. However, Puja Didi and Rani Didi participated in 2021. (See Table 10 for line-by-line analysis of interview III).

Regarding the formation of the groups, the SHGs follow a set criterion, which involves identification of the homogenous people on the basis of some criterion such as geographical proximity, business correlation and homogeneity of members. The interview below elaborates on the criterion for the formation of the group.

Interviewer: How you help the Self-help groups to come together?

Respondent: 640-Craftsman pottery artisans are doing this work. For last 12 years we are working with terracotta artisans' community in Chittoor district, Andhra Pradesh. 640 craftsmen families are doing pottery work in our district. Initially we promoted SHGs among artisans' community among both men and women. It facilitated savings and thrift needs and also providing inter lending to working capital loan for their handicraft needs. But these groups are not working properly. These groups are homogenous groups and close relatives (e.g., son and father, mother and daughter) working together. This is because the concept of self-help groups is from nearby houses covering. We observed three years and there is no enthusiasm among members to attend the meetings for thrifts and etc. These members are close relatives. The concept of self-help group is to work together to meet common wishes and that purpose will not serve. After that we go on to form MAC (mutual Aided cooperative) societies and give membership to 1 family. The structure is working properly and they are doing thrift and credit activity as legal entity. They borrow funds from scheduled bank and in turn these funds are distributed to the members. There is no misuse and till date there is no NPA in the two societies and in each society, turnover crossed 7 crores per annum.

Interviewer: In this society are members are from the same family or from the same vocation?

Respondent: In each society there is one member there is 1 family and 1 membership. They are from nearby and same village. In each society approximately 350 families take membership. On basis of cluster approach, they are located near to each other. SHGs are unregistered and they open joint account in name of self-help group. But the MAC bodies are registered

Table 10. Line-By-Line Analysis and Coding for Interview III.

Line-by-Line Coding	In Vivo Coding	Descriptive Coding	Analytical Coding
We do Sikki handicraft work.	Handicraft and artisian–based business	Practicing Sikki handicraft artists	Sikki artists
We are from Madhubani village, and we train the members on Sikki art.	Group of artisans – Sikki art	Homogenous group	Group of homogenous members, business correlation
As an apprentice, new members slowly and slowly observe the senior members and thus become proficient in this art form.	Peer learning	Learning by observing others	Apprenticeship and peer learning
We have not taken any loan from the bank, but we have been supported by the Jio loan.	No bank loan and corporate credit linkage	Loan taken from corporate only	Lack of credit creation through bank linkage. Corporate credit linkage
In order to make our old house into workshop a loan Rs. 328,000 from the corporate. One lakh rupee was used for purchase of furniture, one lakh for purchase of the raw material and Rs. 128,000 was used for the repair of the house. This house was used as the workshop for making the handicraft.	Utilisation of loan for productive purpose	Loan utilised for purchasing furniture, raw material and repair house.	Productive utilisation of loan
There are 4 SHGs that are joined in the form of SHG Federation.	Clustering and federation	Federation development	Sustainability of SHGs through the development of federation

(*Continued*)

Table 10. (*Continued*)

Line-by-Line Coding	In Vivo Coding	Descriptive Coding	Analytical Coding
This includes Jawala, Bhagwati, Bhairav and Ganesh. All the 4 SHGs combined, 35 members are working together.	Size of group federation and details of groups in federation	Group federation and size of group	Federation and size of group
There is no loan repayment problem in the group.	Payment not an issue	Timely loan repayment	Financial sustainability and control
Tula Mohalla comprises of Jawala and Bhagwati. Bhairav and Ganesh are far off, and we find it difficult to reach them.	Issue of distance	2 member groups at distance	Distance and geographical proximity and access to groups
If there is a problem in repayment, then the Adhyaksh counsels the defaulters to repay the loan.	Peer sanction and enforcement, information sharing	Members counsel members	Peer sanction and enforcement
And sensitise them of the joint liability, in which they are told of the problem of free riding.	Free riding an issue resolved through joint liability	Information and mutual sharing of free riding problem	JLG and communication, control to mitigate free riding problem
Defaulting member is told to repay the loans to facilitate the rotation of savings and progressive funding by the banks.	Peer sanction, peer enforcement of defaulting member.	Internal control through peer sanctioning	Communication of dynamic incentive – progressive lending to facilitate rotation of savings

bodies and maintain proper book of accounts and audit is conducted annually. The audit reports and books of accounts are submitted for renewal. In self-help groups. SHG is a small and group of 10–12 people. SHGs formation is not homogenous and non-activity based. Guidelines allow the coverage of houses on the same lane and some houses are doing pottery and some are doing weaving and next household is doing petty businesses. These non-homogenous take loan under the SHGBLP and one member utilises the loan for pottery and one is utilising it for weaving. This leads to non-repayment of loans. In a SHG which is homogenous, members can monitor each other. Under SBLP, members have different skillset, some are good at baking, firing etc. In a MAC society as well, people have diversified skillsets. There are two kinds of loans. Loan in name of society for purchase of raw material and other kind of loan is the loan on working capital for construction of assets. In SHG members are not able to prepare the books of accounts. SHG is formed by the government societies and they have one structure which is *Sangh Mitra* under which 10–15 SHG are formed into the federations or village organizations. At the group or taluk level, a three-tier system is followed at the village system, taluk level. In the self-help group is formed by the government agencies like DRDA. They have one kind of structure, which is called as Sangh Mitra. 10 to 15 SHGs are formed into a village organization or federation, at the taluk level into mandal Samkhya and district level one federation. In NRLM, self-help groups are responsible for the maintenance of the books of accounts. The member participation in self-help group is extremely less due to the Sangh Mitra, as she is responsible to maintain the books of accounts. Under NRLM, some few SHGs, where the group leaders are active can maintain the books of accounts. Lack of financial literacy is the main reason for the non-maintenance of the books of account. Book account maintenance is not easy and minimum education is required for maintenance of the books of account. Digital literacy is extremely important for the people at the bottom of pyramid. The members are able to monitor each other, as these SHGs are located in the area specific clusters. Each unit has responsibility for the utilization of loans and also providing loans for the setting up the showrooms. These showrooms take the responsibility for the payment of loans. Joint liability groups are not registered groups, but the group head can take the responsibility for the payment of loans. If any of the member is not paying in time, the joint liability group monitors only the group leader. In the cluster 10–15 members are operational. Masters' craftsmen are responsible for monitoring the craftsmanship. All the master craftsmen are formed into apex body and the master craftsmen can exercise the pressure in his group and the other group. This craftsman is responsible for covering all the groups and the craftsmen are brought from all over the world including Benaras and West Bengal. MAC society and MSME have lot of benefits as this can be registered under the company's act. Schedule bank can provide the loan to the banks and MAC members have knowledge about the banks. Self-help group model is extremely difficult and SHPI is outstanding and it allows the members to pursue various kinds of art including the pottery making, weavers and terracotta. Skill building and hand holding support is extremely important. Financial literacy is extremely important for promoting the Karigari among the members of the group.

Interview: How many people in your group and how they are selected?
Respondent: The government has provided us revolving fund Rs 10,000 for CIF. We do Pach work and put them up for sale at exhibitions. We have very good creditworthiness. Money earned increase from Rs. 100,000 to Rs 200,000. For choosing the candidate or members, we call them to home and counsel them to become self-reliant by savings. Meetings are conducted even at higher frequency to make the women self-reliant. Generally, members are from the same village but we give coaching to members from the different villages as well. We all work together. It makes me feel good and they also feel good and are able to pass time. We also make eco-friendly Ganesh ji. We get the mitti in March and then we make the eco-friendly Ganesh ji and then we establish it in September. There are no repayments in problem. We do not take women who are not credit worthy. Komal ben is known all over the village. There has never been an issue regarding the non-repayment of loan. Even if there is a default due to medical reason or any kind of disease in the family, we support them and counsel them regarding the importance of timely repayment. In our group members attend meetings regularly. Komalben manages the distribution of the money. This is Komalben's ancestral business and her mother has taught this skill to them. She handles all the tasks like distribution of money. Pach work has been passed on to Komal ben from the generation to

generation. Members do cooperate with each other and encourage each other. In the initial days, women were constrained by the needs of their members and children. Slowly and slowly, I counselled them and supported them. They owe their success to the money, emotional support and efforts of Komalben. Komalben has travelled over the world from Delhi, Bangalore, Chennai, Hyderabad to make exhibition. And they indulge in Kurti making, bedsheet. This provides them so much happiness and they feel so elated that their work is so good that we try to figure out whether they are willing to learn. Slowly and slowly, they explore whether they are willing to learn. In the Ajeevika melas, we get revolving funds which we utilise for the purchase of raw materials. Our group is not linked to the Federation and we feel that linking to the cluster will help us in becoming self-sustainable. Members of the group are willing to come together to help each other. (See Table 11 for line-by-line analysis of the interview IV).

Challenges to Financial Inclusion Among Natives

In the interview with the member of the SHG, it became clear that the members in an SHG formed by the tribals and the native people do face some challenges. These challenges include the lack of financial literacy and acumen among the members of the SHGs. The poor artisans who are the member of the SHG waste most of their resources in the non-productive purposes, including the wastage. (See Fig. 12).

There are 10 members in the group, and all the members are artisans who are skilled workers. They make jute products. The members are selected on the basis of their profession. They all are from the same village. We have taken loan under the SBLP from the bank. We also pool the savings and pay back the loan taken to the members of the group. If any of the members are unable to repay the bank loan, other members make the payment on their behalf, and we exert pressure on that individual to make sure the debt is repaid in full. The members of the group are covered under Ajeevika and also receive the loan from the programme. They also get to visit the Ajeevika mela and fair on invitation.

We are going through the crisis period for us. During the COVID period, the handicraft sector has been significantly impacted. Our SHPI is specialised in Dhokra art. They make daily utility items such as bottles, cycles, but they do not have any tools. They go to the art centre; they need tool kits, market linkages. We make clusters, and SHGs are formed only through artisans in handicraft sector only, and then these are clubbed into the SHG Federation. Rest is not allowed, and these groups are linked to SBLP and other government schemes such as insurance, medical activities, pension and senior citizen pension scheme. Due to corruption, most of artisans are unable to benefit. There is a need for the behavioural change of the artisans. In the initial period, the SBLP loan granted

Table 11. Line-By-Line Analysis and Coding for Interview IV.

Line-by-Line Coding	In Vivo Coding	Descriptive Coding	Analytical Coding
Government has provided us revolving fund Rs. 10,000 for CIF.	Seed capital in form of CIF	Revolving fund by the government	Government support provides the financial sustainability
We do Patch work and put them up for sale at exhibitions.	Group handicraft put for sale in exhibitions	Market linkages to support sale of indigenous handicraft	Market linkage to support marketing of handicrafts
We have very good creditworthiness.	Creditworthiness of banks	Higher financial performance leads to creditworthiness	Creditworthiness of the group
Money earned increase from Rs. 100,000 to Rs. 200,000.	Income enhancement	Group lending leads to income enhancement	Group lending lead to higher income
For choosing the candidate or members, we call them to home and counsel them to become self-reliant by savings.	Peer support, peer counselling to train them on savings/thrifts	Savings/thrifts increased through peer counselling	Peer counselling to promote savings and thrifts
Meetings are conducted even at higher frequency to make the women self-reliant.	Peer monitoring – frequency of meeting/make self-reliant	Frequency of meeting, peer monitoring to higher repayment of loan	Peer monitoring leads to better loan repayment
Generally, members are from the same village, but we give coaching to members from different villages as well.	Selection of members from same village	Members from the same village	Selection of members – same village
We all work together.	Social cohesion	Social cohesion leads to better repayment	Better repayment due to social ties
It makes me feel good, and they also feel good and are able to pass time.	Social cohesion to work satisfaction	Social cohesion and better work satisfaction	Social cohesion positively impacts financial outcomes

We also make eco-friendly Ganesh ji. We get the mitti in March and then we make the eco-friendly Ganesh ji and then we establish it in September.	Handicraft manufacturing	Handicraft manufacturing over phases	Handicraft manufacturing. Seasonal business
We do not take women who are not creditworthy.	Selection criteria – do not take non creditworthy women	Selection criterion – creditworthy women	Creditworthy women only selected for the group
Komal ben is known all over the village.	Influential group leader	Centralisation and group lending	Leadership promotes better thrift behaviour
Even if there is a default due to medical reason or any kind of disease in the family, we support them and counsel them regarding the importance of timely repayment.	Peer support and counselling to inculcate financial behaviour among defaulting members	Peer support, cohesion and peer learning to support better repayments	Peer support to promote financial behaviour
In our group, members attend meetings regularly.	Peer monitoring through regular group meeting	Regular group meetings to peer monitor	Institutional sustainability
Komalben manages the distribution of the money.	Group leader and his role in distribution of wealth	Better distribution of money by group leader	Centralisation
This is Komalben's ancestral business, and her mother has taught this skill to them.	Ancestral business and craftsmanship	Family business, skills passed from generation to generation	Craftsmanship and family business
Members do cooperate with each other and encourage each other.	Peer support and cohesion lead to better loan repayment	Peer support and counselling	Better productivity due to peer support and counselling

(Continued)

Table 11. (*Continued*)

Line-by-Line Coding	In Vivo Coding	Descriptive Coding	Analytical Coding
In the initial days, women were constrained by the needs of their members and children. Slowly and slowly, I counselled them and supported them.	Peer support and increased social welfare of groups	Peer support and better welfare of group	Peer support and leadership
Komalben has travelled over the world from Delhi, Bangalore, Chennai, Hyderabad to make exhibition.	Successful entrepreneurship by leader	Global market linkages and leadership	Global leader with global market linkages
This provides them so much happiness, and they feel so elated that their work is so good that we try to figure out whether they are willing to learn.	Peer learning and work satisfaction	Self-contentment and social learning	Peer learning to ensure goal attainment
Slowly and slowly, they explore whether they are willing to learn.	Attitude building and measurement of willingness to learn	Exploration of interest to learn	Discovery of propensity to learn
In the Ajeevika melas, we get revolving funds which we utilise for the purchase of raw materials.	Market linkages, fair and seed capital to purchase raw material	Market support to procure raw material	Market linkages to buy raw material
Our group is not linked to the Federation, and we feel that linking to the cluster will help us in becoming self-sustainable.	Sustainability and federation	Federation leads to sustainability	Sustainability through clustering under a Federation

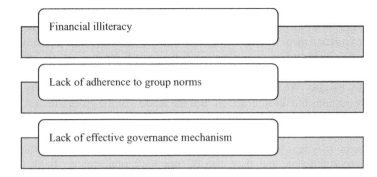

Fig. 12.   Challenges to Social Inclusion of Native People in India.

for a particular handicraft is utilised for their own purpose, for e.g. they buy assets for their own children. The majority of the members are diverse and actively participate in self-help group (SHG) meetings, accounting, and bookkeeping. While this sector is organised, it will require some time to fully organise and streamline its processes effectively. The artisans live in one geography. These people live outside the bank periphery. Bank officers come, and they take us to the field. We have helped them to make the groups, but after the formation of the group they change. The male members are addicted to drink. They are less interested to monitor. The Government officers under NRLM also monitor them. The Government only implement the programme, but they do not follow up. We also have limited resources, and hence, we also do not follow them. We do not have money to go to field again and again. The members regularly submit accounts; they tell them and we do proceedings and then we conduct meetings. There was an artisan, Ram, who was already defaulter from the loan, and Ram's wife was included in the SHG. And because of this, bank denied the loan. The members do not know about the loan paying capacity or loan history of the members. Only when the bank denies the loan do we get to know about them. The individuals prioritize short-term gains over long-term benefits, and this behaviour has become habitual for them. They go for product verification training, and they do not get any skill but look at their immediate benefit. They are concerned about the stipend and their tour and do not care about the organisation. At the time of formation of group, even members do not know about each other's creditworthiness. For e.g. at the time when they form a group, members do not reveal about their prior loans. They work only for immediate benefit and bank only looks at the creditworthiness of the spouses of the members and denies the loan. We have 120 SHGs, and 55 SHGs work well and repay loan in time and they follow up. More than 50% SHGs are working well and the artisans have been given the karigar card. In cases where individuals face difficulties repaying loans and not all artisans possess the required documentation, the state government steps in by identifying the artisans and facilitating their participation in an exhibition at

Pragati Maidan. The state government identifies the artisans and facilitates their participation in an exhibition at Pragati Maidan. But the middlemen gives money to the govt department and unjustified people are allowed loan. The monitoring of artisans is difficult for us, and we can follow up. Following up, mobilising the human resource and training them is important. Most of the artisans are not financially literate. We conduct the financial literacy training for leasers, and he should be responsible for interaction. But the leaders of the groups do not interact with them. The artisans are bank defaulters and are afraid of going to the bank. When they discover that the person visiting the bank is a bank officer, they tend to hide because they fear interactions with the bank. There is a TV, and they spend time in entertainment, and they also do not have opportunity. Bank loan for product order, they misuse that amount. These people are poor and do not have WhatsApp. Some of them have TV, and we are exploring opportunity to conduct meeting at common services centre. We have trained 15 persons to be master trainer, so that they can give training outside. The artisans are not professionally networked, and they do not share business formation. In each cluster, it is recommended to establish a common services center with IT facilities, including the use of WhatsApp, to provide training and support for capacity building. There is one leader, treasurer. These people conduct meeting under the trees, cottage office of village. These members should be trained to be more regular and trained to make minutes of meetings. The members pressurise the defaulting members, they abuse the member and they fight. We are NGO, State and Government are the stakeholders and members trust NGOs more. There is need for financial literacy and capacity-building for members. Financial literacy, women empowerment and product verification are important. They can sell the product in the market, but there is no demand for their product. Technology development, prototype development will help strengthen the project. They make various products, diyas, elephants, cats, boats, etc. Other problem is the utilisation of raw material. There is no record of their raw material utilisation. The product is made through 100 Centigrade health product, and this is a health hazard. The Government provides the training in casting but does not do anything directly and transfers it to NGO. There is need for design development, and there is need for handholding through NGO. Government promotes the project of the person who gives the money. There need for process training casting, cutting to ensure product development. NGO concept is not clear, and we will not be able to fund the federation. SHPI works for the initial period and helps in formation of SHG, but we will not be able to carry on for long. Sometimes artisans are exploited. For e.g. in 2007 in Delhi DC exhibition was being conducted, how the product should be presented, and we proposed that there should be a buyer and seller meet and that has been implemented. But still in Orissa, there is scope for work. With livelihood, the life and standard of people will change. All the information about the scheme is being disseminated through the website, and we send this message to the members. Digital and financial literacy is extremely important, and Kharagpur cluster is doing extremely well. There is need for regular evaluation of the NGOs.

Respondent: My SHG is Jayshree Bahuchari Sakhi mandal. There are 24 members (women) in group. We make decoration material, silver. After making, we sell the material in Saras mela. We get invitation from the Gujarat Government. The money is paid according to the production and output produced. We take women who want to work. Our criteria for selection are the members who stay in the same village. Yes, we have taken a bank loan. In our group we make meeting register. We attend melas in Pragati maidan and our products are popular and the Collector invited us for the meeting. From the member cooperation, the members are able to pay back the loan. I am the Aadhyaksh and there is a treasurer. Bank officials come. Yesterday, there was a meeting regarding interest free loan and interview. All members are able to pay back the loan before time. In my group, savings are deposited 10 days prior. Our SHG products are successful and a book is getting published of our success stories. We make item of 400–500 item from Kodi, make toran with barik materials, we also make items for car, water bottle and we make Jumma. With my bangles we make gift articles. All our handicrafts are made by hand, and none of the products are made with machines. We have make product prior to the Saras mela. We make products that is barik decoration and you will not find this product anywhere. The Government provide us help when need to go to the melas. NRLM provides us financial support and with my NRLM certificate money is credited to my account. NRLM officers and bank officers come for monitoring. Bank officers ask for loan. Two or three women who are monitors assess the loan requirement and provide loan from the collected savings. The groups have helped a lot in making loan and can give back the loan on time. The loan is taken for emergency and members feel privileged that despite the lack of salary they are able to complete the work. In Gujarat state I have been nominated by the state for representing handi crafts.

He determines the art in which the artist is expert and the Mohalla to which the ladies belong. Then we organize the members into a group on basis of terms and conditions are determined and groups are formed. As the members are from the same profession, they can collect and deposit money. A qualified person from the group monitors the group. After some time SHPI leave them and when the group is sustainable it becomes independent. It is a lineage business and individually the banks cannot provide the loan. Members are joined to each other and have social ties and since they have business correlation, they can pay on time. One of the members who is literate maintains the books of accounts. The members can solicit help from our organization. When the income declines, they migrate. Most of the bunkers are women. 50% of the Karkhanas are ancestral and our organization is an NGO. If the member is unable to pay the members deploys the social pressure, which helps the member to discipline the member and pay the loans. Group is an extremely effective method of financing for the illiterate members.

Orissa Rural and Urban Producer Association

What we work for the artisans is a very good experience, as you feel extremely good that because of you, someone got livelihood. As far as federation as things as changed, who so ever they want to help, they do not do so, it is a good experience. Twenty ladies are selected in the form of a group, and after that, an account is opened, and after that, you become permanent and then if you want to register. Training is done for 6 months and also stipend is given to the trainer. Directorate of handicrafts provides a good market. The purpose of selecting the members is so that they can group and meet nearby. Thus, most of the ladies selected should be within a distance of 2 km. This will lead to problem. These people meet regularly and once in a month. In Orissa, the banks do not actively participate; instead, they provide loans to individuals who then distribute the funds among themselves. These individuals repay the loan with interest on time, contributing to an increase in their borrowing capacity. In some places, the ladies do not need these loans. But if they get a chance to form SHGs and our government is based on SHG linkage, why they would leave it. They take loan and do not pay back and consume or utilise it. The group will not be disrupted in those cases, where the group members invest that amount. Many of the groups break away. The Government gives money to SHG, so that they can do some work, so that they will keep some money and moreover they will not sit ideal. In a group if one of the members does not pay back the money, then the rest of 19 ladies go back to his door and put pressure on him. The Government makes the schemes for common good, but beyond a point, money gets into the hands of the wrong people. The cycle of poverty persists because funds meant for the people get intercepted by middlemen, leading to mismanagement and lack of proper follow-up, resulting in continued poverty among the population. There is no follow up and money goes away. The banks are unable to dedicate time to individual self-help groups since they serve a large customer base of 2 lakh customers. Focusing on a single self-help group may not be profitable for banks as it conflicts with their profit-making objectives. I also keep touch with politics and if we do not follow up. If I am a big artist, there is no need for follow up and in case of small groups who cannot pay the loans they break. SHGs owned by private banks lend them money and then take back interest. Private banks are not concerned with utilisation of money, but they are concerned with the recovery of loans. Monitoring can definitely reap good results. Monitoring augurs well for everybody as they do not know the way forward, as they take the money and what to do with money they do not know.

Institutional Processes in a SHGs

Thus, there are two mechanisms that include the internal processes and external processes. The internal processes include the setting up of the governance mechanism for the groups, which comprise of meetings, book of accounts and peer mechanism that comprises of peer selection, peer monitoring and peer enforcement.

The external processes comprise of the financial intermediation by the SHPIs. From the analysis of the data, it becomes clear that groups that have been initiated through the NGOs and the SHPI are generally more sustainable. These NGOs help to monitor these groups and also provide training to these groups. Thus, these groups are formed by the NGOs, that help in mitigating the adverse selection problem by forming the groups of homogenous members. Also, the bank linkages through SBLP help in providing financial support through access to finance. Thus, the financial intermediation by the NGOs helps in improving the financial sustainability of the group. Similarly, clustering of the SHGs in the form of Federations provides an opportunity to the members to learn from each other. Clustering and bridging of groups in the form of federations provide access to more support in terms of financial training. Thus, such linkages and affiliations provide them the platform to communicate with each, share information and control their financial behaviour to achieve financial sustainability. If we analyse the last interview of the members of the groups that are pursuing the Madhubani paintings, we find that this group was not linked to the bank linkage and drew funds from internal savings and Ajeevika. We classified this group in Group B. This group was successful due to the leadership and the social ties. Apparently, there was no support received by the members in the form of social intermediation and financial subsidy from the Government. The study concluded that 'network relations' in the form of 'bridging' and 'linking' play an important role in the sustainability of the group. The leader apprised that member are hard-working and have done well to become financially self-sustainable but are dependent on the *Kosha Adhyaksh* for the maintenance of books of accounts. We suggest 'network relations' as an important peripheral concept that impacts the institutional sustainability of the group. It was also found that 'closure stake holder relationships' or 'relational network' leads to more 'resilience' in the organisation.

Internal Processes and Mechanism

Thus, from the analysis of the data, it became apparent that the regular book keeping, regular meetings, peer monitoring, peer selection, peer enforcement, social capital in the form of existing relationships with the other members of the groups by the view of the profession and geographical proximity are the internal mechanisms that facilitate the inclusion of the poor vulnerable indigenous members. Given below are detailed descriptions of the codes of internal governance mechanism.

Shared norms: The members of the group borrow from each other on the basis of the shared norms. These shared norms pertain to conducting the regular meetings, taking attendance regularly, savings and record keeping to ensure the timely repayment of the loans. (See Fig. 13 for the open codes).

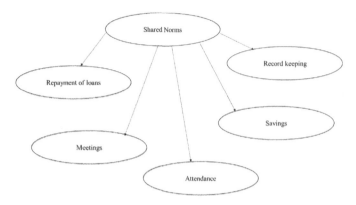

Fig. 13.   Open Codes.

Book keeping: The interviews indicated that the members of the group conduct the regular meeting with the members of the group. The leader is responsible for the book keeping, and the members are trained regarding the procedures of book keeping and its relevance. For book keeping, financial literacy is another factor that plays an important role to ensure financial sustainability of the group. Given below is the code for the internal process of book keeping as derived from the analysis of the interviews. (See Fig. 14 for open codes).

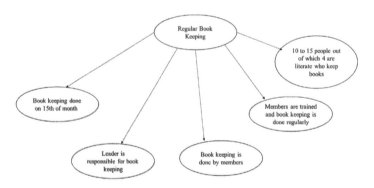

Fig. 14.   Code for Regular Book Keeping.

Regular Meetings: The paper highlights that the success of the community-based groups depends on the regularity of meetings. The meetings should be conducted regularly in which the members get together, and these meetings conducted periodically where by the members conduct the meetings regularly. (See Fig. 15 for open codes).

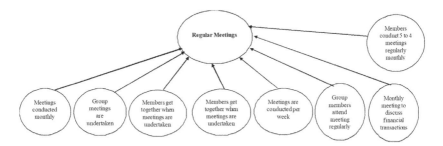

Fig. 15.   Importance of Internal Meetings.

Cooperation: The members of the group tend to cooperate with each other for encouraging the group savings. The members in the group in a social contract agree to assume a joint liability, whereby the members agree to pay on behalf of each other in case of default. If one of the members is unable to pay the loan, the other members in the group put peer pressure. This mutual cooperation leads to the financial sustainability in the group. (See Fig. 16 for open codes).

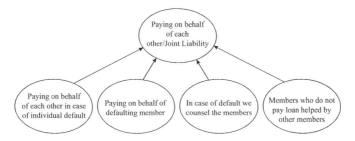

Fig. 16.   Cooperation.

Peer Monitoring: In a group, the members of the group peer monitor each other. These members use the meetings and the book keeping to pressurise the members to pay back the loan amount they have taken. This peer monitoring is used to gauge the behaviour of the members of the group. The members monitor the behaviour of the group members, which helps to reduce the default rate in the group. (See Fig. 17 for open codes).

Peer counselling: In a group with joint liability, if one of the members does not pay the loan, the members get together and visit the home of the defaulting member, where they counsel him regarding the importance of timely repayment of loan. This peer counselling helps to ensure the financial sustainability of the group. (See Fig. 18 for open codes).

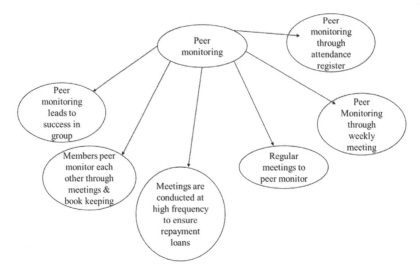

Fig. 17. Open Codes.

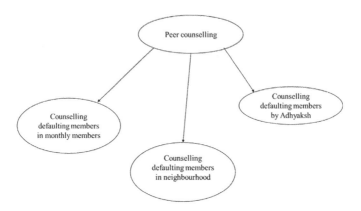

Fig. 18. Open Codes.

Peer sanction: In case if the members of the groups are unable to pay, then other members of the group get together and put peer pressure and also use the peer sanctions to sanction the behaviour of members of the group. If the members do not behave themselves, a warning is given to them, and if they still to not adhere to the group norms, the member is expelled from the group to maintain credit-worthiness of the group. (See Fig. 19 for open codes).

Fig. 19.   Open Codes.

Social capital: The members in a SHG stay close to each other and govern the behaviour of other members of the group by the virtue of social capital. Social capital refers to the relationships among the member of the group. The existence of the social relationship among the members of the group helps to increase the level of bonding among the group. These social relationships enable the member to work cooperatively towards the achievement of the group objectives and financial sustainability. (See Fig. 20 for open codes).

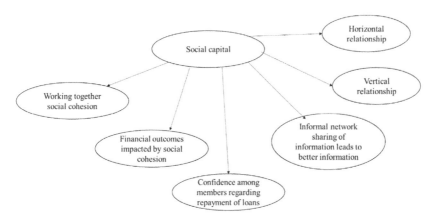

Fig. 20.   Open Codes.

External Mechanism

External mechanism refers to the presence of the external forces such as delegated monitoring by the banks, dynamic incentives offered by the banks to the members of the group in the form of additional loans and credit. Thus, the external mechanism plays an important role in the achievement of group goals. The delegated monitoring is the first factor, which refers to the sanctioning of group by bank, monitoring by the bankers at the different levels of the management mechanism and by NRLM.

Delegated monitoring: The members in a group take loans from the banks on the basis of their social capital. This social capital enables the members to obtain this loan and also motivates the members to get bound by a social contract, where they assume joint liability for each other's loan. The members of the group monitor each other, but a special three-tier body also monitors performance of the members of the group. (See Fig. 21 for open codes).

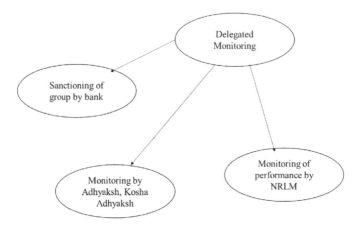

Fig. 21.   Open Codes.

Dynamic Incentive: The members of the SHG get loans from the bank and the bank denies the loan even if one person in the group defaults. Thus, the members of the group are motivated to monitor each other. Thus, the incremental incentives work as motivation to follow the group norms and facilitate the financial sustainability of the group. (See Fig. 22 for open codes).

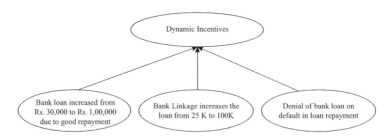

Fig. 22.   Open Codes.

Some more interviews were conducted with the members of the SHG belonging to the natives and indigenous groups.

Interviewer: Can you tell me something about your Self-help group?

Respondent: There are 13 women members and these women are covered under the Ajeevika group.

Interviewer: Have you taken any loan from the bank?

Respondent: Yes, we have taken a bank loan and members are generally the member of the same village. These women know each other and they peer monitor each other. Banks generally do not peer sanction our group. Banks are very cooperative and meetings and maintenance of books of accounts is done by the members of the group. This meeting is conducted once a week. Rarely, the members default on payment of bank loan. In our group pursue this vocation of making the handicraft since the time we came from Pakistan. These women pursue the vocation of making the handicraft since the independence. In many of the Karkhanas, in markets, karigars pursue handicraft as an ancestral artform. We make leather products, Kurtis etc. If some women member is not able to pay the loan, all the members get together and visit the home of the said member. Through cooperation and peer pressure, repayment is retrieved from the defaulting members. Ajeevika block members play an extremely important role in maintaining the self-sustainability of the groups. These block officers come from Ajeevika once every month and bank officers also come, once in a period of 2–3 months to convince the defaulting members to make the payment. They persuade the members to maintain the financial discipline. Bank delay the enhancement of loan due to the COVID pandemic. Our bank is 20 km and there is lot of inconvenience. All the tasks regarding the collection of the money and deposition is undertaken by the chief accountant. These groups play an extremely important role in promoting social welfare objectives such as equity, inclusion. We do not need to submit our account books to NABARD. Due to corona, there is lot of inconvenience and kindly help us to provide the market linkage.

Peer Mechanism Is the Group Formation

The groups are formed on the basis homogeneity, social ties and business correlation. The members in the group peer select each other based on homogeneity, which includes the social ties or business correlation. This facilitates the financial discipline in the group. Thus, the first stage in formation of group is peer selection on the basis of homogeneity. They members are alike and they either are from the same profession or they share the social ties. (See Fig. 23 for open codes).

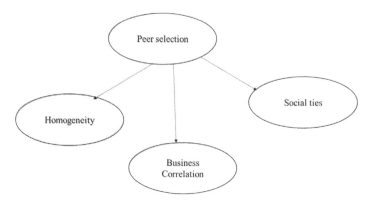

Fig. 23.   Peer Selection of Members.

Financial intermediation: At the stage in the formation of the group, the SHPIs or the NGOs play an important role in the handholding. The members are either incubated by the NGOs or counselled by the NGOs or intermediation is done by the NGOs. This financial intermediation helps to achieve the financial sustainability through mitigation of adverse selection and moral hazard. (See Fig. 24 for open codes).

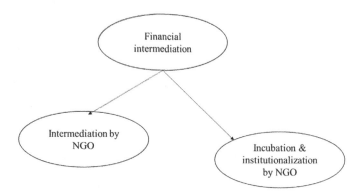

Fig. 24.   Financial Intermediation.

Institutional sustainability: The groups achieve institutional sustainability through accurate financial record keeping and through delegated monitoring. Effective leadership also helps to achieve the institutional sustainability in the group. The SHGs face various problems such as lack of adherence to the group norms such as financial record keeping, attending the meeting regularly and repayment of the loans in the designated time period. This lack of institutional sustainability further leads to lack of financial sustainability among the group members. (See Fig. 25 for open codes).

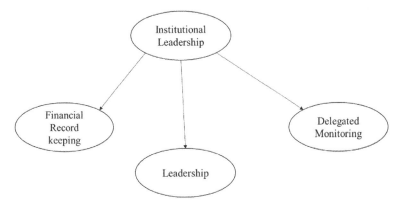

Fig. 25.   Institutional Sustainability.

Conclusion

SBLP is a microfinance initiative that ensures the financial sustainability and institutional sustainability of the members of the groups. Peer mechanism plays an extremely important role in protecting the vested interests of the members bound by a joint liability project, whereby each member has the responsibility to counsel the other member of the group, so that the repayment of the loan is made in time and the financial and institutional sustainability of the group is maintained. There are various reasons for the success of the group, which include the selection of the member as per the predefined criterion, where each member has prior information about the creditworthiness of the other members of the group. This apriori information helps to mitigate the adverse selection problem, and the group also helps to mitigate the moral hazard problem and helps in achieving the goal of financial and institutional sustainability.

Further Reading

Armendariz, B., & Morduch, J. (2007). *The economics of microfinance* (2nd ed.). MIT Press. Paperback.

Ayayi, A. G., & Sene, M. (2010). What drives microfinance institution's financial sustainability. *Journal of Developing Areas*, Tennessee State University, College of Business, *44*(1), 303–324.

Banker, R. D., & Lee, S. Y. (2000). *Mutual monitoring and peer pressure in teamwork.* The University of Texas, Accounting and Information Management Working Paper Series, 2000–11.

Basu, P., & Srivastava, P. (2005). *Scaling-up microfinance for India's rural poor.* Policy Research Working Paper No. 3646. https://openknowledge.worldbank.org/handle/10986/8311

Bec, A., Moyle, B., & Moyle, C. (2018). Resilient and sustainable communities. *Sustainability*, *10*(12), 4810. https://doi.org/10.3390/su10124810

Besley, T., & Coate, S. (1995). Group lending, repayment incentives and social collateral. *Journal of Development Economies, 46*(1), 1–18.

Bourdieu, P. (1986). The forms of capital. In J. Richardson (Ed.), *Handbook of theory and research for the sociology of education* (pp. 241–258). Greenwood.

Charmaz, K. (2006). *Constructing grounded theory: A practical guide through qualitative analysis.* SAGE Publications.

Coleman, J. S. (1988). Social capital in the creation of human capital. *American Journal of Sociology, 94*, S95–S120. http://www.jstor.org/stable/278024

De Aghion, B. A., & Gollier, C. (2000). Peer group formation in an adverse selection model. *The Economic Journal, 110*(465), 632–643. https://doi.org/10.1111/1468-0297.00557

Department of Women and Child Development. (2017). *Process of forming SHG with an external facilitator.*

Dissanayake, D. M. N. S. W. (2012). The determinants of return on equity: Evidences from Sri Lankan microfinance institutions (May 9, 2012). *The Kelaniya Journal of Management Journal, 3*(2), 2.

Gangopadhyay, S., Ghatak, M., & Lensink, R. (2005). Joint liability lending and the peer selection effect. *The Economic Journal, 115*(506), 1005–1015.

Karlan, D. S. (2005). *Social connections and group banking.* Working Papers 913, Economic Growth Center, Yale University.

Mosley, P., & Hulme, D. (1998). Microenterprise finance: Is there a conflict between growth and poverty alleviation? *World Development, 26*(5), 783–790.

Quidt, F. J. M., Fetzer, T., & Ghatak, M. (2016). Group lending without joint liability. *Journal of Development Economics, 121*(C), 217–236.

Spence, M., & Zeckhauser, R. (1971). Insurance, information, and individual action. *The American Economic Review, 61*(2), 380–387.

Chapter 7

Digitisation of the Self-Help Groups

Abstract

Self-help groups (SHGs) are formed by the tribal people to access finance through SHG bank linkage programme. The efforts to govern self-help groups (SHGs) are challenged by the absence of adequate bookkeeping and regular meetings, hindering effective governance despite all endeavors. The members of the groups are tribal people from the marginalised sections of society, and they are unable to maintain the books of accounts and keep track of their money because of illiteracy and banks being at far distance from their place of abode. Digitisation of SHGs has a vast impact on the efficiency of the groups and their financial sustainability. This chapter wishes to look at the digitisation initiative to transition the records of SHGs from manual to electronic mode, where the accounts will be visible to all the members. However, digital literacy is a big challenge, and this chapter aims to look at the challenges in digitisation of group.

Keywords: Digitisation; self-help group; marginalised groups; financial literacy; digital literacy

Introduction

Since 1992, when self-help group (SHG) bank linkage programme was introduced by the National Bank for Agriculture and Rural Development (NABARD), the scholars have remain divided over what is the role of banks as a financial intermediary and social intermediary. According to the extant literature, financial institutions, particularly commercial banks, are wary of lending to the SHGs. Banks have played an extremely important role in transformation of the national economy. SHG bank linkage programme was initiated with the intent of democratisation of the credit. But due to the lack of the creditworthiness of the borrowers, the credit is hardly extended to the borrowers under this particular

Sustainable Pathways, 161–178
Copyright © 2024 Nishi Malhotra
Published under exclusive licence by Emerald Publishing Limited
doi:10.1108/978-1-83549-490-520241016

scheme. Thus, there is a need for monitoring the activities of the client, and this study is aimed at generating the grounded theory.

Literature Review

History of Microfinance in India

Intervention that has touched the lives of millions of people, microfinance has been accepted and lauded as source of sustainable finance for the poor people at the bottom of the pyramid. Graduating to the next stage, microfinance has grown from a mere microcredit movement to microfinance comprised of micro insurance, pension and savings. For the achievement of financial inclusion, microfinance was touted as the major panacea. This movement emerged as the key enabler for the achievement of the Sustainable Development Goals (SDGs) of poverty alleviation and economic growth. Prior to the introduction of the microfinance, outreach to the poor and access to financial services was facilitated by India. At the core of this movement is the history of failure of subsidised and donor-driven model of finance for the marginalised poor. In 1980, the Government realised that there was need for the market-based solutions, and hence, microfinance institutions emerged. The movement focused on granting financial access to individuals at the base of the economic pyramid to establish sustainable livelihoods and fulfill the requirements of the marginalised poor. It thus accelerated the earlier trend of achieving financial inclusion to achieve the objective of poverty alleviation and economic growth. A new concept of social finance has emerged to create a positive impact on environment, society and governments. Thus, social finance became pivotal for the betterment of the society and empowerment of the marginalised poor. As an enabler for the achievement of the SDGs, microfinance emerged as a panacea for economic development.

Not only microfinance as a vehicle of social finance was aimed at meeting the social objective of poverty alleviation but also provides sufficient economic return to the financial institutions. This study aims at discussing the conceptual and policy framework for microfinance in India. Microfinance has been used now for past 40 years to provide access to finance to marginalised poor at the bottom of the pyramid. Since the 1980s, initiatives in this field have been notable, with outstanding organisations like Self-Employed Women's Association (SEWA) leading the way. However, despite wide coverage, the metrics that we use to measure financial progress came from a time when microfinance meant making loans to the poor.

Perspectives on Microfinance

Till 1980s, microfinance initiatives were mainly Government-driven and subsidised by various donors. In 1980s, subsidised credit was criticised as a programme which was not sustainable. Thus, there was a need for market-based solution, and microfinance emerged as a part of financial system. Thus, microfinance institution emerged as an institutional approach that operated on market principles. This financial system approach emphasised the large-scale outreach to the economically poor both to the borrowers who can pay their loans. There was an increasing thrust on institutional self-sufficiency.

From the analysis of data, two distinct perspectives emerged for microfinance: (1) poverty lending and (2) financial perspectives. Poverty lending approach concentrates on reducing poverty through credit. This approach also involved social intermediation approach which comprised of providing complementary services such as skills training to the poor borrowers. Major objective of microfinance under this perspective was to provide credit to the poor at a subsidised rate. Microfinance, although a dominant force in sustainable finance, drew the interest of policymakers. They acknowledged the institutional challenge arising from microfinance provision, emphasizing the need for services to be affordable to clients while ensuring adequate returns to equity (Elizabeth Ryne). The main reasons for increase in cost were the cost structure and delivery methodologies of microfinance institutions. Business models for the microfinance institutions started getting questioned. Initially, SHGs were mainly relying on self-help promotion institutions (SHPIs) or non-governmental organisations (NGOs) to bring together women and eventually linking them to the banks. Despite all efforts, banks are wary to lend money to the poor people (Esther Duflo et al., 2014).

Microfinance Financial Intermediation

Hoping to facilitate access to finance to poor people, microfinance institutions aim to perform the role of financial intermediary. Financial intermediation refers to the provision of the financial products such as savings and credit provision to the poor people. There was an increasing thrust on reducing the dependence of microfinance institutions to the poor people. Financial system comprises of demand and supply of financial services. There are still large institutional gaps in financial services. These institutions as an intermediary were supposed to fill the gaps and comprised of financial and non-financial institutions. Most informal intermediaries are typically weak particularly for the repeated shocks. It often provides adequate only adequate protection to the poor households. So informal players which included moneylenders, relatives and friends mainly do not confirm to book keeping standards, need collateral and lending is not formalised.

SHG Model and Microfinance Institution Model

SHGs, next to more broadly defined savings groups (SGs), are a form of community-based approach to microfinance. SHG has been defined as providing help and support to the members of the group in dealing with their problem and improving their psychological function and effectiveness. It is a group of people with common objective, who are facilitated to come together to participate in development activities, i.e. savings, credit, income generation.

SHGs are conceptualised by the SHPIs. These SHPIs include NGOs, governmental agencies, banks, cooperative and microfinance institutions. These SHPIs provide training, monitoring and other support service. SHGs also are provided with the seed capital on certain occasion, but on most occasions, SHGs borrow from the external sources.

History of SHGs in India

Many literary works argue that Mohammed Yunus created the consciousness from which he built in 1970s the largest revitalisation movement in the history of rural India. This consciousness created strength and unity among the women of rural India when Ela Bhatt in India in 1980s started SEWA. The microfinance institutions aim to act as financial intermediaries to facilitate access to finance for impoverished individual. In 1987, NABARD and the Canadian International Development Agency (CIDA) funded action research into Community Managed Groups (CMGs) established by the Bangalore-based NGO, MYRADA, based on the successful experiences of community banking. SHG movement held great promise for illiterate women in rural India who were again mobilised by other NGO PRADAN in 1987. International Fund for Agricultural Development (IFAD) promoted an informal borrowing lender program by drawing lessons from the success of NGO-driven Self-Help Groups (SHGs).

During this period, many other changes took place in Indian financial sector. One of the biggest milestones for Indian Banking and Finance industry was nationalisation of banks in 1969–1971. Future of rural India was still extricably linked to the judgement and prudence of moneylenders. Realising the plight of rural villagers at the hands of moneylender, India introduced mandatory system of priority lending in 1972 and established Regional Rural Banks. To give impetus to Indian microfinance, India undertook piloting and implementation of SHG movement.

Most of the SHGs were formed on the basis of the concept of Saving First and Credit Later.

In 1992, the Government recognised SHG as an alternative credit model. The model was centered on the Graduation principle, where SHGs progress up the income ladder, emphasizing factors that facilitate this upward movement. SHG bank linkage involves partnership between the SHG, NGOs, and banks.

Microfinance

While focusing on how supply of microfinance will meet the demand for micro-finance, the Government globally introduced Financial Inclusion programme. Within the new paradigm of Market approach, the probability that financial needs get transformed into demand depends on availability of an adequate financial ecosystem, which comprises of clients or borrowers and lenders or financial service providers. Regulations and laws are the main components that impact the structure of the market and nature of competition and delivery channels.

Microfinance has played an important role in transforming the national economy. The microfinance industry is unique in that it solely comprises regulated organisations. India introduced microfinance regulations in 2012. South East Asia is fast emerging as a microfinance industry. This industry is growing at a rate of 13.8% annually. Like a camera with many lenses sweeping through the landscape, the microfinance landscape in India marred with multiple models. The most prominent among these is SHG bank linkage and microfinance linkage model.

Expansion and democratisation of credit through microfinance has been made possible due to the presence of diverse players. Indian microfinance portfolio stands at Rs. 681 billion, and microfinance institutions form approximately 38% of the total loan portfolio. Banks form approximately 34% of total loan portfolio, non-banking finance corporations form 10% of portfolio, small finance banks constitute 17% of total portfolio and non-for-profit institutions form approximately 1% of total portfolio.

In the total loan portfolio of approximately INR 681 billion, banks have a sizeable share despite the growing number of concerns regarding their lack of empathy towards micro borrower. Micro Finance Institutions (MFIs) charge an interest rate of 24%–25% which is much higher than the bank rate which is the Prime Lending Rate (PLR). Due to the lack of creditworthiness and collateral, small borrowers face limitations in accessing loans.

Women Empowerment

SHGs play a dominant role in achieving women empowerment. This empowerment can be in the form of social empowerment, women empowerment and political empowerment. Tankha argues that the SHGs could be of various types. Globally, in rural parts of South East Asia, Latin America and Caribbean, there existed informal groups called as ROSCAs. Kenya has majority of women who participate in community saving through ROSCAs. Rotating Savings and Credit Associations (ROSCAs) originated in West Africa and became integral to African ancestry communities in the Caribbean, serving as a fundamental part of their financial practices and traditions. ROSCAs are part of the ancestral culture in Bahamas, where people contribute a sum periodically to the common pool (Srinivasan H. M.). SHGs are supported by the NGOs and by the government agencies. There are three kinds of SHPAs (1) NGOs, (2) government agencies and (3) banks.

NGO model of SHG is promoting the formation of SHG. The primary function of these groups is to provide loans for various purposes such as consumption, clearing outside debt, social needs, medical expenses, education, business ventures and agricultural activities. A typical household starts with own savings and then is promoted by the NGO (Shiyani).

Micro lending schools and technologies: Micro lending schools can be classified into four major schools (1) solidarity group, (2) grameen (3) SHG, (4) village banking and (5) individual lending.

Solidarity groups: Solidarity groups use the peer pressures to control the credit risk. Generally, the lenders deploy the stepped approach to lending. This approach facilitates the generation of credit history data while minimizing exposure to formal lenders and easily managing risks. Only one account is opened in the bank for the Group.

Grameen model: In this model, self-selected group of 4–5 other groups from the village form a centre, and this structure enhances the financial viability of the project. A compulsory training of 4–5 months is given before the loan. Moreover, the loans are provided to the members in a staggered manner. After 1 or 2 months of payment, the group becomes eligible for the second loan. The savings kept serve as collateral for the members. Also in some cases, the depositors are not allowed to access their savings.

SHG: Under the Self-Help Group (SHG) bank linkage model, members have a single account with the SHG instead of individual accounts with the banks, and the banks do not directly engage with the SHG members. The SHG member decides to make the regular savings contribution and members can borrow from each other, SHG opens a group savings account and deposit funds that are not loaned and the SHG maintains the meticulous record of group attendance, savings and internal lending activities (Churchill, Cheryl Frankeiwiciz & Craiz).

SHG Bank Linkage Programme

SHGs are aimed at providing the access to financial services to the rural power in the marginal area. The mechanism of Self-Help Groups (SHGs) involves starting as a savings group with minimal savings. The savings are collected, and the amount is lent to the members again. A group account is opened with the bank to deposit the surplus savings. NABARD has chosen a two-pronged strategy to combine the principle of SHG and self-reliance. By converting the savings into interest bearing loans, these groups augment business. The SHGs enjoy the institutional autonomy and creditworthiness. The SHGs are free to choose the interest rates and the lending rates. SHGs act as an engine of development by promoting various causes such as social development, rural and agriculture development (Khadka, Hans Dieter Seibel and Shyam).

Methodology

In this study, for the purpose of analysis, constructivist grounded theory approach has been used. This research paradigm is based on the notion that there are multiple world views and ways of knowing. It deals with theorising through practice. It is a more practical way of engaging with the world and constructing abstract understanding about it (Charmaz, 2003). As a part of this methodology, data were analysed using the open coding, focused coding and theoretical coding,

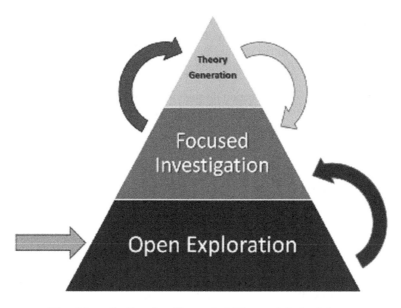

Fig. 26.   Coding for Grounded Theory Methodology.

as shown in Fig. 26. The approach involved simultaneous data collection and analysis.

Coding is the process of labelling things you are using or observing. According to Saldana (2015), in qualitative inquiry, coding most often involves using a word or short phrase to symbolically assign a summative, salient, essence-capturing and evocative attribute to a portion of language based on the provided data. Coding leads to the generation of the emergent theory, which is the contribution of the study in grounded theory methods.

Research Problem

In this study, the type of research problem handled is of the type What is going on? Who are the proponents? SHG bank linkage is a microfinance initiative to facilitate financial inclusion of the most marginalised people in this world. Digitisation of SHG bank linkage is another social process which is aimed at facilitating the access to financial services at the doorstep of the citizens of India. There is lack of studies in domain of how digitisation impacts success of the SHGs. This study aims at generating a theory from the data collected through the interview. Total of 5 interviews were conducted, and two of these are attached herewith.

Data Collection

Preparing for the Interview

For the purpose of analysis, the purposive sampling technique was used for the purpose of analysis. The data were analysed using the three stage approach comprised of open coding, focused coding and theoretical coding. The outcome of this method was the emergent theory. Five districts were selected in the state of Uttarakhand, namely Pauri Garwal, Nainital and Dehradun, India. Interviews were conducted with the District Managers at District Mission Management Units (DMMU).

Before starting the data collection through interviews, we ensured that our data collection takes care of 'Principled sensitivity to rights of others'. While doing research, we took care of four basic tenets of research ethics:

(1) Informed consent,
(2) Avoiding deception,
(3) Protecting privacy,
(4) Telling the truth.

In regard to rules and principles of the institute, the guidelines of Institutional Research Boards (IRBs) were taken care of. For the purpose of data analysis, open-ended questions or qualitative data collection technique was used. The primary function of these groups is to provide loans for various purposes including consumption, clearing outside debt, social needs, medical expenses, education, business ventures and agricultural activities. At the time of data collection, information was recorded during interviews when possible and in other instances, summaries of the interviews were produced (Charmaz, 2003). Interviews provided an opportunity to slow down and listen intensively to the interviewee. Transcribing was done manually using the Word document. While conducting the interviews, privacy of the informants was duly taken care of. Any kind of verbatim in the interview was removed. Also none of the informants were case of opportunistic sampling.

The phenomenon of digitisation of SHG linkage scheme was studied intensively for gathering extensive data. During the collection of data, coding was performed simultaneously. With the permission of the interviewees, the data were transcribed and recorded for the purpose of analysis. Subsequent to transcription, the data were coded.

Open Coding

This stage deals with analysing the transcribed data line by line, to identify what are people saying, what are people doing, what problems are encountered during the analysis and what things are people taking granted for? In this report, gerund coding has been used for the purpose of analysis. The focus is on human transcription and deals with externalisation of internal beliefs.

Transcript for Interviews

First Interview (Uddham Nagar, District Manager)

NM: What is the status of e Shakti implementation in your village?
DM: Yes e Shakti has been implemented in Uddham Nagar.

NM: What are the challenges in implementation of e Shakti?

DM: Basically, e Shakti is aimed at digitisation of women who do not update their books of accounts or the minutes of meetings. There are four districts that have been covered under NRLM (national Rural Livelihood Mission). Major challenge is that under NRLM, one has to fill complete thick registers which comprises of 4–5 thick books. Accounts which comprise of debit and credit is very complicated so women who are illiterate and cannot fill it. NABARD has simpler accounting with extremely simple books of accounts. E Shakti ensures uploading of MIS, generation of Grades, Bank loan application. Currently, women have to update the accounts and animators who are employees of a third party agency, do the data entry. E Shakti is aimed at credit creation and it is a good project but not all self-help groups are active under NRLM (national Rural Livelihood Mission).

NM: What are your views regarding the Financial Literacy?

DM: In direction of digital literacy at least 8–10 times women are trained. In North India as compared to South India, the SHGs are far lagging behind. Even banks are providing training to these women and motivating them to become self reliant and be prepared for the stage when there will be no animators for hand holding.

NM: Regarding the rate of credit generation, do you feel lack of knowledge about the credit?

DM: Women do know about the credit facility from the bank. They also know about the payment norms. Self-help groups members are from extremely poor families. And these groups are from the tribal banks and culturally they are averse to credit and more prone to savings. These women do not know about the livelihood and they also do not know about the market linkages. This is particularly in Khatima and Sitarganj. In many self-help groups, women have been employed as business correspondent. Rural youth or engineering pass outs do not get their employment. Also there is no livelihood and whatever livelihood is there for that there is no market linkage. An integrated value chain or network model can be helpful. Though it is a cluster initiative, at the initial stages the programme should be introduced on Experimental basis. NRLM is a case in point, as MIS preparation was introduced on experimental basis. There was no awareness among the members, who are from remote villages.

Second Interview (Nainital District Manager)

NM: Kindly tell us how the District level is prepared and Monitoring is done at Block level.

SM: Block level is the most important level and it comprises of various small units. Personal bank branch visits are conducted. Quarterly meetings of state Level Bank Committee by LDM are conducted. But there is a need for continuous monitoring through personal visit to SHGs and follow up to ensure that self-help groups do not break down as they need support. When we go for CGL we should visit the SHG to sensitise them regarding the need to adhere to Panchsutras and pursue livelihood to make financial inclusion fruitful. In order to make Financial inclusion more fruitful, there is a need to pay attention to the Minimum Credit Plan (MCP).

NM: What are our views on digitisation? Do you think digitisation will be fruitful?

SM: In the remote areas the women do not have infrastructure and the knowledge. Women hardly know how to prepare the books of accounts or hardly have infrastructure in terms of Mobile, Internet and other digital technology. Rural women are mainly concerned with the use of the informal finance. There is a need for sensitising the women members of self-help groups about the relevance of adherence to Panchsutras. Development should be done in phases. In the first phase, the emphasis should be on strengthening the monitoring through personal visits and in the second phase digitisation can be undertaken. Bankers should be sensitised as many times bankers are wary to provide credit to the SHG members. They give loan on whims and fancies. Women divert funds for social purposes so training should be conducted to make them aware about the disadvantages of the informal sources and benefits of formal sources of finance.

NM: Do you think organising a workshop for women to sensitise them regarding adherence to group norms and livelihood will help to bring out the change?

SM: Definitely motivating the women regarding the relevance of adherence to Panchsutras and maintenance of books of record will be of high relevance. At present there are number of trainings that have been undertaken by the bank and the bankers to sensitise them. Also a large number of Marketing trainings have been undertaken to create market linkages. All these initiatives are covered under the institution building & Capacity building.

NM: What is the state of Grading and use of business Correspondent among the SHGs and how effective these are?

Bank Sakhi Model is highly successful in ensuring financial inclusion. Many business correspondents have done extremely important. They act as a bridge. However, over all the women are not really forthcoming to undertake financial inclusion activities.

The Block Mission Management Unit consists of block officers, CRPs, and Area coordinators who are responsible for checking and monitoring the activities of the coordinators. The activities are regularly carried out by both external and internal coordinators.

Memoing

After generating approximately 15 open codes, the next step was to prepare a memo of the interview. Memoing is crucial for the purpose of qualitative research, as this causes you to stop and think. It gives you an opportunity to analyse your ideas and construct a theory. Memoing not only aids in defining and structuring codes into theory but also serves as the foundation for theory development and publication. As per Barney Glasser, a good idea should be written down before doing anything. Memos also help to reconstruct the data. The method for memoing is to look at the summary of interview, take a code or phrase and write a memo. Memos generally should be able to answer:

- Whom did the interviewer speak with?
- What was the topic of conversation?
- What was the spark?
- What were the words that caught your attention?
- And what were the open codes that you assigned to it?

Open codes are created through various techniques such as the reporting grid, interviews, and transcription.

Reflections

Memoing is important to make reflections. It helps to answer the questions why does the code seem to be significant? What are the implications? Does this event remind you of something similar? Does it surprise you because it is unexpected?

Follow Through

After the reflections have been made, these will serve as guide for the future interviews. It will help in identifying the questions that come to mind and doubts or scepticism that comes to your mind about the reflections. This will serve as guide for future.

After every round of open coding and memoing, the new ideas will be iden-tified, and these points will be kept in mind while taking the next interview, as shown in Fig. 27. Till 10–15 codes have been collected, this process will be repeated again and again.

Every time memoing was done, additional questions were generated, and the same were used for asking newer questions in the next interview. An example of this is shown in Fig. 28. Overall, from the exercise, following open codes were generated.

Focused Codes

Focused coding is mainly concerned with grouping together of the similar codes together. By grouping together similar codes, as shown in Figs. 29–31, we create gerunds that highlight certain action shared among the group of open codes. Computer Assisted Qualitative Data Analysis Software (CAQDAS) software can be utilised for analysis purposes. The process for focused coding is as follows:

Out of the gathered open codes, the 4–5 similar open codes will be selected. These codes will be written on a sheet of paper, and the labels will be kept on table. After writing down the open codes, the next step is to identify the title that

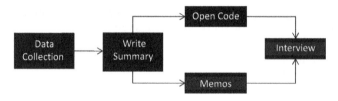

Fig. 27.   Open Coding.

Memo
Title: Updating NRLM Books is extremely tough
Date: 23.06.2021

The District Manager argued that updating NRLM (National Rural Livelihood Mission) books is extremely difficult. He mentions about the bulky registers and formats, which the women members find extremely difficult to complete. He also gave an example that the women find completing NABARD books easier. He mentioned about the trainings given by the banks and motivation by the District Manager, telling women to embrace technology to become future ready. Thus clearly there is lack of appropriate financial literacy and motivation to change the attitudes of the women

Fig. 28.   Memo at the Open Coding Stage.

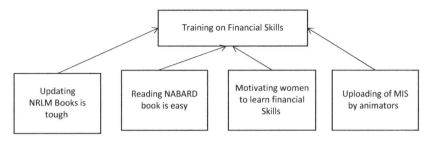

Fig. 29. Focused Codes for the First four Codes (First Interview).

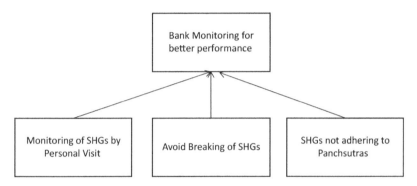

Fig. 30. Focused Codes for the Open Codes (Interview Transcript Number 2).

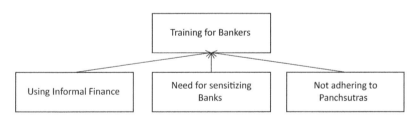

Fig. 31. Focused Codes for Open Codes (Interview Transcript Number 3).

explains what is common among all these codes. This title will be the focused code. This process of selecting the open codes and repeating the process will be carried out repeatedly. Further to substantiate the veracity of the codes, MACE method will be used. MACR method will used to achieve theoretical sufficiency in the method.

- Meaning – Charmaz (2003) in her book has discussed how to define the code so that the code becomes easier to understand. In the above analysis, the informant said that updating the books under NRLM is extremely difficult. This clearly mentions that there is difficulty in comprehending the books and Management of Information Systems (MIS) under NRLM.
- Action – Charmaz (2003) in her book mentions that the open codes selected must describe what action is taking place in the focused codes. It explains how the open codes support and interact to make focused codes. It involves determining, are there other things that focused code does. In the focused code given above, the open codes updating NRLM books and MIS is difficult, reading and updating NABARD is difficult, motivating the women to learn financial skills and uploading MIS for animators, all refer to the difficulty in updating the books due to the lack of financial literacy and financial acumen; this refers to focused code
- Challenges – Charmaz (2003), in his book, mentions that the memos should define the problem that the focused codes are trying to solve. And the memo should also discuss the problems caused by the action and interaction. The memo should also define the barriers faced in carrying out the action mentioned in the focused action
- Results – Charmaz (2003) What happens when the focused coding is taking place and what happens after actions have finished?

After completing focused coding, the relationships in the form of action and relationship will be examined to identify any unanswered questions. If necessary, the researcher can return to the field to collect additional data.

Constant Comparison

At this juncture, in order to develop the focused codes from the open codes, the memos were reviewed on these high-frequency codes. The purpose was to determine whether constant comparison was practised by searching for the opposite cases or other deviations. In the case given in Fig. 32, the informant mentions that NABARD books are easier to maintain, as these are simple. This implies that the informants do not have enough financial literacy, and the process has achieved the focused code.

It refers to the process of refining the theoretical categories. After the process of focused coding has been completed, the researcher referred to the scholarly literature in domain of financial literacy. In the next round of interviews, the subject or informant or data to be selected should be the ones who satisfy the above criterion.

Memo
Title: Financial Literacy
Date: 23.06.2021

The District Manager highlighted that the Women members of Self help groups are illiterate and highly marginalized. They do not know how to update the books of accounts and how to prepare the Minutes of meetings. They are also not aware of the livelihood activities and they lack earning capacity. According to him literacy is an extremely important factor for achieving self sufficiency and realizes complete benefits of Self help group bank linkage programme. Women members are also not aware of the Market Linkages or ways and means of earning sustainable earnings. Since the entire conversation is about the importance of Financial Literacy in generating demand for Credit and Financial Inclusion. The spark of the discussion was when the District Manager highlighted that the women members find the NRLM formats extremely difficult to understand and NABARD formats are comparatively easy to understand. He also highlighted the need to undertake a integrated network value chain, with different stages. An integrated approach will pave the way for the future analysis

Fig. 32.   Theoretical Sampling.

Theoretical Coding

In this stage, the focus is on the development of codes based on the mentioned criteria. Theoretical coding comprises of collecting the data and coding it. During the theoretical coding stage, two focused codes are taken after selection on the basis of similarity. Then the codes are further developed into theoretical codes. Theoretical code is a title that captures the essence of the focused codes. After the generation of theoretical codes or the conceptual categories through theoretical clustering, the theoretical codes will be compared with the memo of the focused codes. Further, the data will be compared with the scholarly literature in this domain for the purpose of conceptual verification.

Constant Comparison

The author mentions that for the purpose of constant comparison, a questionnaire was created, citing the conceptual category. The first question was regarding the purpose of the conceptual category, and second question is regarding how much the participants agree with the additional information collected. Based on the concepts, the Axial Coding framework, which involves examining the context, causes, and contingencies related to the established code, was employed for the analysis process. This led to further refinement in the categories. If there are still some gaps in the data, further data can be collected by moving from the theoretical code to the focused code, but one does not move back from the focused to the open code. Further, in order to explain the relations between various categories, the examination of the data can be done based on coding paradigm that focuses on causal conditions, context, intervening conditions, action/integration strategies and consequences. Thus, this stage focuses on development of codes on the basis of the above mentioned criterion.

The elements shown in Fig. 33 are explained as follows:

- *Context:* Financial intermediation is within the context of the authorities that a lender has and the rights of lender with respect to the borrowers.
- *Condition:* Financial intermediation is in reference to the lack of adherence to the social norms such as maintenance of books of account, maintenance of minutes of meetings and marking attendance.
- *Cause:* Financial intermediation is to be facilitated through monitoring of the activities of SHGs.
- *Consequences:* Financial intermediation by the banks will lead to the higher level of sustainability, which will further lead to reduction in the level of dropout rate among the banks.
- *Contingency:* In the future, monitoring can be improved through better digitisation.

Constant Comparison

For the purpose of further analysis, the data are continuously compared to the academic literature and scholarly material. From the analysis of literature, it becomes clear that there is no theory regarding the impact of bank monitoring on loan participants or the members of SHGs.

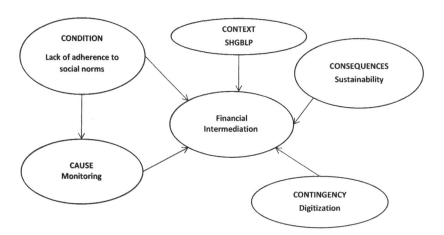

Fig. 33.   Theoretical Coding Worksheet.

A questionnaire includes fundamental questions addressing the main purpose of the survey.

Generalisation

In order to facilitate generalisation of the results, it was ensured that the categories conceptualised were as abstract as possible. This implies that more widely the theory can be applied. Through constant comparison, the theory was revalidated by moving from the theoretical code to the focused codes. This process was repeated till theoretical sufficiency was achieved or theoretical saturation was achieved. Though in this study only 5 interviews are captured, for the purpose of analysis, the theory is extended through more interviews to enhance its generalisability, as shown in Fig. 34.

Theory Generation

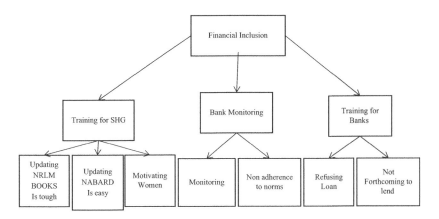

Fig. 34.   Theoretical Coding.

Data Analysis

From the analysis of the given data, it becomes clear that the theory simply states that there is a need for rigorous training and financial literacy of the members of SHGs, bank monitoring, to ensure adherence to the Panchsutras, i.e. maintenance of the books of account, training for the bankers in order to facilitate the adoption of formal mode of finance, lending to the bankers at first priority.

In this study, while drafting the grounded theory, we have taken complete care that the empirical works indeed ensures that the grounded theory actually works in the real-world circumstances. It is highly recommended that the theory is developed from the actual data, and the theory emerges from the real data. Every conceptual code that has been generated, there are sufficient number of incidents that are quoted, which refer to the practice of constant comparison. Also the process of constant comparison is conducted till the time theoretical saturation is achieved in the process. This study is done from constructivist paradigm and within that paradigm, it refers to the basic premise that study cannot be replicated, rather the study is the result of social interactions and the meaning is constructed socially. This meaning keeps on changing from time to time.

Grounded Theory Evaluation

In order to evaluate the theory, the researchers have considered the following points:

- credibility,
- originality,
- resonance,
- usefulness.

In order to enhance the credibility of the study, the researchers have continuously made use of member check, negative case analysis and constant comparison. The theory generation method is followed from the constructivist grounded theory perspective (Charmaz, 2003). Also the study is based on the premise that the concepts and conceptual categories are included because of the perceived utility. And in the study, the authors have been extremely open about the methodological decisions, and all the data cited are highly believable.

Conclusion

This study aims at generating a grounded theory on how financial literacy and monitoring can play an important role in ensuring financial inclusion. Through financial inclusion, this initiative can be effectively used for achieving the goals of economic development and poverty alleviation among the poor people.

References

Charmaz, K. (2003). Grounded theory. In J. A. Smith (Ed.), *Qualitative psychology: A practical guide to research methods* (pp. 81–110). SAGE Publications, Inc.
Saldana, J. M. (2015). *The coding manual for qualitative researchers* (3rd ed.). SAGE Publications.

Chapter 8

Role of the Indigenous Tribes in Conserving Nature: Case Studies on Sustainable Practices by Indigenous Tribes

Abstract

Tribal communities play an extremely important role in the conservation of the natural resources including water and natural resources like air. Indian tribes have an extremely important role to play in the protection of the environment and vital resources. Due to the possession of the heritage knowledge, the tribal people are playing an extremely important role in the management of the natural resources. This chapter discusses about the various traditional practices adopted by the tribal groups in water conservation practices.

Keywords: Tribal people; water conservation; heritage management; sustainable management; traditional practices

Introduction: The Role of the Indigenous Tribes in Conserving Nature

Indigenous tribes are the tribes and the local people who play an extremely important role in the conservation of the nature. They have innate knowledge about the sustainable practices that have been developed over the centuries and passed down from generation to generation through word of mouth. The members of the native communities have access to the indigenous farming knowledge for the protection of the agricultural produce and crops. Similarly, they have knowledge about preserving the climate through various traditional practices. This chapter will provide first-hand access to the various case studies regarding the unique knowledge possessed by the tribes about the conservation of the local resources and natural resources. It will also discuss in detail the importance of indigenous contents, pedagogies and epistemologies in promoting development. Besides that,

Sustainable Pathways, 179–198

Copyright © 2024 Nishi Malhotra

Published under exclusive licence by Emerald Publishing Limited

doi:10.1108/978-1-83549-490-520241018

the indigenous communities and people have relationality with the nature, and they share the relationship with the nature, natural world and the spiritual world, where through the interdependencies, they are able to leverage the leverage the peer mechanism for the welfare of the community. This chapter discusses in detail the role of various indigenous tribes in conserving the nature.

Bricolage and Indigenous Tribes

The indigenous tribes are major resource in ensuring the sustainable development and sustainable livelihood. They have coexisted with the dynamic socio-economic environment through adaptation as an effective response to the changing in the environment. Through bricolage, the indigenous communities have adjusted to the environment to retain their livelihoods. Indigenous communities have their own customs and rituals, which they have changed and adapted to in the form of new practices, and these practices are bricolage, and they are being adopted as sustainable practices all over the period. The research highlights that the indigenous communities have developed various cultural adaptations to the climate hazards, that help in the management of climate change. The Deen Dayal Antodaya National Rural Livelihoods Mission (DAY NRLM) is a unique proposition aimed at enhancing the livelihoods of people in rural India. Bricolage, as suggested by Claude Levi-Strauss, refers to the practice of making do with whatever materials or resources are readily available or at hand. This bricolage is a synthesis of the scientific practices and the traditional practices. This concept of bricolage is adapted to a range of fields, including resource management, entrepreneurship and forest-based livelihood. Self-help group (SHG) bank linkage is a unique social innovation that aims to provide access to financial resources to the poor artisans who do not have collateral and thus bank denies them loan. India has introduced the unique DAY NRLM and thus various usages of bricolage (1) institutional bricolage, (2) entrepreneurship bricolage, (3) social bricolage and (4) productive bricolage. The artisans are the native people, and these local communities of artisans such as Kumhar community, Santhal, Gond community, Damor community found in Rajasthan, India, produce handicrafts through the use of the resources such as mud, clay, wood from the natural resources. These artisans as bricoleur make creative choices through the selection and act within the resource constraint. These local artisans have improvised these art forms and reusing the resources to ensure adaptation to the accepted practices. The entrepreneurs and artisans use the bricolage activity to raise the capital using the social capital and the peer mechanism. Indigenous knowledge is increasingly being considered as the biggest asset, capability that is embedded in the traditional and narrative practices and interpretive processes. The case in point is the weaver community of Banaras and Jharkhand, that weave the handloom using the hand-woven cotton and silk. The women in the bunker community collect the cocoons, and they take out the thread from the cocoon and the men do the weaving using the handloom. The people living in the hills and the tracts are rich in the agricultural practices, and they utilise these practices such as the sun drying of harvested paddy, growing paddy with fisheries in the water-fed fields, winnowing grains using muram. The tribals in the Mathura district use their hands to pluck tulsi flowers and weave those into the tulsimala. However, as bricolage, the IIT Delhi has helped these flower weaving communities to use machine to create tulsimala. Another important practice is the use of the social capital to sell the agricultural produce in Mandis at the fair price. In the Azadpur Mandi, the farmers and agriculturists take their produce, and they use their social capital to align with the other sellers to get the produce in the market. India has introduced the National Agricultural Marketing scheme, under which the agricultural prices are provided to the farmers through the use of the technology, such as phone and computer with internet. This practice has enabled to automate the market and provide the best market prices for the agricultural produce to the local farmers and agriculturists. In literature, there is a vast place for the narratives and metaphors in influencing people's language and knowledge. In the social settings, indigenous people are the local people who retain some or all of the social, economic and cultural practices, that distinguish them from the other sections of population. The folklore is the oral tradition that comprises of the narratives with the social objectives and moral stories, and these narratives are passed on from generation to generation. This tradition takes the form of ballads, stories, myths, games and riddles. One such tradition is the Lambada Bhat's found in the Banjara Hills of Andhra Pradesh and Bhils and Meena of the Rajasthan state. These people lead to nomadic life, and they move from city to city, and they speak the native language called as Goarboli, and this language is not without the manuscript, and this tradition is closely linked to the stitching clothes with miniature work of thread, glass and coins. This tradition is passed from generations to generations and thus form the basis of the bricolage. The Banjara history uses the folklores, tales, fables, fictions, stories, songs and memories to pass the traditions from one generation to another. These Banjaras follow various customs and traditions such as sacrifice of the goats near the temple on the occasion of Diwali and Holi. The Banjaras are the tribals, who have practised the oral tradition for number of years. These tribals have practiced various traditions such as naturopathy for the health of the people. Undoubtedly, the *Banjara* tribe is described by the catchline '*Parvat mala jaae Banjara, Jeevan ko Rah Batae*'. Labhana community is another nomadic community of tribal people, who live in harmony with the nature and natural settings. They are a backward section of the society who have spent centuries in the lap of nature tending cows. These people are the original dwellers of the Sindhu valley and Geerijan because they stay in intimacy with the nature. They also pursue the cow rearing, and they follow the Krishna Bhakti Parampara, and they belong to the Mathura Labhana. They are descendants of the Gour Vansh, Lav Maharaj, Rajput, and they follow their traditions to pass on the rituals and culture from generation to generation. The confluence of the culture across the time periods and centuries leads to sensemaking through the oral language and oral traditions. Thus, the articulation of the culture and practices through oral traditions leads to sensemaking of the practices of tribal people and becomes accepted customs and rituals. The tribal literature is fast emerging as the expression of the lives, bricolage and the cultural life of the tribal people and is unfolding in the form of folk art, music, dance, language and culture. The Indian culture boasts of the rich cultural heritage and art form that has evolved and adapted the foreign and external influences. The traditions, rites and rituals of the tribal people which were earlier in the form of traditions have been articulated in the form literature, which is the mode of self-expression in the form of record of human experiences and teachings. The tribal communities are the form of 'cogent existential reality' and who have been ostracised and excluded by the virtue of their identities, culture and power relations. For most of the migrant tribes, the migration is an outcome of the conflictual relationship with the mainstream by the virtue of their cultural and sociological differences. And the post migrancy is often seen as the new belonging to a new clan or culture, through the intervention by the state. A bricoleur is a person who is a jack of all trades, employing whatever tools and equipment are available to accomplish tasks. This type of individual is resourceful and adept at making use of whatever resources are at hand to solve problems or create new things. The example of bricoleur is the artisan who makes the earthenware or the pots. This artisan is the one person who collects the clay from the river banks; he bakes it to make the terracotta and then provides various designs as per the culture. Thus, this person or artisan is a generalist who follows various traditions and customs. The natives and indigenous people in India are very talented people who have the skill in their hands. They perform all the various activities with their own hands, and they use the oral traditions to propagate their culture. Through the use of language, they articulate the practices and customs, by rationalising them with the narratives about the local traditions. Through the creative practices, the bricoleur puts together his creative and aesthetic abilities. Bricolage is an expression of freedom of the communities and the people, and it is an instrument to ensure the integration of the artisan community with the mainstream.

Methodology

In this chapter, to analyse the impact of bricolage on Indian tribal livelihoods and sustainable practices, various theoretical practices suggested by Langley have been used. The tribals have a great role to play in the independence of India. The chronology of uprisings of Indian tribals is given below (see Fig. 35).

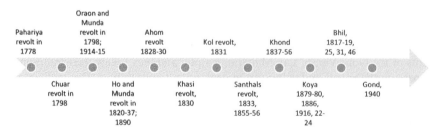

Fig. 35.   Chronology of Tribal Revolts in Pre-Independence Era.

Based on the information provided, theoretical perspectives offered by academia to analyze the contribution to entrepreneurship include Tribal Critical Race Theory, Decolonisation Theory, and Kaupapa Maori Theory. These perspectives likely offer valuable insights into the dynamics of entrepreneurship within specific cultural and sociopolitical contexts. The ethnic markers in the form of language, symbols, insignia and culture are the shared norms that lead to perceived homogeneity in the group. To discuss the ethnic marker, let's look at some of the case studies from Indian artisans and handicraft makers. The social practices and shared norms of the tribal groups are the ethnic markers and cultural identity of the tribal groups. These markers have evolved over the period to constitute bricolage or the narratives of how the indigenous people have adapted to the cultural changes, without losing their cultural identity. The hermeneutical approach was followed to identify the best sustainable art forms and cultural practices that have emerged as ethnic markers among the tribals and indigenous population in India. As part of the methodology, the access was negotiated with the tribal artisans, while keeping in mind the cultural sensitivity of the ethnic groups. A culturally responsive framework was used to collect the data. The semi-structured interviews were conducted with the use of technology, in the form of telephone or digital platforms like the Zoom interviews.

Bricolage Some of the Case Studies From the Indian Tribes and Their Contribution to the Socio Ecological Preservation

Bricolage in Indian Entrepreneurship and Jugaad

The traditional analogy of a Karma yogi on his sojourn to Mount Kailash to meet Lord Shiva the Adi lord faces a dilemma to carry the traditions of his ancestors, the books to the abode of Lord Shiva. Caught between two cliffs, he is unable to identify the solution to the problem, when he meets the Narayan himself. The Narayan guides him to unload the traditions and the baggage of old rituals which he has bequeathed from his ancestors in the form of books and literature. The Karam yogi uses bricolage, and with the use of lever and pulley, he can transport the books to the other world. Indian artisans are known for their ingenuity and craftsmenship. Over the period of time, with the changing requirements, the crafts of the Indian artisans have taken newer dimension. One such invention is the *mitticool refrigerator* by Manuskbhai Prajapati. The artisan, born into an artisan community, embraced the idea of blending modern knowledge with traditional craftsmanship. This fusion led to the creation of a clay fridge that operates without electricity, showcasing a unique and innovative approach to refrigeration. This bricolage has revolutionised the lifestyle of many rural family by offering convenience without the recurring costs. This innovation has become the Indian pride and led to sustained improvement in the life of the rural people. The conceptual framework of inquiry consists of nine dimensions, which include (1) epistemology, (2) ecological, (3) methodological, (4) political, (5) ontological, (6) axiology, (7) relational, (8) institutional and (9) personal. Jugaad as a practice helps to empower people through ingenious practices to fight the oppressive powers. The social life is full of dichotomies, and the Indian tribal communities are no exception to it. In the context of the SHG, the tribal people who have taken loans as part of the community and are unable to pay it face extreme form of hostility in their community. The organic community has a certain order and the villages in India or communities are classified based on the *shrenis and varnas.* There is already a lot of chaos in the mosaic of human civilisation with many gaps pertaining to the advancement of civilisation. In this scenario, the native people have been the torchbearer of the Indian culture. They have indigenous practices and cultures, which they have been pursuing for centuries, and these practices have been passed on in the form of the narratives through use of the oral traditions and the customs and rituals. These oral traditions have facilitated the human development through the process of sensemaking and bring order in the chaos. The natives carry the rich and glorious traditions of their ancestors, passing them on from generation to generation through narratives, stories, and folklore. According to Patton, bricolage is not a theoretical construct but is a matter of practical experience.

The pottery has been the cultural expression of the various civilisations, from the Mesolithic civilisation to Neolithic civilisation. The pottery from the Mesolithic age comprises of the cord-impressed pottery made from clay and terracotta. The Neolithic civilisation comprises of various cultural civilisations that include Ahar Banas culture, Amri Nal culture, Bhirrana culture, Kunal culture, Mehrangarh culture, Sothi Siswal culture and Rangpur culture. The ochre coloured pottery is found in Rajasthan, Western UP and Eastern Punjab, followed the black and red ware culture (1450–1200 BCE) in northern and central Indian subcontinent. Each of these forms of pottery are the ethnic markers. Painted Grey Ware found in Western Uttar Pradesh, Haryana and Eastern Punjab dating back to 1200–600 BCE and Northern Black Polished Ware (700–800 BCE) are the ethnic markers of the various phases of the Indus Valley civilisation.

One of the communities in Gujarat in India is pursuing the Patch art form. The Patch art form is their ethnic marker, and they do this work to exhibit it in the international exhibitions. This art form gives them a cultural identity of their own which is different from that of the other cultural groups in the nation. The group is formed by the tribals who pursue the same profession, and they are homogenous in terms of profession. They are covered under the SHG bank linkage programme to take loan from the banks on the basis of the social capital. The social capital is the binding force among the members of the group. The excerpt from the interview with the head of the master craftsmen is given here 'The Government has provided us revolving fund Rs 10,000 for support. We do Patch work and put them up for sale at exhibitions. We have very good creditworthiness. Money earned increase from Rs 100,000 to Rs 200,000. For choosing the candidate or members, we call them to home and counsel them to become self-reliant by savings. Meetings are conducted even at higher frequency to make the women self-reliant. Generally, members are from the same village but we give coaching to members from the different villages as well. We all work together. It makes me feel good and they also feel good and are able to pass time. We also make eco-friendly Ganesh ji. We get the mitti in March and then we make the ecofriendly Ganesh ji and then we establish it in September.

Lord Ganesha has been worshipped for years as *Vigna harta and Vigna Vinashak*. The remains from the Indus valley civilization speak volumes of the worship of Pashupati nath and popularity of animism as a practice among the indigenous people who descended on the Indian subcontinent much prior to the advent of the Aryans. From the practice of making *terracotta Ganpati* to modern day sustainable Ganeshji, the indigenous tribes using various expressions and insignia of cultural identity have been able to adapt their artform to contribute to the sustainable ecosystem, through bricolage. The Embroidered patch work produced by the women of Gujarat since the pre independence era. This work is an ethnic marker that has enabled the people of Gujarati community to create a social affiliation among the clan and differentiate themselves from the rest of the group. Many artisans who migrated to India from Gujarat have pursued this art form for centuries now and this artform is further passed on from one generation to another.

Further the interview with the leader and the master craftsmen reveals the shared norms in the group, that helps the artisans to achieve financial sustainability. There are no repayments in problem. We do not take women who are not credit worthy. The leader of the group is known all over the village. There has never been an issue regarding the non-repayment of loan. Even if there is a default due to medical reason or any kind of disease in the family, we support them and counsel them regarding the importance of timely repayment. In our group members attend meetings regularly. The leader of the group manages the distribution of the money. This is her ancestral business and her mother has taught this skill to them. She handles all the tasks like distribution of money. Patch work has been passed on to leader of group from the generation to generation. Members do cooperate with each other and encourage each other. In the initial days, women were constrained by the needs of their members and children. Slowly and slowly, I counselled them and supported them. They owe their success to the money, emotional support and efforts of Komalben. Komalben has travelled over the world from Delhi, Bangalore, Chennai, Hyderabad to make exhibition. And they indulge in Kurti making, bedsheet, . This provides them so much happiness and they feel so elated that their work is so good that we try to figure out whether they are willing to learn. Slowly and slowly, they explore whether they are willing to learn. In the Ajeevika melas, we get revolving funds which we utilise for the purchase of raw materials. Our group is not linked to the Federation and we feel that linking to the Cluster will help us in becoming self-sustainable. Members of the group are willing to come together to help each other.' Thus, with the ethnic marker, the Patch work, the members of the native community can express their subjective feelings as social collateral and collaborative and cooperative initiative to finance. Moreover, this ethnic marker enables the members to get the loans from the bank.

Yet another sustainable practice is the promotion of millet as the diet and preferred food replacement for cash crops such as rice. With the support of India, the year 2023 has been declared as the international year of millets. Bricolage implies the move from the theoretical practice to application. The literature has highlighted the importance of agriculture in the life of Malayali people. One such research work is by Narayanan who provides a chronological narrative of evolution of cultural practices among the tribes such as Malayarayar tribe. This work through the discourse highlights the assimilation of the cultural changes that lead to the transformations in the cultural practices. The literary work highlights the evolution from the natural beliefs to cultural adaptations. Various communities in Koli hills of state of Tamil Nadu and other regions of the nation pursue the cultivation of the millets for ages now. The tribal leaders of these groups and communities play an important role to promote this agricultural practice and transmitting this indigenous knowledge through the use of the folklores and the narratives, including the folk songs. The Malai songs are being used for promoting the use of millets, and India has also adopted various programmes to promote the growing of millets as part of the sustainable agricultural practice.

Thus, on a conceptual level, the bricolage can be defined as making use of whatever is available at hand and making modifications to bring the conceptual knowledge into practice (see Fig. 36).

As per the study, joint liability group is an example of bricolage and jugaad in Hindi. India has undertaken various initiatives to provide finance to the poor people, who do not have collateral or do not have access to finance. The marginalised tribes and the artisans do not have any collateral or belongings but have the skill in their hand, which helps the poor tribal artisans to achieve financial inclusion through microfinance. The essence of the joint liability groups and the social capital mechanism is given below:

SHGs are voluntary associations of people formed to attain a collective goal. SHG is a village-based financial intermediary committee usually composed of 10–20 local women. The members make small regular saving contributions for a few months until there is enough capital in the group for lending. Funds may then be lent back to the members or other villagers. These SHGs are then further 'linked' to banks for delivery of micro credit. It lays emphasis on capacity building, planning of activity clusters, infrastructure build up, technology, credit

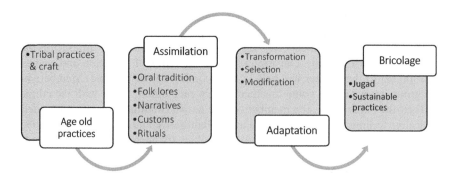

Fig. 36.   Process of Bricolage.

and marketing. Microfinance through women SHGs is a significant medium of poverty alleviation and empowerment of women. In India, self-help groups or SHGs represent a unique approach to financial intermediation. The approach combines access to low-cost financial services with a process of self-management and development for the women who join as members of an SHG (Francis Sinha).

People who are homogenous with respect to social background, heritage, caste or traditional occupation come together for a common cause to raise and manage resources for the benefit of the members of the group (NABARD). The SHG bank linkage programme is a cost effective mechanism for providing the access to finance for the people at the bottom of the pyramid. Banks are wary of lending to the members due to the lack of collateral and information about the creditworthiness of the poor. Due to the risk of higher monitoring costs for the loans given to the poor, the banks are wary of lending to the poor. Self-help group bank linkage programme (SHG BLP) is cost effective for banks since group loans reduce the operating expenses as well as delinquency rates. From the analysis of the data analysis, 'Negotiation' has emerged as the major category. SHG BLP has high recovery performance and leads to reduction of transaction costs for banks and clients ensuring the availability of credit at market rates and opportunity to the banks for developing quality clientele in future. This social innovation has led to higher asset creation through micro credit particularly for the women entrepreneurs. Microfinance acts as an alternative delivery model for promoting micro credit to women. And by joining SHG saving regularly, women dependence on moneylender has reduced. For the women participants who have taken loans from the SHG, a higher degree of asset creation is visible through the establishment of the micro enterprises with the bank linkages. The primary obstacle the bank faces in providing for the impoverished is their dispersion and the high cost of transactions. In developing economies, the high cost of credit and contracting costs frequently results in costs and market failures. Over 1 crore rural families have benefitted from SHG bank linkage and rural women run the most cost effective and the fastest growing microfinance programme in the world as per the report by the National Bank for Agriculture and Rural Development (NABARD).

SHG linkage programme provides loan to the marginalised women such as artisans, through the social contract that is based on limited individual liability and joint liability. If even one of the members fails to pay the loan, all other members pressurise the defaulting member. The incremental loan from the bank acts as the dynamic incentive for the members to pay back their loans in time. The members of the SHGs are the artisans who have been practising this art for centuries. Thus, the peer mechanism has emerged as the heart and soul of this initiative. This microfinance initiative works on the principle of power, collaboration, manipulation and pressure. In the self-help group (SHG), the joint liability creates a system of peer monitoring that contributes to high repayment rates. The reason for the repayment by the poor is the unwillingness to pay, and the members need the incentives to monitor each other. Due to the presence of the joint liability, the members have incentive to monitor each other, and in the event of non-payment of loans, the members cooperate with each other. The SHGs are effective in vulnerability reduction by providing the much-needed access to the non-usurious loans. And the loans from the joint liability groups have helped the households to maintain the consumption. The various SHGs covered under DAY NRLM have been provided various economic benefits in the form of livelihood. 690 Lakh or so women members of around 63 Lakh SHGs across the country are providing economic and social needs of rural people. The SHG covered under linkage provides health responses such as mask making, health messaging, sanitiser, etc. During the COVID-19 pandemic, the SHGs have played an important role in promoting financial sustainability. One SHG of Valsad district had prepared 1.00 Lakh masks and DAY-NRLM, Mehsana, prepared a record 1.78 Lakh masks during the first lockdown. SHG provides necessary services to the senior citizens, Andaman, India. Similarly, during COVID-19, community kitchens were set up for hundreds of hungry people. Society for Rural and Youth Educational Advancement (SRYEA) with volunteers of 15 SHG members from 3 SHGs were involved in 'Food on Wheels'. The Mega Anti COVID-19 Drive run by SHG members across the length and breadth of our country has scripted a golden chapter in the history of mankind. During these campaigns, the members have made immense use of digital technology through eShakti. On a conceptual and theoretical level, this chapter aims to understand how the peer mechanism functions to ensure the financial inclusion of the poor. The study suggests that self-help groups operate through manipulation, collaboration, power dynamics, and pressure akin to the model shown in Fig. 37.

Pressure is appearing to be the most relevant tactic of negotiation for the members of SHG. Knowing that all the members in the group have joint liability,

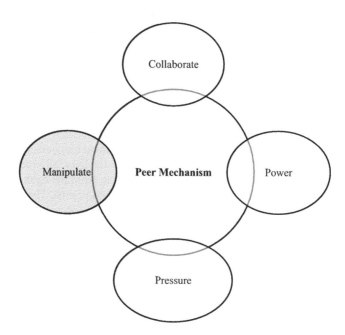

Fig. 37.　Peer Mechanism of Self-Help Groups.

the individual members exercise negotiation in the form of *pressure* on defaulting member. This involves '*competition*', 'closures or expulsions' and 'krunch', *i.e.* pressurising the other member to do better. Through the analysis of the data, we came across all the three forms of tactics.

> In community, members can get money by fighting. They know each other and have been hired by each other. There is social pressure. They conduct meetings every 15th day of every month. And if they misutilize the loans for consumption purpose, they then stop coming for meeting, then there is a big fight and then with lot of fighting we get the money back.

This is '*expulsion*' strategy or tactic for negotiation. The other form of negotiation is '*competition*' between the SHGs. For example, there are SHGs Naya Savera, Usha Kiran, Udaan, and we organise the competition of three groups and then after competition the members decide among themselves to whom loan is to be provided. Besides, the groups also use *power* the SHPI director of one of group highlighted that

> only strongest of the members is made the Adhyaksh and Kosha Adhyaksh in the group. Within the power the members also use '*limits*', which involves setting up the parameter limiting money. SHPI tries to monitor and control its financial performance. Members remain worried for their daughter's wedding and other such social obligations. In order to avoid the misutilization of loan, we provide only 50% of sanctioned loans to the members of SHG. Thus, this way power is used for controlling the loans. *Collaborate* tactic is used too often. The members of the group pool their savings and then these pooled savings are distributed in the form of intraloan. Bank loans are also granted to the group and after that the group divides the loan among themselves. Besides, that SHPI or implementing agencies help the Self-help groups to come together. SHPI help to form the group. We provide them finished product prototype and once they have received the training then we leave them to become independent. (Interview taken from the self-help groups).

Initiatives of SHPI are fuelled by 'community engagement' as all the SHGs formed are integrated to form a federation.

In a group, the fellow members act as a motivator and hence motivate the members to make the payment. In a village there are 3 to 4 groups. Thus, if one group has one leader and other members are not able to pay. Then the other groups or the leaders help them to update their book of accounts. Thus, SHG Federation helps the SHG members to collaborate. In groups members organize themselves and this improves their self-efficacy and increase their bargaining power.

In one of the interaction the SHPI head said,

> If a member is unable to repay a bank loan, the bank must be paid
> on the person's behalf by other members. In our village, there has
> never been a default before. The timely repayment of the loan is
> the responsibility of our entire firm. Members share their worries
> and financial information with one another. The residents are all
> acquainted with one another. They talk about money whenever
> they get together in the village. The entire society keeps an eye on
> things and builds up pressure. Family members and SHG members
> inquire about and supervise the loan amount's use.

SHGs play an important role in promoting the financial sustainability through increased value of assets and saving rate, better access to institutional loans, higher rate of repayment and elimination of informal sources and impressive social empowerment. An interview was done with the leader of the self-help promoting institutions, and the respondent stated that 'We are working in area of women empowerment and motivating them to come in a group for their day-to-day activities. They have various problems and we advise them to become organizations. Banks do not respect the individual member and respect the group. And they are made into groups. There are separate groups for artisans, agriculture labour and agriculture are given training. When they say they have no income and we enable them to attend the Skill development workshops and this enables them to meet certain known income. This provides them an assured income and this will be a main area of focus. We have group of women between 18 to 51 years and if they need credit then one woman from one family can take one loan and that is criteria for loan. If one member in the family does not pay loan then the others get demotivated. Age criteria is also taken into account for writing the proceedings and creating the document list. Whatever artisan group they are maintaining the documents. The focus of the programme is credit. Individual we have grant for woman and they have become the member. Rural women are around 10,000 as part of the Self-help groups. If they are facing the problem, they will definitely come together for a common case and addressing the needs of the women is extremely important. The whole group is responsible for the repayment of the loans and that is how the group dynamics work. While taking the loan, they all decide it together. If you make them responsible, they do take the activity. Ensure they repay back the money but due to the social dynamics and problems such as poverty, divorce in the family, the family members will have to bring back the money. So, the women is exploited in the family. Different members of the family come together and meet fortnightly and they stay in the same place. They come forward to take the liability. Here in Karnataka, there are not many documentary services in place and the women face lot of pressure. The family is not cooperative and the women are facing so many problems. Microfinance has spoiled the women life and members are continuously taking the loan and not using it for the productive purposes. We guide the women about the Government schemes. SABLA as an NGO has established various information networks. The bank cannot invest in the monitoring of the banking of the poor people. However, the Peer influence is not working, wife beating is there and they say it is a family matter and this leads to the society issue. They are working very closely with those women. There are many social action women. All these areas the NGOs are not working. There are lot of problems and the NGOs are conducting an extremely conducive job and they are coming forward. NABARD is helping the NGO in skill building, land development and micro enterprises. The very few agencies are working in these areas and domestic violence are increasing and rape instances are increasing. There are women who are widows and men does not have control over their finances and men is a big hurdle for women empowerment. Where men involvement is not there, men doing well. Lots of experience what is women empowerment, world bank is saying, Amul cooperative and crime against the women is increasing and gender discrimination is increasing. Men are not allowing women to enjoy the power. Lot is to be done. Society fabric is not very conducive to women empowerment. And women is not involved in any of the decision making rights and the women should be given more property rights. More than 4,000 cases are pending in the Court and they ask for the equal property rights. Husband does not cooperate with the women.'

Bricolage involves making do with the materials available at hand, reflecting a resourceful approach to creating and problem-solving. In order to understand the processes of organisational design, the bricolage is extremely important. Bricolage is the response to the changes in the environment. Bricolage refers to the series of action that is used for viewing and collecting the resources. Bricolage forms an extremely important part of the identity of the culture and the identity of the person in the question as the people basically pursue the skill of their hand, which they have bequeathed from their ancestors. Indigenous people have vast experience of working on the sustainable practices that include the preservation of the environment. From the resource-based view (RBV), the bricolage is extremely important in the services like culinary, hotels restaurants, art and art forms, lifestyle goods and crafts. One of the greatest advantages of bricolage is that it facilitates the fusion of the various kinds of cultures, and this enables the synthesis of the culture (modern and the traditional). This bricolage also helps to identify the type of professional as either high risk or the low-status identities. The lack of acceptance of cultural practices has led to a general lack of awareness about the diverse traditions and practices of tribal and indigenous peoples worldwide. However, through narratives and storytelling, there is potential to increase acceptance of these practices and integrate them into everyday life and professional practices, serving as a powerful tool for promoting understanding and appreciation of indigenous traditions. The literature highlights the need for embracing the indigenous practices, for example, in our daily life; people have started adopting the bamboo made furniture, the cane furniture, use of traditional paintings such as Warli paintings, Ayurvedic treatments for treating the ailments. Thus, bricolage also refers to the indigenous people relating to their environment in a more traditional and in naturalist way, and the actors effectively combine the various elements in the environment to create the sustainable practices. Thus, the institutions become extremely important, though they are abstract. There is need for modifying the practices and adopting these activities to the institutions at large. Within the organisation, there are problems of agency, with the need for the social change. The functioning of the organisations is embedded within the social context and the existing social and cultural beliefs. According to the literature, ethnic communities can be identified in three ways: (1) based on objective attributes, (2) through reference to subjective feelings, and (3) in relation to behaviour. Unani medicine has also emerged as an important source of medical treatment. In Indian society's social fabric characterised by unequal distribution of social power between different groups, individuals use tactics like accommodation, negotiation, and resistance to navigate and address the unequal power dynamics in relationships. This includes the inclusive policies to include the indigenous people in the process of negotiation. The tribal communities in the hills of Tamil Nadu have traditionally cultivated millets along the river lines for many centuries and have asserted their claim to the fallow land. Thus, the heads of the group have better negotiating power, and they are usually invited by the state organisation to discuss and negotiate about the rights and relevant claims to the land. NGOs and mutual organisations play another important role in leveraging the social organisations for promoting the welfare of the people. The NGOs do not have any kind of residual claim in the profits of the company and through their hierarchal partitioning that is existing in the organisations for the number of years.

Agency Problem in the Social Organisations

Increasingly, the heritage groups of indigenous people have age-old traditions, and these traditions are promoted and embraced by the people at large for the sustainable impact. Long time before the forts and fortresses had their own khuds, jal kunds and baolis were maintained to conserve the rain water. Bricolage is the use of the traditional methods to recharge the water systems and thus conserve the water using the age-oold methods. Thus, more and more social organisations are coming up with various mechanisms for the rain water harvesting that can be used for water conservation. The Kunds are built in the arid regions of the Gujarat and Rajasthan for the water conservation. Through the pipes, the water is collected from the top of the houses and collected in the tanks. Temple ponds were also being used for the water harvesting. Many of the organisations are conserving these practices, and they are promoting the tourism around these heritage walks. In a social organisation, there can be instances of misutilisation of funds or donor money. The motivation for promoting these practices may stem from various factors, including personal gain, lack of oversight, or the pressure to achieve certain outcomes or targets. The social organisations that are aligned to the historical organisations at the world level like UNESCO or the cultural societies are indulged in promoting the conservation of the age-old practices. Increasing number of the heritage walks around the city are facilitating the revival of the tourism around the sustainable practices. Many of the age-old scriptures such as Brihat Samhita, Puranas, Mahabharat and Ramayana talk about the age-old practices of water conservation through hydrology and hydraulic engineering. The age-old cities of Mohenjo-Daro and Dholavira are known for its unique and historical water conservation, water control and the drainage system. Mohenjo-Daro is the oldest public bath, and the Harappan civilisation is known for the important watershed management. The Vedic texts and the Upanishads also make a mention about the importance of water conservation. The Charka Samihita also refers to the importance of the water conservation through the traditional methods. Of paramount importance are the age-old healing practices that are based upon the conservation of water and important resources. The modern civilisation gives a lot of importance to the use of the age-old medicinal practices and herbs for the treatment of the age-old ailments. The ancient trade routes have been the important source of exchange for the people at large in the ancient ages. Many of the medicinal villages and centres in the ancient world are known as the medicinal practices, and the Buddha himself is known as the healer of the world. The number of age-old practices of Unani and Arabic medicines have made its way into the modern world. Bricolage is observed in the commercialisation of the traditional medicines and practices. The most important example of the commercialisation of the traditional medicine is the medicinal practices promoted by the Department of Ayush, where by very many medicinal practices are being promoted at subsidised cost along the modern medicine. India has introduced the important practice of Ashtavaidyas, who are increasingly adapting their practices to the modern system of medicine. This adaptation and the introduction of new innovations in the medical system can lead to the discovery of newer forms of medicines. In the past, Taxila and Kasi have emerged as the centres of medicine learning, and these centres have won the praises of even Pliny.

Water Conservation Practices Among Indigenous Tribes

The Sustainable Development Goal number six highlights the importance of the water conservation and access to the clean drinking water among the tribals at the bottom of the pyramid in the interior hamlets and villages of the nation. The various Governments are using the innovative techniques for the purification of the water, which also include the use of the 'Prefabricated Zincalume tanks' for the cleaning of the water. The water purification system is extremely low cost, and it has enabled the villagers to access the clean drinking water. The water availability in the hilly terrains of the Palghar, Maharashtra, is an extremely difficult proposition, as the members and the women particularly have to walk miles in order to fetch the clean drinking water. In the hilly terrains, accessing the water table is a huge problem due to the inaccessibility to the water table and difficulty in the recharge of the water aquifers due to the hilly terrains and the steep slopes and hard rock formations. Many of the non-profit organisations have taken over the initiative of conserving the water through the water conserving practices such as building the check dams, cordons, wells, ponds, sub-surface bunds and the farm ponds. Moreover, the Zincalume tanks have been installed in the habitations in population less than 100. The project is encountering challenges due to the absence of essential equipment like rain harvesting pipes. The access to the drinking water has also improved the human development in the region, while increasing the Human Development Index (HDI) for the region.

Jal Shakti Abhiyan and Catch the Rain Programme

India has implemented the famous 'Har Ghar Jal' programme under which the tap drinking water is made available to the people at the bottom of the pyramids. This includes the accessibility to the clean drinking water to the homes of the six crore rural households through the tap water connections. Earlier, the women had to travel miles and miles to get clean drinking water from the village wells. This scheme has made huge difference to the life of the people in the states across the territory of India. This is a community-based programme, whereby the people of the village play an extremely important role in the operation and maintenance of the drinking water facility in the villages. They are responsible for the water harvesting, operation and maintenance at the community level. This way, more than 90 crore people have benefitted a lot for this system. Villages are encouraged to establish Water Samitis and Pani Samitis to enhance welfare at the household level. The women are being trained in the villages to conduct the water surveillance. On priority, water is made available in the anganwadis, schools and ashramshalas to reduce the incidence of the diseases such as cholera, ring worm among the women at the bottom of the pyramid. The water is made the centre of life for almost everybody by involving the SHGs, non-government organisations. The objective is to transform the village into the Jal Prabodh Gaon. In order to bring the transparency in the water management, India has introduced the geo tagging for the assets, linking the tap connection through the Aadhar number and the use of the mobile application for the tracking of the utilisation of water in the village community. According to the report, the increasing number of households have benefitted from the access to the clean drinking tap water. The drinking water has reached approximately 9.18 crore under the Sab ka Saath Sabka Vikas mission. Indeed, this scheme has changed the scenario of water management in the Indian villages.

The case in point is the 'Jal Panchayat' that has been set up in the Bundelkhand region in India. The concept of 'Jal Saheli' is not new to water conservation and management in India. The Parmarth Samaj Sevi Sansthan under the project 'Establishing the Women's First Right to Water Resources' started the Pani Panchayat in the three districts of the Lalitpur, Hameerpur and Jalaun of Bundelkhand region. Generally, in a village, the women have to spend a lot of time in travelling from one place to another in order to get water. Paani panchayat offers the women the panacea to combat the scarcity of water, and various programmes and initiatives have been undertaken to conserve the water wastages by undertaking various practices such as conserving the water ponds, building the check dams and harvesting the rainwater. This community of Jal Saheli plays an extremely important role in creating livelihood by promoting the community-level initiative for water management. In many of the districts in various states like Gujarat, Akodara village and other villages and the cities, India has undertaken the initiative of installing the water reverse osmosis (RO) systems. The villagers by paying a nominal amount can access the safe drinking water from the RO systems. They do not have to go the far-off wells, and the payment for the water can be made using the digital mode that brings in more transparency into the systems. In many of the villages, the people are using the traditional system to purify the water available. An NGO Nimbkar Agricultural Research Institute (NARI) is promoting the use of the low-cost solar water purifiers (SWP), and this system does not need any kind of electricity. The village craftsmen are involved in the cleaning of the water using this traditional method. The water purifier comprises of the slanting tubular solar water heaters. The NARI water systems are producing approximately 30 litres of portable water, and this technology is being scaled from one village to another. This water purification system is based on the RO and ultraviolet (UV)–based water purification system. NARI Phaltan is thinking of expanding this facility to more villages to make possible scaling up this facility for purifying additional 20,000 to 30,000 litres of water.

Another case study for the use of the traditional methods for the purification of the water in the interior of the villages is given by the tribal women in the Banagudi Kurumba village near Nilgiris, that has enabled the sustenance of the successful 'Nanneer Gramam'. Banagudi Kurumba is the first tribal village where an ultra-filtration membrane purification system has been implemented. This technology has been developed by the Bhabha Atomic Research Centre (BARC). Further training is provided to the women in the villages for the use of water purification system.

CMIE Data and the State of Drinking Water in Villages in India

In different villages of states in India, the state of drinking water is continuously improving. However, from the Aspiration dx data from CMIE, there are still many villages in India, which do not have the access to clean and portable drinking water yet. There are many villages in India, that do not have any kind access to the clean drinking water, as the water is available for less than 6 hours in a day. The situation is particularly grim in the northern states like Jammu and Kashmir, where due to the higher elevation and large tracts, the water levels are quite shallow, and it is not possible to provide the regular water supply to the hinterlands and the people in the hamlets. Besides that, in the north-eastern states of Assam, water is available for almost 24 hours in a day. In some of the far off villages in north-east India, there is some issue regarding the access to the drinking water. Some of the states have witnessed tremendous improvement in the access to the clean and drinking water, and Bihar as a state is at the forefront in the access to clean drinking water. Jal Jeevan Mission has been implemented without any fault in the interiors of the villages in Jharkhand and Bihar. Water supply is ensured for almost 24 hours in a day without any delay. Very few of the villages in Jharkhand and Bihar do not have the access to clean drinking water for entire 24 hours a day. Most of the tribal people are located in the villages of Madhubani, Dumka, Gumla, and they can access the tap water for almost 24 hours a day. This has further led to the improvement in the general level of living of the people and improvement in human index. However, the problem of migration remains one of the big problems in the state of Bihar and especially the villages that are inhabited by the tribals and the indigenous people. India has undertaken various initiatives to improve the level of health and sanitation in the interior of the villages in India, and this includes the supply of the healthcare services and the water supply. Chhattisgarh is the largest state that has the largest area in term and the largest agricultural producing state in the country. Gond tribe is the major tribe that resides in the state of Chhattisgarh, and this tribe is the major contributor to the revenues that are generated from the tourism. However, the health and the life expectancy for the people in the tribal villages is still not as per the national benchmark. In this regard, India has undertaken various initiatives including the access to clean drinking water and the health facilities in interior through various schemes and programmes. The Government in the state of Chhattisgarh has undertaken more than 238 programmes for providing clean drinking water to the households that aims to provide the potable drinking water to more than 22 Lakh families in the state of Chhattisgarh. Though most of the households in India have regular water supply for more than 24 hours in a day, still there is deficiency in water supply in some of the villages. India is set to achieve the 24 hours of water supply by the end of the year 2023. This will cater to the demand of approximately remaining 65,636 households in the state of Chhattisgarh. Under the Jal Jeevan scheme, the clean water supply will be provided to these households, and there is also a plan for the harvesting the waste water from the communities and households in the state. This water will be recycled to provide clean drinking water to the households in the state. The water will also be used for the irrigation and for growing the plants and for the agricultural purposes. Overall, the state of drinking water in the country is improving on a regular basis. The Canacona tribe in the state of Goa is facing a major challenge in accessing clean drinking water due to the presence of the hills and mountainous terrain. Due to the steep slope, the labourers find it extremely difficult to access the drinking water, and there are various instances, where the women cite that they have to walk for miles to get access to clean drinking water from the springs. India has undertaken various initiatives to provide the clean drinking water to help the villagers overcome the challenge of having to walk up to the top of the hill and dig the pits in order to access clean drinking water. In some of the hilly terrains of the state of Gujarat, the access to clean drinking water has become nightmare. The case in point is the Lahan Jhadadar villages in the state of Gujarat. The hills in the hilly tract are impossible to recharge due to the steep slope. However, the villages in the state of Gujarat have put in place various initiatives such as the Pani samiti to conserve the water has undertaken the task of constructing the check dams. With the help of the water systems that are naturally recharged from the rain water and the naturally occurring water systems, the Government has taken on itself the task, and through the Jal Jeevan Mission, water is being provided to all the households in the state of Gujarat.

More than 8.6% of the tribal population lives in the tribal villages of Gujarat, and they do not have access to clean drinking water. Van Bandhan Kalyan Yojana (VKY) has been introduced as the scheme for promoting the development of tribes in the state of Gujarat. The state of Haryana is facing issues with accessing clean drinking water, as less than 60% of its population has access to clean water supply. Under this mission, 30% more weightage is given to the regions in the hilly terrains, and 10% more weightage is given to the villages where majority of population is SC/ST dominated.

Ahar Pyne Water Harvesting System

Indigenous tribes in India are in possession of the unique knowledge and sustainable practices. One such practice is the way of harvesting the rain water and using it for the irrigation purpose. The traditional water harvesting system is the hallmark of the communities in South Bihar. This water harvesting system is the best due to the success of this water harvesting system in its ability to swiftly carry or percolate the water to the sandy grounds. Indeed, Ahar harvesting system is a catchment basin that has three sides and the fourth side is left open as land itself. These Ahar beds are the fallow beds that are used for harvesting rabi crop and the kharif crop in rotation. Pynes are the artificial channels that are used to channelise the water into the irrigation fields. In the 19th century under the British colonial regime, this system was discontinued. This was a jolt to the agrarian water economy. Ahar Pyne is the traditional water harvesting system that is practised in South Bihar, India. In order to harvest water, the reservoirs are built with three walls around on three sides. This water system is built at the end of the drainage lines such as the rivulets and the riverine. These diversions from the regular river systems are used for the irrigation purpose, and this water is used for the irrigation purpose. The irrigation in the state of Bihar is the main stay for the peasants due to the peasant tradition. Ahar Pyne is a traditional water harvesting system that existed in India for ages immemorial. However, in the recent past with the coming up of the modern harvesting systems, the old water conservation practices have lost its sheen. The major challenges and transformations in this age-old innovation of water harvesting have been the design innovations and origination of the meanders to prevent the sand deposition. In order to create a sustainable Pyne system, there are various systems that are taken into account. These factors include natural conditions, physical configurations such as uniform terrain, rainfall intensity. This system comprises of no obstruction in the flow of river, and the meander is a unique feature of this Ahar Pyne water harvesting system to reduce the instances of sand deposition. For the success of this system, it is important to determine the variance in the water flow, mean flow of the water into the river system. These factors need to be considered for the appropriate water harvesting and water management.

Bengal Inundation System

Inundation canal is used in West Bengal and particularly in the flooded regions. During heavy rainfall and floods, water collects in the reservoir and then inundates into the fields. Along with the flood water, the fishes also arrive into the water storage system. These fishes are often used for treating the ailments that are linked to the presence of mosquitoes and dengue. Similar to the dams and the dykes, the embankments were constructed to collect the seasonal water and prevent the flooding and inundation of the rivers. The embankments were con- structed with the mud, bamboo and earthen material. The pools are also called as poolbundy and bundis or bunds due to the ability of the embankments to prevent the floods. The bunds and embankments were constructed to protect the inun- dation by floods, but bunds were not able to achieve such protection.

Dighi's

To meet the water needs of the citizens, the capital was shifted from the Aravali hills to the Yamuna Plain. Efforts were made to bring water into the Yamuna plains and supply it to both the army and common people. This system of water pursued was famously known as the *Shahjahani* canals and *dighis*. In the older days, this system was the source of fresh water for the public at large. The dighis are designed with a square or circular architecture, and each *dighi* had its own sluice gates for bathing and washing clothes. The dighis are popular since the time of the Indus Valley civilisation when the public baths were the systems in Mohenjo-Daro and Harrapan for water conservation and maintenance.

Baolis

Many step wells were constructed in the ancient era by the sultans and nobles, and these baolis were where the general public could come and fetch water. There are many such baolis which include the Gandaki ki baolis, Rajon ki baolis. These water sources were the source of water supply to the people and were frequently used for washing and bathing. The indigenous tribes are playing an important role in the water conservation. In the recent past, the Jal Sahelis are playing an important role in the conservation of the water, through the repair and mainte- nance of existing wells in respective villages and advise the villagers. The water panchayats are also playing an important role in running the community kitchens.

Conclusion

Bricolage has emerged as a common practice for the tribal communities. Owing to be in the possession of an important skill of hand and craftsmanship, which is passed on from generation to generation, tribal communities provide a lot of real life solutions or jugaad or sustainable practices. These communities have come to play an important role in the preservation of the nature, climate and ecology. In India, the present Government under the leadership of Sh Narendra Modi is providing a lot of support and training to the communities and engaging them to create sustainable solution for the ecological problems or climate changes. Thus, sustainable practices and tribal communities have come to play an important role in the preservation of the environment.

Chapter 9

Epistemologies and Ontologies in Self-Help Group

Abstract

This chapter discusses about the role of social capital in providing access to the microfinance for the tribal people at the bottom of the pyramid. Marginalised people at the bottom of the pyramid do not have access to finance due to the problem of information asymmetry, and the community groups use the social capital to gain access to the physical capital and financial services. Due to the presence of the lemons and agency problem, the people at the bottom of pyramid are unable to be financially included. The social contract is operationalised through the use of the peer mechanism, and this helps in financial inclusion of the marginalised tribal people at the bottom of the pyramid. Thus, financial intermediation and financial inclusion play an important role in mitigating the woes of the marginalised tribal people who have been financially excluded from the financial system.

Keywords: Social capital; marginalised communities; financial inclusion; peer mechanism; information asymmetry

Introduction

The research shows that the social capital is a well-accepted epistemology to understand how the self-help groups obtain access to loan through the social relationships existing among the members. The theories of power explain the underlying issue of agency and information asymmetry in the context of self-help groups, particularly those composed of illiterate and vulnerable individuals. Banks hold power and exercise it over these groups, exacerbating the problem of information asymmetry and exploiting the vulnerable members.

Community organisations are aimed at providing access to finance to the people at the bottom of the pyramid. Tribals are indigenous people who possess traditional skills and knowledge passed down through generations, including the

Sustainable Pathways, 199–211

Copyright © 2024 Nishi Malhotra

Published under exclusive licence by Emerald Publishing Limited

doi:10.1108/978-1-83549-490-520241020

ancient art form of their ancestors. These organisations basically lack the access to finance due to the lack of collateral and information about the creditworthiness of the poor. The decision about the access to the outside equity or use of retained earnings is an important decision for these artisans. Due to lack of belief in the ability to pay back the loans, the members are hesitant to take bank loans due to their lack of confidence in their ability to repay them. Thus, the banks mainly suffer from the 'Lemon' problem as the banks believe that most of the small entrepreneurs who come for business are basically inferior quality customers, as they cannot pay back their loan or they will default on their loans. Thus, the bankers are willing to grant the loan only if (1) enforcement of the loans is easy and (2) the banker has the personal knowledge about the borrower. The financial intermediation in this process is very costly, as the banks will have to incur very high cost of monitoring the customers. Thus, in the interior of the village, the moneylender is extremely money-minded person, who has intimate knowledge about the borrower. Thus, the financial contracting comes to play an extremely important role in the rural markets of India. Information asymmetry is an extreme problem that can lead to the moral hazard and adverse selection. These members also do not have any confidence in their ability to pay back the loan. Signalling hypothesis is an important theoretical lens. Capital structure theory by Ross (1973) asserts that the financing choices of a corporate signal the funda-mentals of the corporate to the market. Thus, the entrepreneurs who cannot afford the formal loan are motivated to save, and then based on their savings and past loan history, the banks provide loans to the people at the bottom of the pyramid. Entrepreneurs who cannot afford formal loans are motivated to save money before applying for a loan. The bank loan signals the improving credibility and financial prowess of these micro borrowers. This chapter aims to discuss the role of the community lending initiatives and social capital in promoting the financial inclusion of the indigenous people by combating the agency problem in the form of information asymmetry. In this chapter, the data have been collected by interviewing the members of the self-help group using the semi-structured method. The analysis of the data highlights that homogeneity of the members in terms of the profession and occupation, and other social relationships lead to the social trust and social capital among the members of the group. This trust further leads to personal relationships in the form of bonding, bridging and linking which leads to higher level of peer mechanism and leads to sustainability of the group. Since the group is a social innovation, the social capital of the community is an important phenomenon. Due to the social objective, the organisations are not able to generate the economic profits, and hence, agency costs emerge as the important criterion in granting the credit to the artisans of the community organisations. The agency costs are mainly comprised of the monitoring costs to be incurred by the banks and the bonding costs by the private equity or outside equity providers. The strategic intent of the community organisations is to achieve the social objectives such as promoting the welfare of the artisans. The analysis of the data highlights that the members of the self-help group combat agency problem by social contract that requires including people who are a priori known to the other members of the group.

Research Problem

This research study aims to discuss the agency problem present in a joint liability group. The members in a group do not have any credit history, due to which the banks and financial institutions in the formal sector are unwilling to provide credit to the people at the bottom of the pyramid. The self-help groups through social capital and relationships existing among the members help the people to get access to finance and loans.

Literature Review

The agency theory (Jensen & Meckling, 1976) highlights that in a corporation, agency cost is an important factor to decide the capital structure. As the banks are not willing to provide loans to the people at the bottom of the pyramid due to lack of collateral and lack of knowledge about the credit worthiness of the poor, the people at the bottom of the pyramid generally depend on the social capital for getting loans from the banks. The literature highlights that the additional cost of dishonesty in doing business in underdeveloped countries like India can be substantial. In an underdeveloped nation, the microentrepreneurs have the incentive to misreport their correct credit profile and strategically default in a joint line. However, due to the presence of the personal guarantee and the joint liability, the banks are willing to provide the loan to the people at the bottom of the pyramid. The study found that the problem of adverse selection is present in the cooperative loaning structure, where borrowers with lower creditworthiness are more likely to default on their loans. Thus, this paper discusses the presence of the agency problem. In this study, the theoretical framework has been used from Jensen and Meckling to explain the moral hazard and the agency problem. As detailed in Fig. 38, the cooperative structure of a group is constrained by the financial value of the group, i.e. V and the utility of financial earnings for the customers. Members of the self-help group can apply for loans from the group, which is typically granted based on the member's share in the group. Each member is required to have a share in the group, which can be used as collateral for loans. The share can be used for productive or non-productive purposes. The loans are distributed among the members based on their share in the group. The member equilibrium is at point D where member utilises V^* for the non-productive purpose and F^* for productive purpose. Furthermore, even though the member would like to be on point and at a higher level of utility by taking out additional loans and allocating a portion for non-productive advantages and uses, the member has an incentive to redirect the funds for non-productive reasons. The group establishes a social contract among its members, where they agree to mutually support and monitor each other's financial activities. The group assumes joint liability for the repayment of loans, meaning that if one member defaults on their loan, the other members are responsible for paying back the debt. And since penalty is not financial, group gives option to reach back to the normal point of equilibrium.

Thus, there remains an agency problem in the group, if the members indulge in moral hazard and divert the savings for non-productive purpose. And in a group, the benefits of good and hard work are distributed among all the members, and

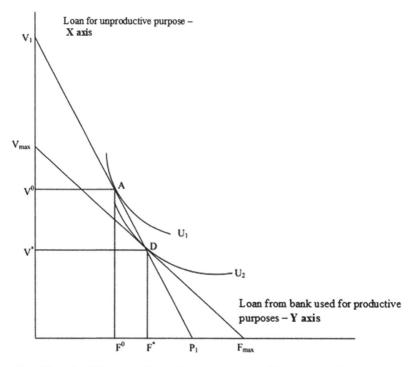

Fig. 38.   Indifference Curve for Members Utility From Diversion of
Loans.

similarly, the financial penalty in form of loan denial is also passed on to all the members, and hence, the utility curve for the members does not shift downward and remains at the initial point D. Thus, the members in a group are peer monitored, and this reduces the moral hazard in the group while maintaining the utility levels. Ross (1973) in his paper has defined the agency problem as relationship between two people in contract with each other, such as relationship of Government and employee, borrower and banks to name a few. Information asymmetry leads to the agency problem. Jensen and Meckling (1976) in their paper have highlighted the issue of information asymmetry as a major issue. In context of the cooperative lending programmes, the credit worthiness of the group members is not known a priori to the bank. This information is with the bank and the leader of the group, which can lead to the problem of asymmetry. Myers and Majluf (1984) in their research paper have highlighted the importance of pecking order theory in financing decisions. Similarly, in groups, the members within the ambit of social contract work to maximise the group returns to ensure repayment of the loan and the pecking order still holds. Though, the set-up is not corporate finance domain for the small entrepreneurs, but the members prefer first to use their retained earnings, followed by the debt.

Findings and Discussion

There are four kinds of tribal groups, and each of these four groups highlight the importance of the social capital.

The tribes in India have undergone various transformations over the period as mapped in Fig. 39. In the first phase of tribal evolution, tribal communities form strong social linkages and bonds with one another, as well as with non-tribal members. In the second classification as per Elwin, the tribals evolve to give up the life of communities and move on to adopt the individualistic life. In the third classification, the tribals make a conversion from tribal community to the religious Hindu clan. The last phase is the phase of emergence of aristocracy among the tribals as chieftains. See Fig. 40 for policy frameworks in community groups.

Many social inclusion initiatives aimed at promoting good health have been started by India. These initiatives include setting up of Shri Sadguru Seva Sangh, Mafatlal Foundation, Raghubir Mandir Trust and Shri Ramdas Hanumanji Trust to ensure human service. Moreover, India has released the stamp in memory of Late shri Arvind Bhai Mafatlal, who undertook various health initiatives for the betterment of the tribal people including the setting up of the eye camp, health check-ups to name a few.

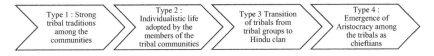

Fig. 39.   Chronology of Evolution of Tribes.

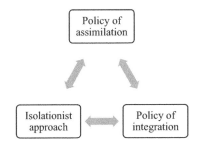

Fig. 40.   Policy Frameworks in Community Groups.

Religious Approach to Inclusion of Tribes

Many different tribes have taken initiatives for the inclusion of the tribes in the mainstream. Various religious groups such as Christian missionary have undertaken the initiatives for the inclusion of the poor and tribal in the mainstream. The protectivist approach aims to ensure that the tribal communities are protected by insulating their ethos, beliefs and value systems. The promotional approach for tribal communities aims to allocate resources and equip them to ensure livelihood for the poor. India has undertaken various initiatives for the inclusion of the tribal communities with the mainstream, which include the conversion of the tribals into the Christian community and Hindus community to ensure access to the financial benefits in the form of subsidy and incentives. Thus, the social capital in the community organisations also comprise of the unique religious affiliations and religious linkages. In the further exploration of the structure of the self-help groups, the task contingencies play an extremely important role in the success of the group. The social capital comprises of the structural, relational and cognitive elements. The network ties that form the structural elements of a society, along with the trust, norms, obligations, and identifications that make up the relational capital, are strengthened through shared codes and language, which in turn form the cognitive capital of the group.

These task contingencies comprise of the following element:

- *Task cooperation:* The task cooperation in an organisation comprises of the embedded ties with repeated exchanges among the members of the group a.
- Economic rationality: The members of the group compete with other purchasers to get loan from the bank.
- Social structure: The group is the social structure that operationalises the social capital.

Data Analysis and Findings

An interview was conducted with the members of the self-help groups, and the excerpts from the interview are mentioned herewith:

> There are 12 members in our group and they indulge in leather works and they have been working for 2 years. All of the members are from same village and in this village, there is a population of 5,000 households. In this group they save Rs 20 per day and we have balance of Rs 30,000. We have not taken loan from bank. If a member needs money they can borrow the amount and pay back the amount with interest. In our group literate member controls the members and every month they conduct the meetings and provide information about financial savings and loan. The members maintain a register of savings and loans. We have Adhyaksh, Kosh Adhyaksh and Secretary. Group has one single savings bank. Our group attends the Saras mela. Members take

loan social cause and this helps them increase the self-efficacy of the member. I was approached by state official to access loan. This is our family business, my grandfather uses to do, my father use to do and we are also pursuing. And also, our children who are studying they also intend to pursue. But literacy helps in improving sustainability of group. Yes, members have joint liability and the treasurer, Kosh Adhyaksh and secretary is responsible for the monitoring of group.

The coding for the interview is given in Table 12:

The interview highlights that in a group, homogeneity of the group membership leads to the social capital. This homogeneity of the group membership comes from the same profession and the same business relations. The structural relations in a group provide a dynamic advantage due to the peer mechanism which refers to the ability of the members and the leaders particularly to peer monitor each other. Due to the presence of the joint liability, the members of the groups are eager to monitor each other and in case of default to pay on behalf of each other. Thus, the members reduce the agency problem in the group by monitoring each other. They peer monitor the behaviour, and thus, they pressurise the defaulting members to pay back the loan in time. The individual members have the limited liability. Due to this limited liability, the members are willing to default, knowing that the other members will pay on their behalf. This leads to the problem of moral hazard in the group. During an interview, group members emphasised the importance of group monitoring in ensuring timely loan repayment.

In yet another interview, the members highlighted that group monitoring is extremely important for the financial sustainability of the groups. The respondent also highlighted the importance of motivation and attitude change to facilitate the financial inclusion and growth. The respondent also highlights that since the members are from the same area, they know each other; this helps to reduce the moral hazard problem in the group.

Interviewer: How you form self-help group of artisans?
Respondent: We get government training and we work on govt project, after these 6–8 days training given on sewing and stitching and then we form the self-help group.
Interviewer: Are the artisans who are included from the same art?
Respondent: Some are from jute and some from textile. They are also from different art form. The art that we have for example embroidery and for that we give training and we form group. These all remain attached to the Ajeevika programme. These groups are from the different regions but the same village. For example, Arifnagar and like this for the same region or district in a village we form a group. There is a team that continuously remain in touch with them

Table 12. Coding Analysis.

Line-by-Line Analysis	In Vivo Coding	Description Coding	Analytical Coding
There are 12 members in our group, and they indulge in leather works, and they have been working for 2 years	Size of the group and age of group	Group size and age of group	Group size and age
All the members are from same village, and in this village, there is a population of 5,000 households	Homogeneity of group and selection criterion	Homogeneity of group and selection criterion	Homogeneity of group and selection criterion
In this group, they save Rs 20 per day, and we have balance of Rs 30,000	Savings and thrift	Savings and thrift	Savings and thrift management
We have not taken loan from bank. If a member needs money, they can borrow the amount and pay back the amount with interest.	Intralending	Intralending	Intralending
In our group, literate member controls the members, and every month, they conduct the meetings and provide information about financial savings and loan. The members maintain a register of savings and loans.	Literacy and group monitoring through meetings and financial savings	Group monitoring through the meetings, information sharing. Literacy improves financial management	Institutional processes, monitoring – meetings and record keeping. Literacy

We have Adhyaksh, Kosh Adhyaksh and secretary. Group has one single savings bank.	Leadership	Leadership and accounting	Leadership management and financial accounting
Our group attends the Saras mela.	Market linkages	Marketing through exhibitions	International marketing through exhibitions
Members take loan social cause, and this helps them increase the self-efficacy.	Social welfare and positive impact of group lending	Improvement in quality of living	Social welfare
I was approached by state official to access loan.	Access to loan	Financial inclusion and access to loan	Financial inclusion and credit linkages
This is our family business, my grandfather use to do, my father use to do and we are also pursuing. And also, our children who are studying they also intend to pursue.	Craftsmanship, family business	Craftsmanship, heritage art	Craftsmanship and family business
But literacy helps in improving sustainability of group.	Literacy and sustainability of group	Importance of financial literacy to improve financial sustainability	Financial literacy
Yes, members have joint liability and the treasurer, Kosh Adhyaksh and secretary are responsible for the monitoring of group.	Leadership peer monitors the group	Peer monitoring by the leaders, accountants	Peer monitoring

and our team works in different area. Our team help the artisans to improve their business and it is not that we leave these villages, our different teams work in different area. There are two different loans i.e., banks and Ajeevika. They help them acquire machines. There is a regular meeting of groups and our one person also remain present in their meetings. There is need for intense motivation of these groups. For around 3–6 months, we must remain attached with them and only then they come on line. When we make SHG it is not that if there are 10 or 14 candidates then all are illiterate or literate. We put at least one or more member in the group who can read and write. Today nobody is illiterate, everybody let us say in a group of 15 members, at least 12 can do something.

How These People Communicate and Many Groups Break?

Area is divided. Let us say an area is chola, and we know their homes are connected to each other. And we make groups for these people, and it is not that once we made group with one from Bhopal and one from Indore. It does not happen those ways. Due to the geographical proximity of the areas, the people in one area (or 'chola') are connected to each other and are grouped. It is not a case of randomly grouping people from different cities, such as Bhopal and Indore, together. The groups are formed based on the shared geographical location of the people.

The interview highlights the phenomenon of social trust generated among the group members through peer mechanism. The respondent says that 'it is not that we leave them. Our team members are in constant touch with the members of the group'. Moreover, when the respondent says that 'we make group of members from the same area and it is not that one is from Indore and other from Bhopal', he implies that the homogeneity of the members in terms of geographic proximity pays an important role in reducing the adverse selection in the group.

Further, an interview was taken with yet another group. This interview clearly highlights the agency problem. When the members say that 'If the individual members approach the group the banks are skeptical, whether the members will repay back the loan or not', this shows the problem of moral hazard and adverse selection faced by the banks. The groups mitigate the agency problem by stating that 'the members who default are peer monitored by the other members and peer sanction in promoting the financial discipline in the group'. The excerpts from the interview are given below:

Interviewer: Whether your group is linked to bank under SBLP?
Respondent: No, we are thinking of taking loan
Interviewer: In your group there are how many members?
Respondent: There are 10 members in the group
Interviewer: How your group select the members in the group?

Respondent: There is a criterion. In a village the members solicit cooperation and membership from the villagers

Interviewer: Do members know each other?

Member: Yes absolutely

Interviewer: How it helps in case of a group?

Member: Absolutely, members of a group are trusted by the bank and if an individual member approaches the bank from the group the bank remains sceptical that they might not pay. Banks are further motivated by the regular monthly meetings. Our group conducts weekly meeting in which we decide the amount of loan to be taken and the savings amount to be collected. One member in the meeting is selected as the leader of the group. In our group there are no instances of loan default. If the member does not pay, he is expelled from the group. Peer monitoring and social sanction help in reinforcement and better repayment of loans. As all the members take the loan for productive activities and are aware of the joint liability, they peer monitor and individually member know that they might need the loan and in case of default might be expelled from the group. So, they work sincerely for the success of the group. Since member are from the same society and village, they discuss the financial problems with each other. From the savings of all the members, loan is given to the needy person. By virtue of social network and relationship, member peer monitors each other. If member takes the loan and use it for non-productive purpose, we call the meeting and advise the leader to penalise the member.

Thus, the interview highlights that the agency problem does exist in a group. The group fears that the member might take the loan and not pay it back in time. And the members of the group mitigate this agency problem through peer mechanism, which takes the form of peer monitoring and peer selection. Thus, in the paper, peer mechanism emerged as an extremely important phenomenon that helps to combat the agency problem in the form of moral hazard and adverse selection.

Theoretical Lens and Findings

From the analysis of the data, it becomes apparent that the community groups develop resources and capabilities to achieve above average returns and competitive advantage through social capital, the benefits of which are shared among the members equally. Community organisations generally do not possess any kind of tangible assets or fixed assets and investments, which also refers to the capabilities and organisational routines. The other major resource in an organisation is the learning capacity of the human potential in the organisational and institutional settings. While transaction cost economics explain why organisations exist, the Coase theory provides a framework for understanding the problem of pricing goods and services based on the utility maximisation of consumers. Artisans have a higher utility for non-productive consumption, which leads to higher prices for the loans they take out under various schemes. However, India has introduced various schemes to support the cause of the artisans and provide them loan at subsidised terms and reduced rates of interest. The strategic management in an organisation aims to achieve the competitive advantage by acquisition and deployment of resources. The unique resource in an organisation or the dynamic capability is the resource which is rare, valuable and non-imitable resource. The acquisition and use of the resources capabilities is mediated by the social context. The entrepreneurship in a social organisation like self-help group is motivated by the social context of resource and capabilities. Thus, the leadership capabilities in a group impact the ability to acquire the resources and exploit those resources to achieve the organisational ability. The resources of an organisation comprise of structural resources, and capabilities and institutional capabilities comprise the social capital. Resource-based view comprises of opportunity refinement, competency leveraging and championing competency. Thus, the strategic management gets to play an extremely important role in leveraging the champion competencies. The size of network relations as mapped in Fig. 41, which are the source of social capital determine the line of power and conflicts in a

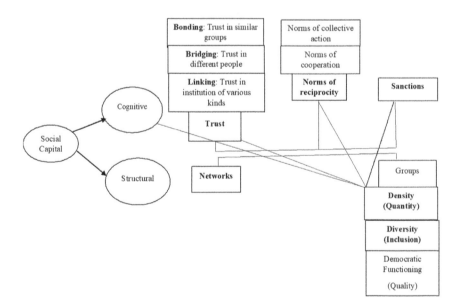

Fig. 41.   Network Relations.

social organisation. Members of social community organisations and banks face agency conflicts, where the interests of the organisation and the individuals within it may not align. The vertical relationship in the community organisation refers to the relationship with the bank, and the horizontal relationships in the community organisation refer to the relationship among the members of community groups. The bright sides of social capital are exaggerated due to the optimistic bias.

Social capital refers to social relations of trust, reciprocity, common rules, norms and sanctions. The social capital is relevant if the social norms in a community organisation promote sustainable livelihood. Thus, trust improves the cooperation and exchanges and ensures reciprocity in simultaneous exchange. The internal mortality of the system comprises of the shared norms and connectedness of the groups. The horizontal linkages in the group refer to the relationship within the group, and the vertical linkages refer to the relationship with the banks. Social capital is promoted by personal relationship and shared norms, and it refers to the shared values and the feelings and comradeship. The literature in domain of social capital highlights the importance of homophily, which refers to the similarity of relationship between the people. According to the existing theories of social capital network, densely embedded network linking direct ties and social structure in a closed structure impact positively the output. Since group is an open structure with sufficient open opportunities, it provides venue for financial intermediation by the brokerage firms and other agencies.

Conclusion

From the study, the agency problem remains one of the biggest problems in the group. The groups address the agency problem through social capital and unique phenomenon called as peer mechanism. The members in the group have knowledge about the creditworthiness of the other members within the group. Due to the social capital and social contract within a group, members peer monitor each other and, in extreme cases of default, also peer sanction each other, leading to financial discipline within the group.

References

Akerlof, G. A. (1970). The market for "lemons": Quality uncertainty and the market mechanism. *Quarterly Journal of Economics, 84*(3), 488–500. Oxford University Press.

Jensen, M. C., & Meckling, W. H. (1976, October). Theory of the firm: Managerial behavior, agency costs and ownership structure. *Journal of Financial Economics, 3*(4), 305–360. Elsevier.

Myers, S. C., & Majluf, N. S. (1984). Corporate financing and investment decisions when firms have information that investors do not have. *Journal of Financial Economics, 13*, 187–221. https://doi.org/10.1016/0304-405X(84)90023-0

Ross, S. A. (1973). The economic theory of agency: The principal's problem. *The American Economic Review, 63*(2), 134–139. http://www.jstor.org/stable/1817064

Chapter 10

How Various Factors Impact the Financial Behaviour of the Members of the Self-Help Group of Indigenous Groups and Natives or Tribal Communities

Abstract

This study explores the profound influence of social and cultural factors on the financial conduct of indigenous tribes and groups. Anchored in Vygotsky's sociocultural theory, the analysis delves into the intricate interplay between cultural elements, such as bricolage, and the immediate availability of financial resources, illuminating their collective impact on the tribes' financial behaviour. Typically residing in proximity, these communities exhibit homogeneity by forming groups exclusive to their clans, lacking access to conventional financial services and tangible assets that dissuade banks from extending loans. Crucially, the social capital embedded within the group dynamics, often referred to as the peer mechanism, emerges as a pivotal conduit for members to secure capital and bank credit. The synergy of bricolage, representing the adept use of available social capital, facilitates access to finance and credit. Despite the existence of social capital and financial literacy programmes, a stark reality persists – a significant proportion of indigenous people remain financially excluded. This chapter endeavours to scrutinise the ramifications of these factors on tribal financial behaviour, employing the Partial Least Squares Structural Equation Modelling (PLS-SEM) method. Proposing a paradigm shift in financial attitudes, the research underscores the imperative of fostering financial inclusion within indigenous tribes and communities.

Keywords: Indigenous financial behaviour; sociocultural factors; bricolage and finance; peer mechanism; financial inclusion in tribal communities

Sustainable Pathways, 213–231
Copyright © 2024 Nishi Malhotra
Published under exclusive licence by Emerald Publishing Limited
doi:10.1108/978-1-83549-490-520241022

Introduction

The social factors and cultural factors seem to have a vast impact on the financial behaviour of the indigenous tribes and groups. Vygotsky's sociocultural theory emphasises the significance of cultural factors and the availability of financial resources in shaping the financial behaviours of indigenous tribes and other indigenous populations. Indigenous people or the tribes generally stay near each other. They form the group with only the members of their clan, and thus as a group, they are homogenous. They do not have access to finance, and they do not have any tangible asset due to which the banks are not willing to provide loan to them. The social capital or the social relations existing between the members of the group called as peer mechanism enable the member to access capital and bank credit. Bricolage or the availability of social capital at hand enables the members to access finance and credit from the bank. However, despite the presence of the social capital and various financial literacy programmes, the ground reality is that not many indigenous people use financial services and are financially excluded. There is a need for financial attitude change to facilitate financial inclusion of the indigenous tribes and people. This chapter aims to study the impact of these factors on the financial behaviour of the tribes and indigenous people using Partial Least Squares Structural Equation Modelling (PLS-SEM) method.

Objectives

UN Sustainable Development Goal of financial inclusion of indigenous tribes is an extremely big challenge. Indigenous tribes and native people stay away from the mainland and reside on the outskirts and move in small communities. These small communities do not have access to the collateral, and they are not able to raise funds from the bank and formal sector. In this scenario, the socialisation and peer effect have a major impact on the financial literacy of these tribes. Despite innumerable financial literacy interventions introduced by the banks and the Government, the financial inclusion of the tribes is a distant tribe. In this regard, changing the attitude of the tribes and the dispositions of the tribes towards knowledge becomes extremely important. This study mainly aims to identify the impact of financial literacy and other socio-cultural factors on the financial attitude and financial behaviour of the members of the groups of indigenous tribes. Besides another major issue with financial literacy, cultural factors and bricolage, access to local resources has an impact on the financial behaviour of the members of the community. The members of the indigenous tribes are organised in the form of groups, where the leaders are responsible for the proper functioning of the groups. The leaders have an agency issue because there is a likelihood that the leader of the group might misuse his position to get benefits for himself.

Hypothesis

Data Collection

The study is a quantitative empirical study, and the data are collected using the cross-section data survey questionnaire. The sampling is done using the purposive sampling method (Cheah et al., 2021; Sarstedt et al., 2018). To collect the data, the respondents were contacted personally through negotiating access with the prospects, who were selected through the convenience sampling method due to the superiority of the method in collecting the data (Yao et al., 2015). The study aims to investigate the relationship between financial literacy and financial behaviour among indigenous tribes. The data was collected from 50 respondents using a questionnaire with six constructs namely bricolage, culture, socialisation, agency, financial attitude and financial behaviour. One being strongly disagree and 7 being strongly agree. During the period Nov 2023–Dec 2023, interviews were conducted with the members of indigenous tribes, which was approximately 50 members using a standard questionnaire.

Hypothesis for the study are:

H0. Bricolage has an impact on financial behaviour of the indigenous people.
H1. Culture has an impact on financial behaviour of the indigenous people.
H2. Socialisation has an impact on financial behaviour of the indigenous people.
H3. Agency has an impact on financial behaviour of the indigenous people.
H4. Financial Attitude mediates the relationship between bricolage, culture, socialisation, agency and financial behaviour.

Data Analysis and Empirical Analysis

Measurement Model

To empirically validate the conceptual framework given earlier, most of the indicator items in the questionnaire have been adapted from the existing literature on social-isation, cultural impact, bricolage, agency, financial attitude and financial behav-iour. The operational definition for the various reflective indicators of the constructs is provided along with the questions asked as part of the questionnaire.

Indigenous tribes in India have distinct cultural values and religious beliefs that are passed down from generation to generation, which in turn influence their financial knowledge, financial behaviours, and financial attitudes. These cultural values and beliefs include respect for nature, collectivist society, passive financial attitude, limited financial knowledge, limited access to financial services, cultural barriers and spiritual beliefs. The basic premise is that financial services are not part of certain cultures. In certain cultures, the financial services are considered to be a misfit, and in certain tribes, the traditional methods of financial management are considered to be superior. The Bonda tribe is a group located in the Jeypore region of Onkadelli, India. Tribals mainly sell goods of daily utility such as vegetables, fruits, medicinal plants, mahua drinks, groceries, variety of snack and beverages. Tribal people belong to the primitive tribes that have existed for more than 1000 centuries now. They belong to the Particularly Vulnerable Tribal Groups. They do not practice any financial savings and financial habits to save money or get financially included in the system. Bonda people are unaware of the money as they have never interacted with the outside world. Thus, the financial inclusion of the Bonda people shows that the culture has a deep impact on the financial inclusion of the tribal people and indigenous tribes. Due to this reason, the survey was conducted with tribal people who have been using financial ser-vices for some period. So towards this cause, research mainly aims to find out the impact of culture on financial behaviour. This includes cultures where financial services are considered to be misfit and where financial services usage is not part of cultural identity. Where the Government is trying towards financial inclusion and banks and financial institutions are not interested in them due to the lack of Return on Investment (ROI), the peer mechanism and social capital have a relevant role to play in the financial inclusion of the indigenous tribes and the native people. The peer mechanism or the social capital refers to the social relationships within the members of the community that are leveraged to facilitate financial inclusion. The tribe's financial inclusion is influenced by the level of social interactions and peer mechanisms within the group. Let us assume that there are members in the group, who stay in close proximity and they go for fetching water from the well together in a group. In these groups, the financial inclusion through the peer mechanism plays an important role. The resilience of indigenous people and tribes, as well as their practice of bricolage (making do with whatever is available), has a significant impact on their financial inclusion. The literature further highlights that in an excluded society, the sole possession of a group of members is the relationships that they have and the social capital. This impacts the financial inclusion and financial behaviour of the members of the group. For them, the reality is socially constructed, and the bricolage is the mutual trust and the relationships. Thus, if bricolage through the leveraging of social relationships plays an important role, social capital becomes extremely important in the financial inclusion of the poor marginalised members of the tribes and group of natives. Thus, socialisation and peer mechanism play an

(1 = Strongly disagree, 2 = Degree, 3 = Somewhat disagree, 4 = Neither agree and neither disagree, 5 = Somewhat agree, 6 = Agree and 7 = Strongly agree)

Culture and Financial Behaviour

I feel that using financial services is not part of our culture.

I feel a cultural misfit between the financial services and own culture.

Using financial services is not part of our culture and cultural identity.

I feel more comfortable to use the traditional methods rather than using the financial services.

Socialisation and Financial Literacy

Peers and community inspire me when it comes to financial management.

I always discuss the money management with my peers and the members of society.

I feel in financial control when my peers and family help me to control my spending.

Community and my peers are proud of financial behaviour, i.e. savings and loan repayment.

I save money because I feel that it helps me network better.

I save money as I think that it improves my status in the family.

I pay my debt in time as I feel that it enhances my social reputation and credit standing.

Bricolage and Financial Literacy

I believe that necessity and the need for empowerment leads me to be financially literate.

I feel that need for social status motivates me to gain financial literacy.

Due to need for money and motivation for financial autonomy I do take financial literacy programmes

I feel that my social relationships have helped me to gain financial knowledge and implement it.

I feel that social network has helped me to gain financial attitude to undertake financial literacy.

I feel that since I am from a woman self-help group, I have higher probability of getting microloan.

As per my thinking, my women self-help group has helped me to get access to microloans.

My internal savings and the retained earnings have enabled me to get microloans.

Agency

I believe that the leader of the group works in the interest of the members of self-help group.

I believe that the members of the group cooperate with each other in payment of group loan.

In a group loan, I believe that some of the members strategically default that leads to moral hazard.

I feel that there are chances that some of the members might not cooperate in the repayment of group loans.

I feel that higher level of monitoring helps me to improve my financial savings and repayment in group.

I feel that higher level higher level of monitoring helps me to improve my financial well-being.

Financial Behaviour

I repay the money that I owe in time.

I have money available to pay loans in case of difficulty.

To invest, I plan to manage my expenses.

I save my money to make investments.

Financial Attitude

When I get money, I spend it immediately.

Buy now, pay it later describes me.

I see it, I like it, I buy it describes it.

important role in promoting financial behaviour among the members of the groups of indigenous people and tribes. The financial attitude refers to the personal disposition of the members of the group of indigenous people. The study aims to assess the relationship between financial attitude and financial behaviour among members of a self-help group consisting of indigenous people.

Common Method Bias

Common method bias refers to data from a single source (Avolio et al., 1991) that might cause quantitative data analysis issues. Common technique bias reduces data validity and structural relationship (MacKenzie & Podsakoff, 2012). Statistical and procedural control diminishes study method bias. Allowing respondents to respond anonymously, placing the demographic question at the end and piloting the questionnaire before data collection ensures procedural control. Two statistical control approaches were used: the Harman one-factor test. The pathologicalVariance Inflation Factor (VIF) was below 5, hence the data had no Common Method Bias (CMB) (Kock, 2015; Sharma et al., 2021).

Measurement Model

According to Hair et al. (2017), the measurement model showed strong convergent validity and internal consistency in the data because the outer loading, composite reliability and average variance extracted are all above 0.708 and below 0.95. To assess discriminant validity, the Fornell Larcker and Heterotrait Monotrait Ratio (HTMT) criteria were utilised. The data have sufficient discriminant validity because the HTMT was far below 0.85 (Henseler et al., 2015). The measurement model results are shown in Tables 13–17, as well as Fig. 42 (Kock, 2015; Sharma et al., 2021).

Table 13. Measurement Model.

		Cronbach Alpha	Composite Reliability (rho_a)	Composite Reliability (rho_c)	Average Variance Extracted (AVE)	R Square
A01*	0.916	0.977	0.983	0.981	0.895	
A02	0.942					
A03	0.949					
A04	0.966					
A05	0.943					
A06	0.960					
BFL1*	0.947	0.976	0.989	0.979	0.855	
BFL2	0.942					
BFL3	0.928					
BFL4	0.888					
BFL5	0.928					

Table 13. *(Continued)*

		Cronbach Alpha	Composite Reliability (rho_a)	Composite Reliability (rho_c)	Average Variance Extracted (AVE)	R Square
BFL6	0.930					
BFL7	0.921					
BFL8	0.913					
CFB1*	0.946	0.963	0.964	0.973	0.901	
CFB2	0.953					
CFB3	0.951					
CFB4	0.948					
FA1*	0.880	−0.829	0.899	0.599	0.810	0.450
FA2	0.930					
FA3	−0.889					
FB1*	0.925	0.919	0.939	0.943	0.806	0.532
FB2	0.920					
FB3	0.932					
FB4	0.808					
SFL1*	0.965	0.982	0.983	0.985	0.901	
SFL2	0.921					
SFL3	0.956					
SFL4	0.959					

Note: A0 stands for Agency; *BFL* stands for Bricolage; *CFL* stands for Cultural factor; *FA* stands for the Financial Attitude; *FB* stands for Financial Behaviour and *SFL* stands for Socialisation factor.

Table 14. Fornell Larcker Criterion.

	A0	BFL	CFB	FA	FB	SFL
A0						
BFL	0.135					
CFB	0.571	0.179				
FA	0.641	0.103	0.711			
FB	0.476	0.176	0.739	0.607		
SFL	0.815	0.218	0.715	0.691	0.631	

Note: A0 stands for Agency; *BFL* stands for Bricolage; *CFL* stands for Cultural factor; *FA* stands for the Financial Attitude; *FB* stands for Financial Behaviour and *SFL* stands for Socialisation factor.

Note: The off-diagonal values in the above matrix are the squares correlations between the latent constructs and diagonals are AVEs. HTMT <0.85 (Kline, 2005).

Table 15. Average Variance Extracted (AVE).

	A0	BFL	CFB	FA	FB	SFL
A0	0.946					
BFL	−0.132	0.925				
CFB	−0.558	0.177	0.949			
FA	−0.607	0.101	0.655	0.900		
FB	0.456	−0.182	−0.706	−0.563	0.898	
SFL	0.800	−0.218	−0.695	−0.656	0.609	0.949

Note: A0 stands for Agency; *BFL* stands for Bricolage; *CFL* stands for Cultural factor; *FA* stands for the Financial Attitude; *FB* stands for Financial Behaviour and *SFL* stands for Socialisation factor.

Table 16. Structural Model.

	Original Sample	S.E.	T Statistics	Remark	R Square	VIF	F Sq.
CFB>-FA	0.387	0.191	2.021***	Sig	0.527***	1.939	0.163
CFB>-FB	−0.493	0.210	2.351***	Sig	0.538***	2.255	0.233
SFL>-FA	−0.220	0.225	0.976	Not Sig		3.784	0.027
SFL>-FB	0.262	0.206	1.270	Not Sig		3.887	0.038
BFL>-FA	−0.045	0.090	0.498	Not Sig		1.057	0.004
BFL>-FB	−0.039	0.113	0.349	Not Sig		1.061	0.003

*** denotes significance level is 97.5%

Table 17. Mediation Analysis.

	Mean	Standard Deviation (STDEV)	T Statistics	p Values
A0 -> FA -> FB	0.03	0.071	0.421	0.674
BFL -> FA -> FB	0.006	0.022	0.28	0.78
CFB -> FA -> FB	−0.052	0.075	0.692	0.489
SFL -> FA -> FB	0.03	0.061	0.487	0.626

Structural Model

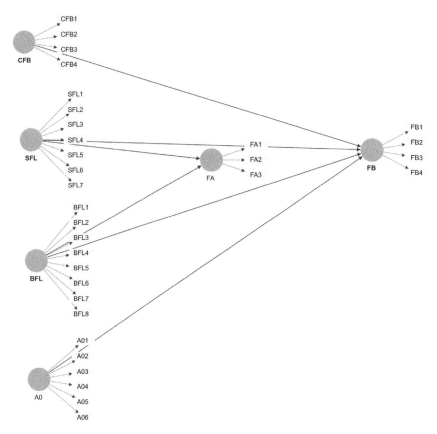

Fig. 42.   Structural Model.

Structural Model

The next step in the assessment of the structural model is to validate the hypothesised relationship (Hair et al., 2017). The data showed that there is no multi-collinearity issue in the data, with the VIF all below the value of 5. At the same time, I evaluated the significance of the path coefficients, the R square and the predictive relevance of the Q square. The data from the bootstrap analysis show the direct relationship between *cultural factors and financial attitude* ($\beta = 0.387$; $t = 2.021$; $p = 0.043$), cultural factors and financial behaviour ($\beta = -0.493$; $t = 2.351$; $p = 0.019$), *socialisation and financial attitude* ($\beta = -0.220$; $t = 0.976$; $p = 0.329$), *socialisation and financial behaviour* ($\beta = -0.262$; $t = 1.270$; $p = 0.204$), bricolage and financial attitude ($\beta = -0.045$; $t = 0.498$; $p = 0.619$) and bricolage and financial behaviour ($\beta = -0.039$; $t = 0.349$; $p = 0.727$). The results of the structural model are given in Table 16.

Mediation Analysis

The transmittal approach is used for evaluating the mediation relationship (Rungtusanatham et al., 2014). The transmittal approach mainly aims to develop the hypothesis that M mediates the effect of X on Y or that X has an indirect effect on Y through M without needing to articulate hypotheses relating to X to M and M to Y ((Rungtusanatham et al., 2014). As suggested by Hair et al. (2017), a bootstrapping with 10,000 subsamples was used to estimate the 95% bias-corrected confidence interval of the indirect effect. Further, the decision tree suggested by Nitzl et al. (2016) has been used for the mediation classification. The results of the mediation analysis show that there is no mediation effect in the model. None of relationships are mediated by the financial attitude. Thus, the cultural factors, social factors, bricolage and agency factors directly impact the financial behaviour in the case of indigenous tribes and native people. These factors are really not impacting the financial attitude. Maybe this is because of lack of financial literacy, and there is need for more sensitisation to build the financial attitude and then impact the financial behaviour.

Discussion and Analysis

From the PLS-SEM analysis, it becomes apparent that cultural factors have an impact on the financial attitude and financial behaviour of the members of the indigenous groups and natives and tribals. The cultural factors or the beliefs and attitude of the members have an impact on the financial behaviour of the members of the group. Indigenous groups and tribes generally have their own culture, in terms of norms, social beliefs, social norms, languages and dressing norms, which has an impact on the financial attitude and financial behaviour of the members of the group of tribals and natives.

Conclusion

The analysis of the study shows that cultural factors have an impact on the financial attitude and financial behaviour of the members of the self-help groups or the indigenous tribes or the natives. Thus, the cultural dispositions, social norms and beliefs have a strong impact on the behaviour of the groups.

Further Reading

Aamodt, A., & Nygård, M. (1995). Different roles and mutual dependencies of data, information, and knowledge—An AI perspective on their integration. *Data & Knowledge Engineering*, 191–222.

Adam, A., & Sizemore, B. (2013). Parasocial romance: A social exchange perspective. *Interpersona: An International Journal on Personal Relationships*, 7, 12–25.

Aggarwal, P., & McGill, A. L. (2012). When brands seem human, do humans act like brands? *Journal of Consumer Research*, *39*(2), 307–323.

Andersen, K., & Clevenger, J. T. (1963). A summary of experimental research in ethos. *Communication Monographs*, *30*, 59–78.

Antheunis, M. L., Valkenburg, P. M., & Peter, J. (2012). The quality of online, offline, and mixed mode relationships among the users of social networking site. *Cyberpsychology: Journal of Psychosocial Research on Cyberspace*, *6*(3). Article 6.

Ashfaq, M., et al. (2020). I, Chatbot: Modeling the determinants of users' satisfaction and continuance intention of AI-powered service agents. *Telematics and Informatics*, *54*.

Auter, P. J. (1992). TV that talks back: An experiment validation of the parasocial interactions. *Journal of Broadcasting & Electronic Media*, *36*, 173–181.

Aw, E. C. X., & Labrecque, L. I. (2020). Celebrity endorsement in social media contexts: Understanding the role of parasocial interactions and the need to belong. *Journal of Consumer Marketing*, *37*, 895–908.

Bartneck, C., Kulić, D., Croft, E., & Zoghbi, S. (2009). Measurement instruments for the anthropomorphism, animacy, likeability, perceived intelligence, and perceived safety of robots. *International Journal of Social Robotics*, *1*(1), 71–81.

Bearden, W. O., Netemeyer, R. G., & Teel, J. E. (1989). Measurement of consumer susceptibility to interpersonal influence. *Journal of Consumer Research*, *15*, 473–481.

Becker, J. M., Klein, K., & Wetzels, M. (2012). *Long Range Planning*, *45*(5–6), 359–394.

Becker, J. M., Ringle, C. M., & Sarstedt, M. (2018). *Journal of Applied Structural Equation Modelling*, *2*(2), 1–21.

Bhattacharjee, A., & Sanford, C. (2006). Influence processes for information technology acceptance: An elaboration likelihood model. *MIS Quarterly*, *30*(4), 805–825.

Blut, M., Wang, C., Wünderlich, N. V., et al. (2021). Understanding anthropomorphism in service provision: A meta-analysis of physical robots, chatbots, and other AI. *Journal of Academic Marketing Sciences*, *49*, 632–658.

Bond, B. J. (2021). The development and influence of parasocial relationships with television characters: A longitudinal experimental test of prejudice reduction through parasocial contact. *Communication Research*, *48*(4), 573–593.

Bonus, J. A., Matthews, N. L., & Wulf, T. (2021). The impact of moral expectancy violations on audiences' parasocial relationships with movie heroes and villains. *Communication Research*, *48*(4), 550–572.

Burleigh, T. J., Schoenherr, J. R., & Lacroix, G. L. (2013). Does the uncanny valley exist? An empirical test of the relationship between eeriness and the human likeness of digitally created faces. *Computers in Human Behavior*, *29*, 759–771.

Burnkrant, R. E., & Cousineau, A. (1975). Informational and normative social influence in buyer behavior. *Journal of Consumer Research, 2*, 206–215.

Chow, A. R. (2023, Feburary 23). AI-human romances are flourishing—And this is just the beginning. *TIME.* https://time.com/6257790/ai-chatbots-love/

Ciechanowski, L., Przegalinska, A., Magnuski, M., & Gloor, P. (2019). In the shades of the uncanny valley: An experimental study of human-chatbot interaction. *Future Generation Computer Systems, 92*, 539–548.

Cohen, J. (2013). *Statistical power analysis for the behavioral sciences.* Academic Press.

Conway, J. C., & Rubin, A. M. (1991). Psychological predictors of television viewing motivation. *Communication Research, 18*, 443–463.

Croes, E. A., & Antheunis, M. L. (1972). Can we be friends with Mitsuku? A longitudinal study on the process of relationship formation between humans and a social chatbot. *Journal of Social and Personal Relationships, 38*(1), 279–300.

Crolic, C., Thomaz, F., Hadi, R., & Stephen, A. T. (2022). Blame the bot: Anthropomorphism and anger in customer–chatbot interactions. *Journal of Marketing, 86*(1), 132–148.

Dai, Y., & Walther, J. B. (2018). Vicariously experiencing parasocial intimacy with public figures through observations of interactions on social media. *Human Communication Research, 44*(3), 322–342.

Darics, E. (2017). E-leadership or "how to be boss in instant messaging?" The role of nonverbal communication. *International Journal of Business Communication, X*, 1–27.

De Cicco, R., Silva, S. C., & Alparone, F. R. (2020). Millennials' attitude toward chatbots: An experimental study in a social relationship perspective. *International Journal of Retail and Distribiution, 48*(1), 1213–1233.

Deutsch, M., & Gerard, H. B. (1955). A study of normative and informational influence upon individual judgement. *Journal of Abnormal and Social Psychology, 51*, 629–636.

Díaz-Boladeras, M., Saez-Pons, J., Heerink, M., & Angulo, C. (2013). Emotional factors in robot-based assistive services for elderly at home. In *EEE RO-MAN: The 22nd IEEE international symposium on robot and human interactive communication. Gyeongju.*

Dixson, M. D., Greenwell, M. R., Rogers-Stacy, C., Weister, T., & Lauer, S. (2017). Nonverbal immediacy behaviors and online student engagement: Bringing past instructional research into the present virtual classroom. *Communication Education, 66*, 37–53.

Edwards, C., Edwards, A., Stoll, B., Lin, X., & Massey, N. (2019). Evaluations of an artificial intelligence instructor's voice: Social identity theory in human-robot interactions. *Computers in Human Behaviour*, 357–362.

Epley, N., Waytz, A., & Cacioppo, J. T. (2007). On seeing human: A three factor theory of anthropomorphism. *Psychological Review, 114*(4), 864–886.

Erebak, S., & Turgut, T. (2019). Caregivers' attitudes toward potential robot coworkers in elder care. *Cognition, Technology & Work, 21*, 327–336.

Esposito, et al (2021). Elder user's attitude toward assistive virtual agents: The role of voice and gender. *Journal of Ambient Intelligence and Humanized Computing, 12*, 4429–4436.

Faul, F., Erdfelder, E., Buchner, A., & Lang, A. G. (2009). Statistical power analyses using G- power 3.1: Tests for correlation and regression analyses. *Behavior Research Methods, 41*(4), 1149–1160.

Ferrario, A., Loi, M., & Viganò, E. (2020). In AI we trust incrementally: A multi-layer model of trust to analyze human-artificial intelligence interactions. *Philosophy & Technology, 33*(3), 523–539.

Fetscherin, M. (2014). What type of relationship do we have with loved brands? *Journal of Consumer Marketing,* 430–440.

Field, A. (2009). *Discovering statistics using SPSS.* SAGE.

Foster, G. (2005). Making friends: A nonexperimental analysis of social pair formation. *Human Relations, 58*(11), 1443–1465.

Fournier, S. (1998). Consumers and their brands: Developing relationship theory in consumer research. *Journal of Consumer Research,* 456–472.

Geisser, S. (1974). A predictive approach to the random effect model. *Biometrika, 61*(1), 101–107.

George, D., & Mallery, M. (2010). *SPSS for window step by step: A simple guide and reference 17.0 update* (10a ed.). Pearson.

Giles, D. C. (2002). Parasocial interaction: A review of the literature and a model for future research. *Media Psychology, 4*(3), 279–305.

Go, E., & Sundar, S. S. (2019). Humanizing chatbots: The effects of visual, identity and conversational cues on humanness perceptions. *Computers in Human Behavior, 97,* 304–316.

Gobron, S., Ahn, J., Thalmann, D., Skowron, M., & Kappas, A. (2013). Impact study of nonverbal facial cues on spontaneous chatting with virtual humans. *Journal of Virtual Reality and Broadcasting, 19,* 1–17.

Gong, L., & Nass, C. (2007). When a talking-face computer agent is half-human and half-humanoid: Human identity and consistency preference. *Human research communication, 93,* 163–193.

Gorry, G. A., & Westbrook, R. A. (2011). Once more, with feeling: Empathy and technology in customer care. *Business Horizons,* 125–134.

Grant, G., & Ball, R. (1991). Television shopping: A media system dependency perspective. *Communcation Research, 18*(6), 773–798.

Hair, J. F., Risher, J. J., Sarstedt, M., & Ringle, C. M. (2019). When to use and how to report the results of PLS-SEM. *European Business Review, 31*(1), 2–24.

Han, S., & Yang, H. (2018). Understanding adoption of intelligent personal assistants: A parasocial relationship perspective. *Industrial Management and Data Systems, 118*(3), 618–636.

Heider, F. (1958). *The psychology of interpersonal relations.* Wiley.

Hellweg, S. A., & Andersen, P. A. (1989). An analysis of source valence instrumentation in the organizational communication literature. *Management Communication Quartely, 3,* 132–159.

Henkel, A. P., Čaić, M., Blaurock, M., & Okan, M. (2020). Robotic transformative service research: Deploying social robots for consumer well-being during Covid-19 and beyond. *Journal of Service Management, 31*(6), 1131–1148.

Henseler, J., Ringle, C. M., & Sarstedt, M. (2015). A new criterion for assessing discriminant validity in variance-based structural equation modeling. *Journal of the Academy of Marketing Science, 43*(1), 115–135.

Hertzog, M. (2008). Considerations in determining sample size for pilot studies. *Research in Nursing & Health, 31*, 180–191.

Horton, D., & Wohl, R. R. (1956). Mass communication and para-social interaction. *Psychiatry, 19*.

Huang, D.-H., & Chueh, H.-E. (2021). Chatbot usage intention analysis: Veterinary consultation. *Journal of Innovation & Knowledge, 6*(3), 135–144.

Huang, M. H., & Rust, R. T. (2021). A strategic framework for artificial intelligence in marketing. *Journal of the Academy of Marketing Service, 49*(1), 30–50.

Hulland, J., Baumgartner, H., & Smith, K. M. (2018). Marketing survey research best practices: Evidence and recommendations from a review of JAMS articles. *Journal of the Academy of Marketing Science, 46*(1), 92–108.

Indriasari, E., Gaol, F. L., & Matsuo, T. (2019). Digital banking transformation: Application of artificial intelligence and big data analytics for leveraging customer experience in the Indonesia banking sector. In *2019 8th international congress on advanced applied informatics (IIAI-AAI), Toyama, Japan* (pp. 863–868). https://doi.org/10.1109/IIAI-AAI.2019.00175

Janarthanam, S. (2017). *Ands-on chatbots and conversational UI development: Build chatbots and voice user interfaces with Chatfuel, Dialogflow, Microsoft Bot Framework, Twilio, and Alexa skills.* Packt Publishing Ltd.

Joseph, W. B. (1982). The credibility of physically attractive communicators: A review. *Journal of Advertising, 11*, 15–24.

Keller, E., & Berry, J. (2003). *The influentials: One American in ten tells the other nine how to vote, where to eat, and what to buy.* Simon and Schuste.

Kepuska, V., & Bohouta, G. (2018). Next-generation of virtual personal assistants (Microsoft Cortana, Apple Siri, Amazon Alexa and Google Home. In *2018 IEEE 8th annual computing and communication workshop and conference (CCWC). Las Vegas, NV* (pp. 99–103). IEEE.

Kim, K. S. (2018). The effects of interpersonal attraction on service justice. *Journal of Service Marketing, 32*, 728–738.

Kim, H. C., & Kramer, T. (2015). Do materialists prefer the "brand-as-servant"? The interactive effect of anthropomorphized brand roles and materialism on consumer responses. *Journal of Consumer Research*, 284–299.

Kim, J., & Rubin, A. M. (1997). The variable influence of audience activity on media effects. *Communication Research, 24*, 107–135.

Kim, J., & Song, H. (2016). Celebrity's self-disclosure on Twitter and parasocial relationships: A mediating role of social presence. *Computers in Human Behavior, 62*, 570–577.

Kompatsiari, K., Ciardo, F., Tikhanoff, V., Metta, G., & Wykowska, A. (2019). It's in the eyes: The engaging role of eye contact in HRI. *International Journal of Social Robotics*, 1–11.

Kong, H. (2013). Face interface will empower employee. *International Journal of Applied Cryptography, 5*, 193–199.

Kulathunga, J. C. (2018). Factors affecting online purchase intention: Effects of technology and social commerce. *International Business Research, 11*.

Labrecque, L. I. (2014). Fostering consumer-brand relationships in social media environment: The role of parasocial interaction. *Journal of Interactive Marketing, 28*(2), 134–148.

Le, X. C. (2003). Inducing AI powered chatbots use for customer purchase : The role of information value and innovative technology. *Journal of Systems and Information Technology, 25.*

Lee, M., & Park, J. (2017). Television shopping at home to alleviate loneliness among older consumers. *Asia Marketing Journal, 18*(4), 113–134.

Levinger, G. (1980). Toward the analysis of close relationships. *Journal of Experimental Social Psychology, 6,* 510–544.

Lim, C. M., & Kim, Y.-K. (2011). Older consumers' tv home shopping: Loneliness, parasocial interaction, and perceived convenience. *Psychology and Marketing, 28*(8), 763–780.

Lo, S. K. (2008). The nonverbal communication functions of emoticons in computer-mediated communication. *Cyberpsychology and Behaviour, 11,* 595–597.

Lunardo, R. (2016). The interacting effect of virtual agents' gender and dressing style on attractiveness and subsequent consumer online behavior. *Journal of Retail Consumer Services, 30,* 59–66.

McCarthy, J. (2007). *What is artificial intelligence.* Stanford University.

McCroskey, J. C., Hamilton, P. R., Weiner, A. N., McCroskey, J. C., Hamilton, P. R., & Weiner, A. N. (1974). The effect of interaction behavior on source credibility, homophily, and interpersonal attraction. *Human Communication Research, 1,* 42–52.

McCroskey, J. C., Larson, C. E., & Knapp, M. L. (1981). *An introduction to interpersonal communication.* Prentice Hall.

McCroskey, J. C., & McCain, T. A. (1974). The measurement of interpersonal attraction. *Speech Monographs,* 261–266.

McCroskey, L. L., McCroskey, J. C., & Richmond, V. P. (2006). Analysis and improvement of the measurement of interpersonal attraction and homophily. *Communication Quarterly, 54*(1), 1–31.

McCroskey, J. C., & Young, T. J. (1981). Ethos and credibility: The construct and its measurement after three decades. *Communication Studies, 1981,* 24–34.

McCruskey, J. C., & McCain, T. A. (1974). The measurement of interpersonal attraction. *Speech Monograph, 41,* 261–266.

Miller, D. T., Downs, J. S., & Prentice, D. A. (1998). Minimal conditions for the creation of a unit relationship: The social bond between birthmates. *European Journal of Social Psychology, 28,* 475–481.

Mittal, B., & Lassar, W. M. (1996). The role of personalization in service encounters. *Journal of Retailing,* 95–109.

Montaño, D. E., & Kasprzyk, D. (2015). Theory of reasoned action, theory of planned behavior, and the integrated behavioral model. *Health Behavior: Theory, Research and Practice, 70,* 231.

Mori, M. (1970). The uncanny valley. *Energy, 7,* 33–35.

Mou, Y. (2017). The media inequality: Comparing the initial human-human and human-AI social interactions. *Computers in Human Behavior, 72,* 432–440.

Nass, C., & Moon, Y. (2000). Machines and mindlessness: Social responses to computers. *Journal of Social Issues, 56,* 81–103.

Newberry, C. R., Klemz, B. R., & Boshoff, C. (2003). Managerial implications of predicting purchase behavior from purchase intentions: A retail patronage case study. *Journal of Services Marketing, 17,* 609–620.

Ng, et al. (2020). Simulating the effects of social presence on trust, privacy concerns & usage intentions. In *IEEE European symposium on security and privacy workshops* (pp. 190–199).

Niculescu, A., Hofs, D., van Dijk, B., & Nijholt, A. (2010). How the agent's gender influence users' evaluation of a QA system. In *Proceedings of the international conference on user science and engineering (i-USEr 2010)*. IEEE.

Noor, N., Rao Hill, S., & Troshani, I. (2022). Artificial intelligence service agents: Role of parasocial relationship. *Journal of Computer Information Systems*, 1009–1023.

Novak, T. P., & Hoffman, D. L. (2019). Relationship journeys in the internet of things: A new framework for understanding interactions between consumers and smart objects. *Journal of the Academy of Marketing Science, 47*(2), 216–237.

Novikova, J. (2016). *Designing emotionally expressive behaviour: Intelligibility and predictability in human-robot interaction*. University of Bath.

Pelachaud, C. (2009). Modelling multimodal expression of emotion in a virtual agent. *Philosophical Transactions of the Royal Society B: Biological Sciences, 364*, 3539–3548.

Pornpitakpan, C. (2004). The effect of celebrity endorsers' perceived credibility on product purchase intention: The case of Singaporeans. *Journal of International Consumer Marketing, 16*(2), 55–74.

Price, L. L., Feick, L. F., & Higie, R. H. (1987). Preference heterogeneity and co-orientation as determinants of referent influence in the choice of service providers. In *Working paper, department of marketing, Katz Graduate School of Business, University of Pittsburgh*. University of Pittsburgh.

Putri, A. (1998). What sample size is "enough" in internet survey research ? In *Interpersonal computing and technology: An electronic journal for the 21st century AECT. 6*. AECT.

Rawlins, W. K. (2017). *Friendship matters: Communication, dialectics and the life course*. Taylor n Francis, Routledge Press.

Rihl, A., & Wegener, C. (2019). YouTube celebrities and parasocial interaction: Using feedback channels in mediatized relationships. *Convergence: The International Journal of Research into New Media Technologies, 25*(3), 554–566.

Ring, L., Utami, D., & Bickmore, T. (2014). The right agent for the job? The effects of agent visual appearance on task domain. In *Proceedings of international conference on intelligent virtual agents (IVA 2014)* (pp. 374–384). Springer International Publishing.

Ringle, C. M., Wende, S., & Becker, J.-M. (2015). *SmartPLS 3*. SmartPLS GmbH. http://www.smartpls.com

Rubin, R. B., & McHugh, M. P. (1987). Development of parasocial interaction relationships. *Journal of Broadcasting & Electronic Media, 31*, 279–292.

Rubin, A. M., & Rubin, R. B. (1985). Interface of personal and mediated communication: A research agenda. *Critical Studies in Mass Communication, 2*, 36–53.

Rubin, A. M., & Step, M. M. (2000). Impact of motivation, attraction and parasocial interaction on talk radio listening. *Journal of Broadcasting & Electronic Media*, 635–652.

Rust, R. T. (2019). The future of marketing. *International Journal of Research in Marketing, 7*(1), 15–26.

Rzepka, C., Berger, B., & Hess, T. (2022). Voice assistant vs. Chatbot–examining the fit between conversational agents' interaction modalities and information search tasks. *Information Systems Frontiers, 24*(3), 839–856.

Salem, M., Eyssel, F., Rohlfing, K., Kopp, S., & Joublin, F. (2013). To err is human (-like): Effects of robot gesture on perceived anthropomorphism and likability. *International Journal of Social Robotics, 5*(3), 312–323.

Sarstedt, M. C. M. (2017). Treating unobserved heterogeneity in PLS-SEM: A multimethod approach. In R. Noonan & H. Latan (Eds.), *Partial least squares structural equation modelling: Basic concepts, methodological issues and applications* (pp. 199–217).

Sheehan, B., Jin, H. S., & Gottlieb, U. (2020). Customer service chatbots: Anthropomorphism and adoption. *Journal of Business Research, 115*, 14–24.

Shin, D. (2021). The effects of explainability and causability on perception, trust, and acceptance: Implications for explainable AI. *International Journal of Human-Computer Studies, 146*.

Shmueli, G., Sarstedt, M., Hair, J. F., Cheah, J.-H., Ting, H., Vaithilingam, S., & Ringle, C. M. (2019). Predictive model assessment in PLS-SEM: Guidelines for using PLSpredict. *European Journal of Marketing, 53*(11), 2322–2347.

Sienkiewicz, A. (2021, January 16). *Chatbot statistics and trends you need to know in 2021.* https://www.tidio.com/blog/chatbot-statistics/

Sokolova, K., & Kefi, H. (2020). Instagram and YouTube bloggers promote it, why should I buy? How credibility and parasocial interaction influence purchase intentions. *Journal of Retailing and Consumer Services, 53.*

Sparrow, R. (2020). Do robots have race? Race, social construction, and HRI. *IEEE Robotics and Automation Magazine,* 144–150.

Stone, M. (1974). Cross-validatory choice and assessment of statistical predictions. *Journal of the Royal Statistical Society: Series B, 36*(2), 111–133.

Straßmann, C., & Krämer, N. C. (2017). A categorization of virtual agent appearances and a qualitative study on age-related user preferences. In *Proceedings of international conference on intelligent virtual agents (IVA 2017)* (pp. 413–422). Springer International Publishing.

Stroessner, S. J., & Benitez, J. (2019). The social perception of humanoid and non-humanoid robots. *International Journal of Social Robotics, 11*(2), 305–315.

Su, B.-C., Wu, L.-W., Chang, Y.-Y.-C., & Hong, R.-H. (2021). Influencers on social media as references: Understanding the importance of parasocial relationships. *Sustainability, 13,* 10919.

Tesser, A. (1988). Toward a self-evaluation maintenance model of social behavior. *Advances in Experimental Social Psychology, 21,* 181–227. https://doi.org/10.1016/S0065-2601(08)60227-0

Thomas, M. J., Mirtz, B. W., & Weyerer, J. C. (2019). Determination of online review credibility and its impact on consumer purchase intention. *Journal of Electronic Commerce Research, 20*(1), 1–20.

Tillmann-Healy, L. M. (2003). Friendship as method. *Qualitative Inquiry, 9*(5), 729–749.

Winterich, K. P., & Nenkov, G. Y. (2015). Save like the Joneses: How service firms can utilize deliberation and informational influence to enhance consumer well-being. *Journal of Service Research, 18,* 384–404.

Wünderlich, N. V., & Paluch, S. (2017). A nice and friendly chat with a bot. In *38th international conference on information systems, association for information systems* (pp. 1–11).

Xiang, L., Zheng, X., Lee, M. K. O., & Zhao, D. (2016). Exploring consumers' impulse buying behavior on social commerce platform: The role of parasocial interaction. *International Journal of Information Management, 36*(3), 333–347.

Xie, T., Yang, X., & Rose, D. (2023). *Converse task-oriented dialogue system simplifies chatbot building, handles complex tasks.* Salesforce AI Research. https://blog.salesforceairesearch.com/converse-task-oriented-dialogue-system/

Xu, K., & Lombard, M. (2016). Media are social actors: Expanding the CASA paradigm in the 21st century. In *Presented at the annual conference of the international communication association, Fukuoka, Japan.*

Yuan, C. L., Kim, J., & Kim, S. J. (2016). Parasocial relationship effects on customer equity in the social media context. *Journal of Business Research, 69*(9), 3795–3803.

Zhang, T., Kaber, D. B., Zhu, B., Swangnetr, M., Mosaly, P., & Hodge, L. (2010). Service robot feature design effects on user perceptions and emotional responses. *Intelligent Service Robotics, 3*(2), 73–88.

Zheng, et al (2020). Role of technology attraction and parasocial interaction in social shopping websites. *International Journal of Information Management, 51,* 102–104.

Zhou, T. (2021). Understanding online health community users information adoption intention: An elaboration likelihood model perspective. *Online Information Review, 46*(1), 134–146.

References

Avolio, B. J., Yammarino, F. J., & Bass, B. M. (1991). Identifying common methods variance with data collected from a single source: An unresolved sticky issue. *Journal of Management, 17*(3), 571–587.

Cheah, J. H., Roldán, J. L., Ciavolino, E., Ting, H., & Ramayah, T. (2021). Sampling weight adjustments in partial least squares structural equation modeling: Guidelines and illustrations. *Total Quality Management & Business Excellence, 32*(13–14), 1594–1613.

Hair, J. F., Jr, Hult, G. T. M., Ringle, C., & Sarstedt, M. (2017). *A primer on partial least squares structural equation modeling (PLS-SEM).* SAGE Publications.

Kline, R. B. (2005). *Principles and practice of structural equation modeling* (2nd ed.). Guilford Press.

Kock, N. (2015). Common method bias in PLS-SEM: A full collinearity assessment approach. *International Journal of e-Collaboration, 11*(4), 1–10.

MacKenzie, S. B., & Podsakoff, P. M. (2012). Common method bias in marketing: Causes, mechanisms, and procedural remedies. *Journal of Retailing, 88*(4), 542–555.

Nitzl, C., Roldan, J. L., & Cepeda, G. (2016). Mediation analysis in partial least squares path modelling: Helping researchers discuss more sophisticated models. *Industrial Management & Data Systems, 116*(9), 1849–1864.

Rungtusanatham, M., Miller, J. W., & Boyer, K. K. (2014). Theorizing, testing, and concluding for mediation in SCM research: Tutorial and procedural recommendations. *Journal of Operations Management, 32*(3), 99–113.

Sarstedt, et al (2018). The use of sampling methods in advertising research: A gap between theory and practice. *International Journal of Advertising, 37*(4), 650–663.

Sharma, A., Dwivedi, Y. K., Arya, V., & Siddiqui, M. Q. (2021). Does SMS advertising still have relevance to increase consumer purchase intention? A hybrid PLS-SEM-neural network modelling approach. *Computers in Human Behavior, 124.*

Yao, W., Baumann, C., & Tan, L. P. (2015). Wine brand category choice and confucianism: A purchase motivation comparison of Caucasian, Chinese and Korean consumers. In F. Martínez-López, J. Gázquez-Abad, & R. Sethuraman (Eds.), *Advances in national brand and private label marketing. Proceedings in business and economics.* Springer.

Printed and bound by CPI Group (UK) Ltd, Croydon, CR0 4YY

01/10/2024

14566648-0001